Paul Hewitt is a tec[...]
company. This is his f[...]

Jane Warren is a featur[...] *Daily Express*. She was runner-up Youn[...]ournalist of the Year in the 1993 British Press Awards. Before joining the *Express* she was a freelance travel writer. She is also the author of *Igor – The Courage of Chernobyl's Child.*

A Self-Made Man

The diary of a man born in a woman's body

Paul Hewitt with Jane Warren

HEADLINE

First published in 1995
by HEADLINE BOOK PUBLISHING

First published in paperback in 1996
by HEADLINE BOOK PUBLISHING

10 9 8 7 6 5 4 3 2 1

ISBN 0 7472 4998 9

Typeset by Keyboard Services, Luton, Beds

Printed and bound in Great Britain by
Cox & Wyman Ltd, Reading, Berks

HEADLINE BOOK PUBLISHING
A division of Hodder Headline PLC
338 Euston Road
London NW1 3BH

To Karen Hewitt: my inspiration

'Man is a creature who lives not upon bread alone, but principally by catchwords; and the little rift between the sexes is astonishingly widened by simply teaching one set of catchwords to the girls and another to the boys.'

Robert Louis Stevenson: *Virginibus Puerisque*, 1881

Contents

Author's Note

In response to criticism of the first edition, I would like to emphasise that this book is not intended to be homophobic. I am living happily as a heterosexual male but would be the first to admit that my own sexuality is not cast in stone. If a particular heterosexual stance has been taken in this book it is because society has forced me into this stance, not because it is one I truly believe in. I am a heterosexual who has so far not expressed the desire to sleep with men, but I see people as much more than two different sets of genitalia, so nothing is impossible. The gay community has allowed me to express myself and to grow during my time of personal evolution and for that I am grateful.

Paul Hewitt, Spring 1996

Acknowledgements

Thanks to Karen for being a tower of strength, always practical while I was emotional, to Wendy for having the broadest shoulders in Reading, to 'the girls' for making me laugh when all I wanted to do was cry, to Jane, Richard, Andrew Lownie and Headline for having a faith in me which was sometimes intimidating (we could have produced this book in half the time if I had not been so distracted by Jane's legs), to Mum and Dad and Jill for being there when it counted, to Nessa for not freaking out when I told you I was transsexual, to Dr Russell Reid and Ellis Snitcher for understanding my needs.

Gender, legal and medical facts were checked by Fran Springfield RGN Clinical Nurse Specialist, Gender Counsellor.

Thanks are also due to the FTM (Female to Male) Network run by Stephen Whittle in Manchester (who can be contacted through BM Network, London WCIN 3XX), and to Dr Malcolm Dodson for his sympathetic ear, quiet strength and integrity. Thanks to Jilly for her inspiring bravery and to Laura and Margaret Kelly for believing me to be 'every inch a man'. And to Susan Warren for helping me to reach my dreams.

If you would like further information on transsexualism please contact Gender Identity Consultancy Services, a professionally run resource centre providing information, publications, counselling and referrals exclusively for transsexuals and those involved in their care, at BM Box 5434, London WC1N 3XX. Tel and fax 01323 470230. Alternatively, contact Dr Russell Reid, FRC Psych, at the London Institute of Human Sexuality, 10 Warwick Road, London SW5 9UH. Tel 0171 373 0901. NHS treatment can be obtained through consultation with a GP.

Foreword

by Alex Carlile QC, MP

'Transsexualism is not a whim. There is no choice.' These words, from Chapter One of this important book, contain the clear message which Paul Hewitt sends to all of us whose understanding of the psyche of transsexuals is incomplete.

When in 1983, shortly after my election to the House of Commons, I was first confronted by the issue, I wondered if I was simply dealing with a branch of freakism. I admit that it was curiosity which led me to inquire further. What I found was something moving and real, a significant group of people trapped by both biology and convention in roles which simply were not theirs. The confusion running from those causes, and the personal consequences for each individual involved, convinced me that politicians should confront transsexualism as a political issue involving many aspects of government – obviously health, but also education, employment, justice and occasionally the prison system.

I cannot claim any great successes so far. Political parties are reluctant to debate transsexualism at their party conferences because they fear trivialisation by the media. My own efforts in partnership with Press for Change, an organisation driven forward by the energy and commitment of female-to-male transsexual Mark Rees, have involved some robust confrontations with and challenges to journalists. At least a score of times I have been faced with an incredulous journalist asking why I should even be interested in the issue, as though somehow the promotion of *these* civil liberties is a perversion in itself.

However, slowly a respectable group of journalists have realised that transsexuals are not only good copy, but also a genuine story of a failure of our times.

Up to a generation ago it was barely possible even to contemplate successful operative intervention which would enable a person to live effectively in what many scientists now recognise to be the subject's true gender. That treatment is available and, for some at least, extremely successful is a phenomenon of today.

For April Ashley, Caroline Cossey, Mark Rees, Paul Hewitt and many others, however, the law, politicians and the public perception led by the media have not kept up with scientific and medical progress. In that context it is encouraging to see that the *Daily Express*, and above all journalist Jane Warren who has collaborated in the writing of this book, have translated their popular and effective style into serious support for the genuine and justified quest by transsexuals for a fair deal in our contemporary society. I share their belief that in the approach to the twenty-first century we should achieve greater tolerance, though sometimes the evidence for this optimistic view is sparse.

Chapter Three of the book contains evidence of the kind of bureaucratic and legal nonsense experienced by even the most successful transsexuals. The name on the passport may be changed, but not the gender, until all the surgery is completed. The National Insurance records can never be changed, which of course means that the state retirement pension will accrue only at the sixty-fifth birthday of a male-to-female transsexual, and a female-to-male will have to retire as a 'woman' at age sixty from many occupations. The NHS medical card will always include a tell-tale symbol, totally unnecessary as the medical records are likely to be more complete than most and tell the medical and surgical story in graphic detail. The birth certificate can never be amended, nor even a new 'ghost' certificate issued for the person's lifetime. Employment rights are not protected in any way connected with gender or sexuality. Marriage is neither contractible in the UK nor recognised if contracted elsewhere, though this may change shortly in the light of legal changes in the New Zealand marriage laws. The prospect of wedding and honeymoon in New Zealand will be an attractive but prohibitively expensive prospect for some couples; yes, and heterosexual couples at that, in which one partner is a transsexual in the acquired but natural role. For this book demonstrates beyond any doubt that normal, attractive, sexy, well-orientated women fall in love and want sexual relations with female-to-male transsexuals, and there is ample demonstration that the same applies to men with male-to-female transsexuals. I have met some of them, and there is no doubting their sincerity.

Also in Chapter Three we read of the nightmare that a prison sentence was for minor fraudster Deborah Hart. Recent correspondence following parliamentary questions has shown the Prison Service to be prepared at least to consider in some cases that the appropriate prison is that in the acquired gender. So far as I am aware, at the time of writing there has been no case in which this has been given practical expression, but at least they are not saying 'Never!'.

One measure of a society is the extent to which it is prepared to de-brutalise its penal institutions: by reputation and especially by political rhetoric as a country we are low in the league of enlightened criminology, though it has to be said that the governors of prisons are often far more enlightened than their political masters. It is on issues like this that politicians should be prepared to voice enlightened views. Such politicians remain difficult to find, though Dr Lynne Jones MP and Jerry Hayes MP have been especially clear in their support for justice for transsexuals. I hope that one of us may have the opportunity to bring to the House of Commons a private member's bill from near the top of the annual ballot, to redress some of the often unintended and historical prejudice which transsexuals face.

A Self-Made Man is an extremely courageous book, prepared to be racy in order to inform, bold in its detail in order to fulfil the need for understanding. If after reading it you feel sympathy or compassion for Paul Hewitt he will be half-way to his goal. If you feel anger, not with him but for him, then the book will have hit its target. It is required reading for all with an interest in the subject, and a revelation for those whose starting point is merely curiosity.

House of Commons
February 1995

Prologue

Every man has to go through hell to reach his paradise

Tuesday 12 April 1994
There were three of them. They were sitting behind me on the top deck of the bus, each of them playing the fool.

The double-decker lurched round a corner. Rain splattered down on the windows and Reading town centre became obscured behind the rivulets of grime and steamed-up glass.

The gang stood up *en masse*. I could hear the tinny wailing of their Walkmans and the squeaking of their leather coats. I tensed up, sensing trouble brewing. Then one of them slunk past my seat, half-way down on the right-hand side, and deliberately dragged his duffel bag over my head. I felt riled, but hid it.

Troublemaker two turned round to face me as he sauntered past with number three. In taunting mock apology he drawled in black man's language: 'Don't worry about it, man! They're animals.'

Something unfamiliar snapped inside me. 'Well, you're with them, so what does that make you?' I goaded, my eyes alive with menace. Then I baulked at my own defiance and began to tremble, the implications of my comment causing my heart to pump fight-or-flight messages around my tiny frame.

Then he got angry.

A huge fist in my face completely obscured my vision. For a moment I thought Mike Tyson had been let out early. Although my challenger was only sixteen or seventeen years old, he towered over me, and his knuckles were making intimate contact with my nose. His friends had paused on the stairs and all eyes were on me. I kept absolutely still, well aware that I had bitten off much, much more than I could chew. My palms were sweating.

'Just 'cos you got a nice suit, you think you're it,' my aggressor hissed. His voice was hard now. I wisely resisted the urge to say, 'At least I haven't got a stupid haircut.'

The bus slowed to a halt. The fist quivered, then dropped away impassively. The boy spat on the floor before stepping on to the pavement with his mates. As the bus pulled away we made eye contact through the dirty window.

It took several minutes for my pulse to return to its normal rate. One day my big mouth is going to get me into serious trouble.

It was only three years ago that the 'look' through the window would have signalled something quite different: possible sexual interest. Three years ago I was a woman, Martine, and the bully could have been eyeing me up as a possible female conquest. For twenty-six years I had been used to having an advantage over these boys – but my power then was sensual, not physical. I would have slunk past their seats and attracted *their* attention. I would have heard a wolf-whistle, not a threat. I would have been the object of flirtation, not aggression.

Now, robbed of my power, I suddenly felt weak.

I certainly never expected that one day I would pose a threat as a rival male to young men on buses. Sometimes I feel a stranger here, thrust without social training into the tribal world of the male. For while I continue to see things through the same old eyes, society is reacting to me from a fresh perspective. I dress as a man now. I have facial hair. I no longer have a waist. And, yes, I can be bullied by gangs on buses.

I stand poised at the gates of manhood and the boys are beckoning me in. Beyond lies a whole world of macho ideals. He who dares wins.

Although I felt intimidated, the gang couldn't dampen my spirits – my artificial penis is in the post as I write.

I was born perfectly female, the ideal biological specimen in fact. I could appreciate my body, although I knew it not to be mine. Others loved my body far more than I ever did. When I wore a skirt I looked slinky and attractive and male attention was aplenty. And yet I have traded my feminine self for a substandard male body which will never function properly. Because of this, people find it hard to understand my motivation. But to remain as a woman would have been to deny myself my dreams and my peace of mind.

I was a man looking out through female eyes, but I played my role well. Most people, except the very perceptive ones, only ever saw me as a woman. Blending in was just part of survival, or so I thought.

I will never be Arnold Schwarzenegger, yet now I feel as fully male as he. I have to accept that I will always be five feet two inches, yet inside I feel six feet tall. I have wanted to step out of my female skin all my life; there is nothing left for me there.

I am a victim of a medical condition invisible to the human eye. Women prefer to be held. I don't. I prefer to hold, and I feel a huge sense of protectiveness towards my twin sister. For a year I patiently played a waiting game for hormones to take effect. I used to liken myself to the man in the iron mask, looking out on the world through two narrow slits. He was a prisoner in a lonely tower, I was a prisoner in my own body. How could I communicate trapped in a body which certainly wasn't mine?

The truth about my real self has caught up with me with such pace that it has taken my breath away. Gasping for air in all the confusion, I have found a quiet spot in which to rest to gather my strength for the succession of operations that are to follow.

My decision to embark on a programme of gender reassignment was an act of pure survival. There have been times when I have felt suicidal, but I am too proud to quit.

This is the eighteen-month diary of my sex change, the physical and emotional transformation from the female to the male gender role.

In the writing of it I hope to achieve two major aims: to turn a negative situation into a positive success story, and to blow the lid on the ignorance which rules the world of the transsexual. This book is written as a tribute to the little boy Paul whom I abandoned all those years ago when I made the unconscious decision to conform in a society defined by rigid rules and shallow stereotypes. This little boy has suffered in silence for far too long, and now he is reborn a man.

Although this is the story of my sex change, my dream can never biologically be realised. In spite of the introduction of artificial testosterone, every cell in my body will continue to host a set of chromosomes which are XX. I live under an assumed male name, and all my documents are testament to this change. But in accordance with the maddening current legal system, on my birth certificate my gender will always be given as female.

I have a beard, more body hair than many natural-born males and thick muscles, but the final kick in the teeth will come upon my death.

Unless the system is changed, my death certificate will read:

Paul Hewitt, female.

This will be despite everything I have achieved. I hope someone continues to fight this fight for me when I am unable to fight for myself.

Chapter One

Saturday 7 August 1993 (3 months before the start of masculinising hormones)

My eyes alighted on a scrumptious babe, a definite ten, when I popped out to Kwik-Save today with my chest tightly bound, my hair short and my female body encased in male clothing. She had long hair and a pear-shaped bottom squeezed into her Levi's. She gave me a shy smile as I bumped into her, quite coincidentally, near the cucumbers. Although I know there are not too many of us left, I know I am a gentleman, so I apologised with a cheeky grin as we collided, while erotic thoughts ran through my head. Let me open the door for you, let me caress you tenderly. So much passion burns inside me, it exudes from my pores like gum from a rubber tree.

I felt I wanted to talk to her, to communicate my unique knowledge, having lived as a woman for so long. As I romance a girl I feel I know exactly what is going on in her head. I have only to flash my mind back to the things I did not like when a man tried to seduce me. And the things I did like. I find myself wanting to reassure her: 'It's all right, darling, I'm not like the others.'

Yet I could use this intimate knowledge of the female psyche with a certain amount of cunning. I know all the right moves to make, and can plot my seduction. Women like to be romanced, to be cherished and to feel special. They need to know that you don't care about the size of their boobs or their cellulite hips. They need the assurance that they are not part of a 'same performance, different woman' routine you practise every night.

If you'd met me three years ago you wouldn't have expected me to express male chauvinist sentiments such as these. Instead, you might have been a careless motorist, observing me crossing at the traffic-lights. You'd have been distracted by my curvy body squeezed into Lycra hot-pants or mini-skirts smaller than your top pocket handkerchief. If you'd have asked you'd have discovered my name was Martine, and the word 'flirt' would probably have sprung to mind as you took in my long dyed-blonde hair and dangly *faux*-gold earrings. If you'd seen my birth certificate, dated 15 September 1967, you'd have read my full name as Martine Carole Hewitt. I always hated my middle name, but then doesn't everyone? The Latin meaning of my first name I discovered is 'warrior', which seemed to tell much more about the real me.

I was born half an hour in advance of my twin sister Karen at Battle Hospital, Reading. The midwife cooed, 'Two beautiful baby girls.' Although that's what she clearly saw during her brief examination of infant genitalia, her instant assessment could not have been less accurate.

As I begin writing this diary, my outward appearance has markedly changed. Not in an overnight transformation, but in a steady sequence of social signals. Now I wear my hair cut short and manly with a slight quiff for a fringe. I am dressed in an open-necked shirt from Top Man which buttons left to right. I wear a signet ring and a single slim gold earring. There are cotton ties in my wardrobe today, three of them. They are my prized possessions, collectively symbolising everything I have missed out on during these past twenty-six years. All three came from Top Man, a bargain at under £10 each. These slender but significant social markers are worn with a strong mix of pride and injustice. And, yes, I use the men's toilets.

Four weeks from now I will change my name by Statutory Declaration, marking for me the beginning of a new life as a man.

My new name will be Paul Hewitt, yet I was born a woman. My sister will have a twin brother. My parents a son.

I have a dream. I want to be a real man. Am I to be confined inside this foreign body with breasts forever? A female android, I mechanically sashay about, while, inside, the man stomps around this soft white body like a headless chicken shouting: 'Let me out, you bastards!'

I am twenty-six years old. I have an honours degree in biochemistry. I am also a female-to-male transsexual. A man born imprisoned in a female body. I suffer from a recognised medical condition called gender identity disorder. My decision to embark on a programme of gender reassignment comes down to a choice between life and death; it's an act of pure survival because my female body has always felt alien. It is not that I *want* to be male. I *am* male and, like all transsexuals, I experience an overwhelming urge to bring the gender of my body into line with the gender of my mind.

This has little to do with sex. It is not a sexual preference but an ineradicable conviction about my emotional and psychological identity. I have reached a crossing-point in my life where I have been stripped of everything. Everything except the courage to face the truth, and the courage to act upon the information I have now learned about myself.

I am not a freak. One in fifteen thousand people is transsexual, and sufferers are united by their total conviction that they have been born into the wrong body. Only twenty-five per cent of all gender reassignment patients are biological women who believe they are men; the rest are men who believe they are truly female. A hundred female-to-males like me undergo treatment every year.

The emotional pain of what I am facing is intense. It has forced me to draw on reserves of courage I never knew I had, but can it really be called courage, when I have no option? I may currently have breasts, but I ignore them. I feel as much a man as Sly Stallone – though rather more articulate. I burned my bras ten months ago and have not looked back since. Each stage I have progressed through has been symbolised by a door that has locked behind me, and since I no longer hold the keys for these doors my only way is forwards. I still can't believe this has all happened to me. The strength of my own convictions frightens me.

Now I bind up my ample 34D breasts in an elaborate chest-binding device every day and hide them beneath a suit or casual male clothes. It has taken months of experimentation and practice to create a binding device sufficient to allow me to face the world with confidence and without fear of discovery. Eight elasticated metres of the widest crêpe bandage I could find, wound from my underarms down to my stomach, flattening the breasts which I view with contempt. When they appeared late on in puberty, how could I possibly have foreseen that I would grow to hate them so much?

For so long my real self, Paul, has lain dormant and oppressed, forced into the indignity of dressing as a woman, obliged to stick to the rules, and manipulated as one of society's obedient wooden puppets. But now I am discovering reserves of power. I will be that obedient puppet no more and the world had better watch out. Fathers, lock up your daughters.

Initially, my male self wasn't as confident or expressive as it is now. When I first started cross-dressing a year and a half ago, the part of me which was Paul was happy to make a part-time appearance. Social conditioning was so deeply entrenched that, like a dog, he used to be happy with the titbits he was passed under the table. But now Paul insists on eating at the table with the rest of you. I feel as if I am being reborn, witnessing my own evolution. In two months' time, when I have lived as a man for one year, I will begin a lifetime course of fortnightly high-dosage testosterone injections. After a year of drug therapy, I plan to have a double mastectomy.

Most women get suicidal at the thought of losing a breast. To me, my enthusiasm and conviction that this is right are profound evidence of my transsexualism. It will be the final staging-post of my bid for maleness. This will be the day I will finally be liberated from my biological chains.

This diary will be a way of keeping track of the changes I am facing. For years I didn't understand who or what I was. The day I stepped into my first suit, the smallest size in the catalogue, was the most emotional day of my life. I looked at myself in the mirror on 16 November 1992 and a small boy seemed to be apprehensively gazing back at me. Tears welled up in my eyes. I had a sudden flashback to the movie *Big*, starring Tom Hanks as a little boy who wishes he was grown up and consequently gets trapped in an adult male body. At the end of the movie he suddenly becomes a boy again, and we see him walking back towards his house with his sleeves flapping over his hands and rolls of material at his ankles. Looking into that mirror, I could see the little boy I'd abandoned all those years ago. I could see him beginning to become a man, and after years of confusion I was certain that I had found myself. Much, much more than a way of dressing, I'd found me.

My twin sister Karen and I were brought up in a normal middle-class household where sex was always a naughty word. We wore Clark's shoes and matching pretty dresses which our nan used to make. There were clues to my condition, but of course these were not recognised and instead I was stuck with the convenient label: tomboy. At five, I sulked when squeezed into the lace frills of a ballet tutu, preferring to wear outsize football strip. At six, when dressed in a nurse's uniform for a fancy-dress party, I sulked all afternoon. While Karen was happy to play with dolls, I preferred Action Man and my Scalectrix set. There were other, bigger clues to my transsexual nature in my adolescence, teens and early twenties. But it wasn't until twelve months ago that I stumbled across the term transsexual.

I was driving through Tilehurst in my little blue Fiesta with a psychiatric nurse in the passenger seat. She was an acquaintance I occasionally played football with whom I was driving home after a coincidental meeting at the local pub. I wasn't happy, and in response to her sensitive line of questioning I began to drop my defences during the course of the journey. I was desperate to talk about my feelings, to release the confusion running riot in my head, and our conversation continued as I pulled up alongside the stone wall outside her house, slipping the gear-stick into neutral. The weather was dramatic, as it always is in films at moments like this, the rain coming down in torrents as my admissions unfolded before a virtual stranger.

'I know I like women, I can't deny that, but I don't feel like a lesbian. When I am with a woman I feel heterosexual. I see them from a man's point of view. I am playing out the male role.'

She turned to me and said, very matter-of-factly: 'So you think you're transsexual?'

I looked blankly at her white face part-hidden by wide glasses. I didn't know what she was talking about. Transsexual sounded like something sinister and deviant.

'What's one of those?' I said meekly.

She scratched the side of her face, then I felt myself retreating back into my own proud world, reluctant to admit I needed help from anyone. Her black cat tried to climb into the car as she stepped out and disappeared up the winding path. Transsexual. A term existed to describe my predicament. A sense of unease had begun to germinate inside me.

I tossed the word about in my head but it didn't mean much. Two weeks later I plucked up the courage to mention it to my mother. It was a Sunday afternoon, and I had just returned from a football match. I had scored four goals, but I still wasn't happy. I sat half-way up the red-carpeted stairway in a state of exhaustion, having run myself into the ground over ninety minutes. I felt driven by a force within, too strong to deny. 'You look shattered. What's up?' my mother questioned.

It came out in disjointed bursts: 'I'm a man. I was born in the wrong body, and I can't go on living like this much longer.' The words sounded pathetic and inadequate. I could feel only bitterness and injustice inside me. As a woman, I felt I had no purpose. I was as redundant as my appendix. The pain was inexorable, like a growing parasite inside me. The words 'why me?' were rolling like credits in my head. A solitary tear welled and trickled down my left cheek. I clenched my teeth tightly between my lips, but no force could withhold the torrent of tears which followed.

My mum, mortified by my pain, rushed up the stairs, kneeled down and put comforting arms around me. I was dimly aware of a howling sound, and as she held me tightly in her cardiganed arms I realised it was the sound of my wailing. Great racking sobs. As Mum clung to me I tried to absorb some of her strength, and for the first time I felt that we had made a connection, that she understood the world from my perspective, that she was on my side. I let the tears flow. Miraculously, she responded with the words and actions which were to change my life: 'My best friend Julia has a friend who is a female-to-male transsexual. I think it is time you met him.'

My mum arranged for me to meet him that evening. His name was Brian. He was forty-two and until five years previously he had been a woman. As I sat opposite this bearded, stocky man with salty tears still drying on my face, I immediately asked him to define the word transssexual for me. 'A female-to-male transsexual,' he said carefully in a deep, masculine voice, 'is a man born in a woman's body, or a genetic female with the brain of a man.'

My feelings as a five-year-old came flooding back to me. To hear this definition, one that I could have written down on paper for my teachers as a small child, was to hear all the answers to the confusion of my life so far in a single straightforward sentence.

Monday 9 August 1993

I bought myself a new waistcoat today. Each time I buy an item of men's clothing it helps to swell my male ego. It's only a tertiary sexual characteristic, not genitals, not hair, but it's all I have. Looking back, I see there were markers as to my true gender throughout my early life.

As a child I had a natural flair and innate instinct for football which allowed me to show up many boys. I started off, barely toddling, flattening the roses with my father Jim in the back garden. When I was a little older he would sweep me into his arms and drive me to the local park, which would accommodate my longer stride. Sometimes my twin sister Karen came too, but she was motivated more by the fun of being with her father than by any satisfaction derived from the game itself.

Certainly, I was a typical tomboy. All my friends were boys. Indeed, at that time I'm not so sure I noticed I was any different from them. I simply found the conversations and games which satisfied me most were to be found among those wearing shorts and trousers. I empathised with boys' competitive nature, the eternal struggle to be top of the pecking order, and the way they fought for respect rather than communicated interest in one another, like girls. I thought I was a boy, or perhaps I never thought about it. I was too busy dreaming I was Tarzan, diving off waterfalls and wrestling with lions. My spirit and my body dressed as one. I was the adventurer, the explorer, Tarzan's mate in the jungle. The animals were my friends and the evil Emperor Ming my darkest enemy. Flash Gordon was my hero . . . even if he did have only twenty-four hours to save the earth.

At six, we were enrolled in ballet classes. Karen was the perfect little ballerina, spinning round in her tutu and earning high grades. But I became sulky and uncoordinated every time I was squeezed into the stupid frills and girlie pink ballet shoes with silk ribbons. I hated prancing around trying to arrange my unresponsive feet. Not surprisingly, my ballet career was short-lived. Six months later I gave it up, and my father suggested I try judo instead. Thus, the Wednesday night routine was set; Mum took Karen to ballet, Dad drove me to judo. I suppose my father was delighted. After all, my tomboy nature made me the ideal surrogate son, and Dad had always wanted a son. I have always identified strongly with my father. He was, and will continue to be, my everlasting hero. I loved it when people saw us and would mistakenly refer to me as son or lad. He also had a pet name for me which stuck from an early age. I was Bill. He adopted it when I was in nappies, but to this day is unsure why.

Tuesday 10 August 1993
Living in an attic room does have its advantages, but having to climb three flights of stairs to get there is definitely not one of them. I am assuming I was paid a visit by Bob the Gremlin as I slept last night. I think he took my energy reserves because I had none when I awoke this morning.

I am still overwhelmed by loneliness and pain, but things must start improving soon. If I'd known my life was going to be this tough I might well have gone back for a rethink before making my entrance at 8.03 p.m. on 15 September 1967.

Dad called round to see me tonight and it was great to see him. I doubt he'll ever know how much he means to me. He's always there when I'm in trouble. He called me Paul tonight ... we really are making progress!

He now lives in Norfolk with his fiancée Jill and their son Simon, who was born in 1984. He was down in Reading for a business meeting. Talking about my childhood, he mentioned the irony of my decision to change sex. Irony? I pressed him for more details.

Not quite looking me in the eye, he explained that when my mother told him she was expecting twins he had felt sure this would increase his chances of having a boy. He had always longed for a son.

'I definitely had this feeling that a boy was going to appear somewhere along the line,' he told me hesitantly. 'One evening when your mother was pregnant we played with names. June chose Paul, after Paul Newman, and I remember strongly approving of that. Martine was her choice for a girl. Then we had twin girls. I was disappointed, but only for the first five minutes. After that I was overjoyed.

I had a family and you both had the correct number of fingers and toes.

'You were both very different as children. A real case of chalk and cheese,' he told me. 'Karen liked doing the girls' things and you liked doing the boys' things. You loved football and had a real ability from a very early age. I also remember your sulks. My new son Simon is exactly the same. He puts his head down when he doesn't get his own way. I see a lot of you in him. When you were young you had to be the winner, whether it was in races or just running training. Simon is exactly the same. He always has to be first. If I beat him he hates it, and that's just like you.'

I was born after a twenty-hour labour and Karen followed thirty minutes later with the help of a vacuum extractor. Karen weighed only five pounds one ounce and was rushed to the pre-med unit as she was so small. I weighed six pounds four ounces and was allowed to stay with my mother, although Dr Nipps, who had supervised the delivery, was apparently concerned that I was suffering from yellow jaundice. After a few minutes' deliberation, however, he decided against a blood transfusion.

My mother, June Hewitt, née Filer, had been working as a telephonist at the Reading telephone exchange for ten years when she met my father, who was then twenty-nine. He was a steel-work construction engineer with his own company based in Reading. Their courtship had been brief, and within eight months of meeting at the Majestic Dance Hall in Reading, where they were both keen members and avid jivers, Jim proposed. Actually, June did the jiving while Jim did some fancy footwork with a pint of Guinness. He was not known for his dancing prowess.

Both my parents were keen to have children and started trying immediately they returned home from an August honeymoon in Malta. They had moved into a rented two-bedroom flat in Southcote, four miles outside Reading town centre, and were saving for their first home. After three months my mother realised she was pregnant. It was a difficult pregnancy and she put on a great deal of weight. At five months she had an X-ray, but had no idea why the doctor had sent her. A week later he phoned to tell her she was expecting twins, unheard of in her family. When Dad got in from work she told him.

His father – my grandfather – Reginald, was a bookmaker's clerk who liked to place his own slender bets. His mother, Doris, was a cheerful and contented housewife. My father was the middle child of three boys.

My mother's parents, Violet and Harry Filer, had married in their late teens. Harry had been a silver-service waiter at London's Savoy Hotel in the 1930s before becoming manager of a public house in the East End. Within a few months of meeting my grandmother he proposed. By the age of eighteen Violet had given birth to her first child, June, my mother. Harry became a supermarket manager with a large branch of Waitrose in Wokingham, and Vi was soon a dressmaker for Courtaulds. There were three other children, my two aunts and my much younger uncle.

Today I am feeling reflective. I look back over my life and can see the signposts at every junction. Sometimes I can't believe that transsexualism is a fact of *my* life. I was brought up to believe in a black-and-white world, to believe in extremes: right and wrong; male and female; God and Satan; football and netball; Saint and Greavsie.

But I have now been forced to realise that each of us is a blend of these extremes. There is male and there is female in all of us. It is society that provides rigid and naive codes of restrictive conduct, further widening the gulf between the sexes. One style for the boys, another for the girls. We are quickly discouraged from expressing all sides of our personalities. Big boys don't cry. Girls don't get dirty and nice women don't have orgasms, or at least they don't talk about them.

When Karen and I were thirteen years old our parents decided we were responsible enough to have grown-up bicycles. Two weeks before Christmas 1980 we all trooped into Reading to vet a couple of girls' racing bikes Mum had seen while shopping. We went into the shop and over to the window display. Karen touched the handlebars in disbelief, turning round to her parents for confirmation that this marvellous five-gear machine might soon be hers.

I felt sick and I remember standing rigid, a sense of unexplained horror welling up inside me as I stared at the bicycle. Dad was discussing specifications with the salesman and Mum was preoccupied with Karen. I couldn't move. I heard Dad finish his questioning and then he must have noticed me, for he came over and circled me with his arm.

'What's up, Bill? Don't you like it?' he asked.

'I can't have it, Dad.'

'Of course you can. We want you to. It's your Christmas present, one for each of you.'

'Dad, I just can't.' Tears pricked my eyes and I clenched my fists. 'It hasn't got a crossbar. It's a girl's bike.'

No amount of joshing or cajoling would cheer me up. We traipsed back and forth across town, with civil war threatening to break out in the Hewitt household. We marched from one shop to another looking at girls' bikes but I remained icily resolute. 'I want a boy's bike,' I said quietly at intervals. This was not an act of defiance or the actions of a spoiled child. I simply saw no reason why I couldn't have a boy's bike.

'I would rather not have one at all than have a girl's bike,' was my final sentiment. After two hours of negotiations my parents were drained. Dad said: 'Martine, let's find you a bike with a crossbar, but I don't want to hear another word.'

Wednesday 11 August 1993

I began my self-discovery as a part-time Paul two years ago. He cross-dressed, but skirts and blouses still filled his wardrobe. Weren't those the clothes that society expected of a person with breasts and no dick? But although I was born female I could never now describe myself as a woman, even though today I ovulate and try not to think about it.

Now I go about my life and I wonder what I can do further to bring about my masculinisation. Because I still look female, women often let their guard drop with me, and I find myself lulling them into a false sense of security. Yet while they treat me as confidante, drawing closer and whispering secrets, I am thinking crude thoughts of a masculine and sexual nature. I feel like an impostor and a fake. I try hard to keep my gaze focused on their faces and out of their cleavage, but sometimes feel I am in danger of falling in.

Although as a woman I was a feminist, as a man I frequently overwhelm myself with this sort of base attitude! As I undress my friends with my eyes, I justify such superficial lust with the fact that I have a lot of catching up to do. I have only recently discovered women. I went twenty-three years without a proper sex life and, after all, boys will be boys.

But although maleness has unleashed a primitive programme in my head, deep down it won't stop me believing in equality. Aside from my part-time primeval instincts, I am dogged in my support of women. I've experienced sexism and chauvinism, and it would be intensely hypocritical of me, in my state of gender turmoil, to make value judgements about other people based on their genitalia alone.

Nevertheless, such intellectualising doesn't entirely preclude me from showing certain stereotyped male characteristics, and these stretch back as far as I can remember.

As a child I certainly showed a typical boy's opinion of girls – i.e. I wasn't interested in them. I thought they were silly.

My friends were all boys and I blended in like a fish in a shoal. At five, I struck up a friendship with Paul Coles, a member of my infant class. He had ruddy-red cheeks and a chubby little body dressed in starched grey shorts. We played marbles in the playground and with my Scalectrix set in the evenings. I was the only girl invited to Paul's sixth birthday. I remember his mother Pam assuming I was her son's first girlfriend and smiling at me indulgently. When I left the party she gave me a purple handbag with frills which she had made on her sewing-machine. I appreciated the gesture, but as an action man I had little use for a handbag. It made me feel girlie, so I hid it in my cupboard. It was never once used, but I often wonder what became of my rough-and-tumble playground buddy. Come back, Paul Coles, you forgot your handbag!

During my whole primary-school career I made only one close female friend. Amanda Fenn was a tomboy with long hair and a stocky frame who was big for her age while I was small, a fact which continues to annoy me. It is difficult to feel like a real man when you are little more than a dwarf with man-sized ambitions. Amanda and I were inseparable until she left our school when she was ten. Immediately she went, I filled the gap by growing closer to my twin, despite the fact that I loved to tease her mischievously and seemed able to make her cry at will. I was the proverbial annoying little brother.

We took some stick at school, my sister and I. But only because we were good. I took a certain amount of pride in standing out from the crowd. Motivation was not a problem; whatever I did I just had to be the best, and I was obsessed by the desire to be as good as, if not better than, my twin. Winning was everything to me. Life has always felt like a series of battles. I refuse to be flattened; I fight at all costs but not with my inadequate fists.

Both Karen's and my schoolwork was exemplary. I shone in mathematics, science and technology. Karen was good at languages and art. We both had work highly commended on a regular basis, and homework was never a problem.

Although I was viewed by teachers at Calcot Primary School in Berkshire as the more outgoing twin – fiercely competitive, quick to answer questions and always first into the playground at break – this masked a dependency I had upon my sister.

When we first went to school the teachers followed through the policy decision of always separating twins into different classes. But I refused to accept this and craved Karen's company. I would fearlessly creep out of my classroom and into the one next door where my sister studiously sat, crawling into the Wendy house to escape detection. Retributions followed but were systematically ignored, until the teachers decided to reunite us.

Karen was popular, but my dynamism meant she was often overshadowed. She stuttered slightly until she was eleven, but my parents brushed it off. Even the teachers said she couldn't get a word in edgeways due to her boisterous sister. But what they didn't know was that I was the one who suffered most from feelings of insecurity. Controlled by inadequacy, I was certain that my sister was loved more than I was. Although my father was careful to treat us equally, I was convinced that my mother preferred Karen to me. I was always at fault. Perhaps the reality was that my mother could relate better to Karen than to me and it showed.

Being a twin, albeit of separate eggs, inspired intense competition. I love my sister and I hate her all at the same time. I love her for her strength and for the bond I feel with her. My hate stems from the fact that I could never measure up. I couldn't stand the competition. I have always followed her around like an emotional limpet, but I masked this well. By copying her I could see how to behave. I would beg her to do my hair for me; I certainly seemed to have no idea of my own. But my façade was a success. Other people saw me as the stronger sister, and in my early school reports I overshadowed her, bursting with personality and bubbling with enthusiasm.

Friday 13 August 1993
Last night I had another nightmare.

> *A pack of unseen slavering dogs is pursuing me. Clawed wolf-like creatures with fangs already blooded, they are crashing through the undergrowth of a bewilderingly dense forest. Barely able to see in the gloom, I am feverishly tearing a path of escape. Vines grasp my legs like hands, and talon-like thorns claw my face, tearing my skin. The relentless hungry baying of the dogs gets alarmingly closer as I stumble blindly onwards. I am aware that I am a marked man, their quarry, and know that my tiny fists will be woefully inadequate protection against these hounds of the Baskervilles. But I don't give up the fight. I am convinced that if I can keep moving I will escape their moist, vicious jaws. My heart is pumping so hard I fear the blood will force itself right out of my body before the first incision tears my pale skin. I can hear the pounding of animal paws behind me. I can smell rancid dog breath under my flared nostrils. My feet find an obstruction and I fall, crashing into damp leaves and moss. As I look up, the jaws of the dog flash into the air in suspended animation. They beckon me in, then time slows down. The canine-toothed cavern, with its tunnel blackness, takes an eternity to reach me . . .*

Then suddenly I awoke. The palms of my hands were glistening with sweat, even though frost was sparkling like diamanté on the window-pane outside. I have spent many nights like this, balanced on an emotional knife-edge between life and death.

My greatest wish is to become in real life the man I am in my dreams. Then I can really start living.

Monday 16 August 1993

Today I went down to the library to research my life's ambitions fully. I raided the shelves for medical textbooks.

Transsexuals are likely to feel they have been trapped in the wrong body from a young age. We are born like this, but it is only when a transsexual child develops sufficient faculties of self-awareness that he feels a sense of not belonging or of 'being different', typically from the age of three as before this children have no sense of sexuality. We are different from transvestites or homosexuals. Their profile typically emerges in adolescence after their bodies have been exposed to sexual influences.

Transsexualism is a recognised medical condition. Its clinical name is gender identity disorder – sometimes known as gender dysphoria, dysphoria meaning profound unease or confusion. But really in the end there is no confusion. I have never been more sure of anything. Now that the choking fog has cleared, I have no doubt about what and who I am. I am a man with a plan.

Transsexuals like me have a conviction that our mind has been born into a body of the opposite gender. We are unable to accept our biological sex as it does not reflect our internal sense of who we feel we are. Once we discover that our feelings have an accepted psychological basis and that corrective treatment is available, most of us develop a desire to have a gender reassignment which will bring our bodies into line with our minds. We want to alter the physical sex characteristics of our bodies as far as is medically possible.

Transsexualism is not a whim. There is no choice. We are convinced about our predicament to the extent that we will eventually eagerly proceed with uncomfortable hormone treatment and the pain of the surgeon's knife, not to mention suffering people's harsh words. They are the unkindest cut of all. Where treatment is impossible or denied, tragically some transsexuals view suicide as their only remaining option.

But not me. Now that I know what I am I feel a sense of relief. Mind you, I'm not sure how much longer I could have continued with such an internal sense of confusion. Now I have made my decision I sense an in-built compass needle which points me in the right direction.

In the simplest terms, treatment means that I will take male hormones so that my voice breaks, facial and body hair grows and my curvy female figure is replaced with a more muscular physique. But first of all the NHS requires that I must live in the role of a man for a minimum of one year. This is what I am now facing. It means assuming a male name and dressing as a man full time. This provides me with a comfort too powerful to describe.

Once transsexuals have lived full time in their new gender for a minimum of twelve months they can hope to have surgery. I am terrified of hospitals, my only memories being of visiting relatives who have subsequently died. But surgery is nevertheless a huge hurdle I must overcome to reach the paradise I see beckoning me. A hysterectomy will follow my bilateral mastectomy. Removing the womb and ovaries is a way of protecting against the risk of ovarian cancer once my periods stop altogether. Plastic surgery to construct an artificial penis is also an option. But I am Undecided of Reading about whether I would actually trust a surgeon with such sensitive regions of my anatomy. This part is also very expensive, and I doubt there is such a thing as a free willy on the NHS! If word got out, everyone would want one.

So the first part of my journey down the female-to-male transsexual road will be taking hormones. Testosterone is a sex hormone, an anabolic steroid which builds the body mass right up, and which produces the side-effects of masculinisation when taken by female athletes for illegal advantage. What are unwanted side-effects to the female Eastern-bloc athlete are exactly the effects I am looking for. I often say jokingly these days: 'I'm a bit worried about the side-effects of these hormones – they're turning me into a man!'

Male-to-female transsexuals take female hormones which give them a more curvaceous shape and encourage their breasts to grow while slightly inhibiting hair growth. Plastic surgery can remove their unwanted penis and create a vagina from the left-over skin. Silicone implants boost breast size while electrolysis can get rid of any unwanted body hair.

By going through the female-to-male process I'll be coming into contact with a wide-ranging group of specialists who enable the painful, expensive and prolonged process of gender reassignment to take place. The team includes urologists, gynaecologists, endocrinologists (hormone specialists), plastic surgeons, psychiatrists and psychologists. But thankfully, in my case, it's all paid for by the NHS. The bureaucrats have finally realised this is a life-threatening disorder. Some doctor somewhere has also convinced the medical industry that physical changes are the best way to help people like me to live a happier life. My eyes nearly popped out of my head when I read it, but until recently the medical profession tried to 'cure' transsexuality rather than use surgery. Aversion therapy, electroconvulsive therapy (ECT) and drugs were all used to try to reinforce the original biological gender of the patient, but none of these was ever successful. This to me functions as proof that human beings are a body controlled by a mind, and not the other way round. Fortunately, since the Second World War transsexuals have been able to benefit from the array of informed disciplines which try to help them rather than make them conform. I am truly grateful to be a child of the late 1960s rather than the pre-1950s.

It is a psychiatrist who will recommend me for a programme of gender reassignment. But my first stop was my GP, who made the referral in March 1993. He admitted to being unused to dealing with transsexuals, but showed a quiet understanding. I guess I was lucky. Many don't understand gender dysphoria and dismissively decide that their patient is a repressed homosexual or transvestite. There are no guarantees when you are a transsexual even of a sympathetic and informed approach from the medical profession! But we have to fight for our own identity; no one else is going to. We also suffer misunderstanding, ignorance and lack of support, sometimes from our immediate family and closest friends, but we keep going. We don't have any choice.

I feel as ready as I'll ever be to go through all this potential hassle and social and physical discomfort despite the fact that my original body is a perfect specimen of my birth gender. I have breasts which Samantha Fox would have been proud of, but which I hate. She is welcome to them. I have long, slender legs, which grow only soft down, not real coarse hair. In fact, my body is so good that I had even been recruited by a company director to do modelling test shots for his bathroom catalogue. Plumbers' playmate of the month, July 1989! Many men tried quite unsuccessfully to seduce me. I was never going to be just another notch on anyone's bedpost bar mine!

It may be difficult to accept that a petite, seven-and-a-half stone, oval-faced and sexy woman, who could have the pick of the men she fancied, actually perceives herself as male, but this condition has nothing to do with physical appearance. In fact, my body has been a complete hindrance to my personal development. Of course, I'm completely aware that I will be trading in a fully functioning female body for that of a semi-functioning male, but my mind is closed to discussion on this point. It is not that I desire maleness. I am male.

In the same way, male-to-female transsexuals – like the model Caroline 'Tula' Cossey, or April Ashley, the world's most famous transsexual to date – felt psychologically female despite their perfect male bodies.

Gender in this context has nothing to do with sexual orientation. I could be straight or gay just like anybody else. As with any other section of society, transsexual sexual preferences vary. I've found out that approximately fifty per cent of post-operative male-to-female transsexuals are heterosexual (i.e. attracted to men), thirty per cent are lesbian (i.e. attracted to women), ten per cent are bisexual and ten per cent asexual. For post-operative female-to-males the figures are eighty per cent heterosexual (i.e. attracted to women), ten per cent bisexual and ten per cent asexual.

Me? I'm terminally horny and red-blooded, but there are worse ways to die! I have a healthy interest in women. I think they are the most fascinating creatures on the planet Earth.

But whom I am attracted to is not really the issue. I am changing gender for reasons that make my sex life pale into insignificance. This is not about who I can and cannot sleep with. This is about me. Marriage and a heterosexual partnership still fit into my game-plan but are not my reasons for having a sex change.

Some transsexuals are completely asexual. Jan Morris, the travel writer and male-to-female, is a case in point. She has publicly stated on several occasions that sexual intercourse was a somewhat tedious ritual which couldn't compare with the delights of the arts. Personally, I'd much rather spend the day in bed with a gorgeous babe, fridge in close vicinity, than gaze at a Leonardo da Vinci, but we are all made differently.

Transsexuality is not homosexuality. Homosexuals are content with their birth gender but happen to find themselves attracted to members of the same sex. They would no more welcome gender reassignment surgery than a frontal lobotomy. But appearances can be deceptive. When I was still living as Martine I went out with women. I didn't do this because I was a lesbian, but because I was a heterosexual male, albeit in the wrong body. Because I felt male, despite my biological gender, the thought of having a sexual relationship with a man repulsed me. I could have surrendered my body, but I could never have surrendered me. If you are confused, then perhaps you have some idea of the emotions that have been flying around in my head.

Wednesday 18 August 1993

Today I saw my social worker. I pulled up a chair in front of her and looked deep into her baby blues. 'Your mannerisms are all male,' she told me as she scrutinised my body language during our monthly chat. 'And your eyes are making me feel slightly uncomfortable. If you were a physical man sitting in front of me looking at me like that, I'd want to pull my skirt down over my legs.' I felt instantly guilty and apologised. Naughty eyes. I hadn't realised they were being so intrusive.

'That's all right,' she said softly. 'It's obviously something you do quite naturally.' I avoided eye contact for the rest of the interview and fixed my gaze safely on a flaking tile threatening to fall off the ceiling.

We talked round and round in circles, but answers seemed to evolve naturally over time rather than be forced. Only I could find my way out of this confusion, and when I finally recognised that fact, I set my social worker free.

I went shopping in Next. I chose a brushed cotton shirt, and as I buttoned from left to right in the changing-room I stood tall – well, as tall as it is possible to stand when you are head and shoulders below the average man. I remembered the emotions of eight months ago when I fulfilled my fantasy and added a male outfit to my wardrobe full of bodysuits and clinging skirts. Male clothing had felt so natural, so right. Nothing had ever come close to the feelings I was experiencing at that moment. The gentle transition from feminine to masculine had begun. These past weeks I have grown to love my ties more than I love myself. I am simply dressing my own fragile identity. Dressing me. Just as I had when I was a child.

Saturday 21 August 1993

I went to see my mother today. There were certain things I wanted to ask her in an effort to understand myself better. She is still insisting on calling me Martine and ignores my secondary sexual characteristics. My haircut and my tie might as well be figments of my imagination, worn by someone else.

I have never been close to my mother. I feel that I cannot really blame her as she was caught up in a loveless marriage which certainly made her sore. Deprived of love by my father, she had little to give us, and she also had little time as she was a full-time mum working part time at the Reading telephone exchange. I was unable to talk to her so I got used to routinely bottling up my feelings. But she did idolise both

Karen and me and tried to do her best by us. One Christmas when we were still pre-schoolers, she bought us books of stories. My stories were action adventures about spacemen aimed at boys, and Karen's were tales of ponies and fluffy white rabbits.

After tea I disappeared upstairs and scaled the rickety steps to the loft. I remembered how I used to watch in admiration my dad's acrobatics as he would swing his legs skywards and complete this feat without the aid of the steps and without a safety net.

I rummaged through boxes of old toys and children's clothes, remembering how I was always happiest and most outgoing when wearing my rough-and-tumble play clothes. There was no rebellion; just a ritual undressing after school. I would throw off my gymslip skirt, white socks and Milwards leather shoes before changing into jeans, T-shirt and trainers. Karen would stay inside and chat to Mum while I raced next door to play with Lee. I had no interest in his sister Andrea, Karen's friend, with her games of magic and make-believe. Karen and Andrea formed their own exclusive pet club, while Lee and I became looting and pillaging Indians, sneaking through overgrown back gardens.

As Lee and I fired toy rifles and scaled ever-higher trees, coming back with torn trousers, scratches and spattered with mud, people egged me on with that familiar label I had come to accept as a definition of me – tomboy.

But clothes were an area of contention from very early on. Dressing twin girls, or boys, alike was very much the vogue in the late 1960s and early 1970s. Even as a small child I showed no interest in feminine frocks. I felt awkward and ungainly in them. As soon as I was out of babies' flannelette my curiosity was apparently drawn to trousers and boyish jumpers during shopping trips to Mothercare and Marks & Spencer in Reading town centre.

The trials of enforced femininity were legion. I distinctly remember going to a fancy-dress parade dressed as a nurse. I must have been five or six. I hated the triangular-shaped hat with the blue cross on it and the starched white skirt. The costume felt even more uncomfortable than school uniform. Did Mum think this was fun? I'm sure I looked a sight, with my mottled Twiglet legs poking out of the skirt, gangling and awkward. Mum, I remember, made me pull on white socks up to my knees, but I allowed them to fall to my ankles in visual defiance. Of course, Karen didn't mind; she loved being dressed up like this. I felt betrayed, but stayed silent, pulling faces and praying the wind wouldn't change, until I was allowed to take it all off after the parade and escape into my football strip.

Mum gripped her china teacup as we reminisced together. 'I dressed you and your sister the same,' she said. 'You looked beautiful with your blonde curls, but Karen was more willing to wear frocks and look pretty. Even when you were about three years old you wanted to wear trousers. Sometimes if I put you in a party dress you would pull faces. Looking back, you're right, I can see that your face said you were in the wrong thing. I didn't get cross when you were grumpy like that. You were both my life. I idolised you.'

My childhood was symbolised by little sulks. To this day I remember my mum promising to buy me a present if I ever stopped sulking. I never stopped sulking, and I never got that present.

'My mother, your grandmother, was a talented dress-maker. When you were both about three years old she made you each a beautiful velvet dress, one in green and one in blue. When you put yours on and made that grumpy face I thought you were just being difficult. And when you didn't show much interest in dolls I thought the same. Action Man was your favourite toy for a long time.'

I felt a confusing cocktail of joy and sharp stakes piercing me as we talked of my childhood. The past is painful to remember, and now I realise that I simply chose to forget. We ended up sitting in front of piles of photo albums, and as she peeled back the fading pages I could see subtle indicators that I was gender dysphoric even as a tiny child. In most photographs my body language is masculine. My legs are astride, regardless of what I am wearing, and my features are set, never cute. In one picture Karen and I, aged about seven, are sitting on a tree stump in Prospect Park in West Reading. Karen looks coy, with her hands clasped between her legs and her blonde hair in a ponytail. She is wearing a girlie blouse, frilly skirt and long white socks. I am sitting beside her. My right arm is placed protectively around her shoulder. With my trousered legs astride, my other hand is planted firmly on my knee. My hair is long and scraggly, looking as if the comb had yet to be invented, and my T-shirt is plain. In many ways this photo tells more than can be explained in a page of writing. It brings all my painful memories to the fore, and today I feel no further forward than I was as the little boy in that photo. The years in between seem somehow not to have happened; for one little boy time has in effect stood still.

We kept turning pages as our tea grew cold and skin formed on the surface. My mother was hardly uttering a word now and instead was letting the pictures speak for themselves. I noticed a marked contrast between pictures of me dressed in more masculine clothes and those where I am dressed like a girl, in which I look like a paler, more uncertain shadow of my sister with an awkwardness about me. Even as two-year-olds, it is Karen who looks angelic, clutching a fluffy white toy bear, while I am less compliant, looking coldly at the camera, my hands empty.

As we sat over our tea my mother told me about Uncle Tony, my father's younger brother, who was an artist who copied photographs using chalk pastels. I remember when he produced an Action Man from the folds of his coat. I was elated. It wasn't that I consciously recognised a toy I could relate to; it simply made an instant connection with my imagination. A year later I was given an Action Man helicopter and enticed Karen to help launch it on its maiden flight out of the bedroom window. It was me, tears welling up in my eyes, who picked pieces of the patio out of Action Man's face and gazed into his strong, flinty eyes when his parachute failed to open. I retreated to read Warlord comics, hidden in my Warlord box with the secret compartment, while Karen studied Twinkle. I was happy, back in my escapist world.

Karen and I were always considered by our parents to be 'perfect' children. Mum was intent on bringing us up in her mould: prim and strait-laced to the point of exasperation. My parents were careful never to let us see them naked; bathroom doors were firmly shut. I may have seen my father's penis once, as he sprinted across the landing. I felt wildly jealous. Why didn't I have one? We found out about reproduction from biology lessons at school and our classmates but never from home.

I remember one evening at the British Legion club in Tilehurst. We had been taken there by our dad and his father, our grandad. As seven-year-olds, my sister and I had spent the evening drinking Cokes and munching packets of Golden Wonder crisps. As darkness fell I followed my grandad round the back of the club, without his knowledge, curious as to where he was going. I hid in the shadows as he urinated against a wall, and then I scampered back inside. I felt intensely guilty, as though I had just witnessed something that I shouldn't. I kept my secret to myself, but suddenly I had discovered the difference between men and women and all my worst fears were confirmed; I was not male.

Tuesday 24 August 1993
I went shopping again today with my sister. I was wandering around the women's department of Top Shop and she found a purple Lycra bodysuit she wanted to try on. She persuaded me to go into the changing-rooms with her, but once inside I felt desperately out of place. I half-expected to be outed and ejected from this female environment. Karen told me later that she had felt awkward too. She had noticed me looking around at all the half-naked women. I will never go into female changing-rooms again.

My new life as Paul is expensive. He has an immaculate taste in clothes, and I always seem to come home with the most expensive shirt in the shop. As a kid I was no different. My dad would chide me as I always disappeared into the shop freezer to reappear with the most expensive ice-lolly. Old habits die hard. I was deeply wounded to be called 'miss' at the checkout in Top Man this afternoon.

I wish I had more money to equip myself with a full male wardrobe, but I gave up work two months ago. I was trying to hold down a job as a financial adviser with an insurance company, but trying to do this and start gender reassignment proved to be as crazy as launching myself out of an aeroplane without a parachute. It was emotional suicide.

While working, I reached the crisis stage where I could no longer face the world as a woman. I would go out in my smart skirt to sell policies, before dashing into the nearest phone box, like Wonderwoman, emerging in a cloud of smoke dressed as a man. I decided that to stay sane I had to drop the bombshell at work. I wanted to dress as a man. My body and mind were caught on opposite sides of the San Andreas Fault; the earth had shifted, and now they were miles apart.

My regional manager acted dismissively as if this were a choice I was making, one that could wait until I had established myself financially. But Paul could not wait. In desperation, after a few more weeks of struggling along trying to please the manager, I felt I had no option but to issue an ultimatum.

With shaking hands and a trembling heart I rang him at ten o'clock one morning. Trying to sound authoritative, I said: 'You either let me come along dressed as myself or not at all.'

But we were two personalities clashing bitterly and there was no way he would come round to my point of view. 'You know my feelings on this,' he said quietly. 'We've been through this all before.' No to my *request* felt like no to *me*. I was choking before I'd even put the phone down, and I ran out of the house in a state of turmoil, not knowing where to go or what to do. I felt as though the whole world was prohibiting me from being myself. Angry enough to kill and desperate enough to boost the suicide statistics, in the end I got very drunk and shed tears for the man I thought I'd never be. I met Debbie, my on/off girlfriend, in the pub. She put a comforting arm around me and slowly I calmed down.

Luckily, I had allies within the company who were more understanding. I received words of encouragement from a lady I admired high up in the company, and also from some sales reps. Finally, the message came back to me that I was to be allowed to work as Paul, to see my clients as Paul, to be myself at last. I impatiently awaited the arrival of new business cards. Mr Paul Hewitt.

Once they turned up I had the next hurdle to overcome. The weekly sales meeting in Ringwood. My colleagues switched intermittently between my female and my male name. My regional manager avoided talking to me altogether. The meeting was embarrassing and stressful but also a liberation. But I came out caring little about triumphs of persistence, just wanting to curl up and die.

On Monday 19 July 1993 I made my first business

appointment as Paul. I stood around for twenty minutes staring at the phone, willing it to find the words on my behalf. The words were simple enough, but the confidence took some time to muster, knowing I was in effect lying through my teeth as I said: 'Hi, this is Mr Paul Hewitt, calling on behalf of Easy Life and Pensions. I understand you have an accident policy with us...'

I replaced the receiver in its cradle and punched the air in triumph. One down, twenty-five to go. I then made five more appointments in quick succession, realising that the knack was to sound confident.

It didn't always work.

'This is Paul Hewitt...' I began.

'Did you say Paula or was it Pauline?' was one reply.

'This is Mr Paul Hewitt from Easy Life,' I said to another potential client a few minutes later.

'You don't sound like a Paul,' came the sharp response.

Once the calls had been mastered, my next step was actually to turn up at the allocated appointment time. It took a week before I no longer needed a twenty-minute psyching-up session in my car before I strode manfully up the driveway and rang the bell. I prayed my courage would not desert me as *God Save the Queen* rang out through the client's hallway.

Overcoming these fears began to create a warm, contented glow in my heart. For the first time in my life I had a sense of purpose, an identity, rather than no identity at all, but for all my colleagues' support, working as a man without the protection of hormones and in my current state of health was to prove about as tough a challenge as climbing Mont Blanc with only one leg.

I spent a distressing two weeks seeing out old clients as Martine and taking on new ones as Paul. This was nothing short of a nightmare. I was fed up having to keep changing outfits – skirt, heels and tights for the clients who knew their broker as Martine, suit, brogues and tie for those who knew Paul. My car looked like a theatrical costumier's.

After yet another wardrobe change I received a phone call from the vice-president of the company. He invited me to breakfast, a test, I later found out, to see how I would appear in front of my clients. I could feel the sweat on my brow as I sat opposite him feeling self-conscious to the core. As we ate cornflakes and toast together – I had to force them down as I had never felt less hungry – he did what many people have done since. While the Forte Posthouse chef was grilling the sausages, David was grilling me. But I felt comfortable talking to him. He seemed to have an innate understanding of my situation and immediately grasped its importance.

But even with his backing I soon realised I couldn't keep working at a time when my emotional stability was crumbling before my eyes. Soon I was not well enough to get out of bed. I had withdrawn totally and felt intensely bitter about the hand I had been dealt. My instincts were instructing me to dive under my quilt and stay there until further notice. The big world outside was a threatening place for a biological error. I started see-sawing between periods of depression and episodes of an almost theatrical display of togetherness.

Finally, I was forced to admit that I was many things, but together was not one of them.

It was the realisation of what I had lost which finally brought me to my senses. One morning I awoke to an empty space next to me – Debbie, my on/off girlfriend who had stayed the night, had left for work – and I had a sudden realisation that this space symbolised the huge chasm in my life. I no longer recognised myself, and Debbie had lost interest in me.

I pulled the duvet around my shoulders, fearful of facing the harsh world outside my warm cocoon. My mind felt numb, barren of thought or enthusiasm, and my legs lay quite lifeless and limp beneath me. My heart beating told me I was technically alive, but I felt literally dead. Being this drained and fearful was no way to carry on a life. Somewhere along the line of my twenty-six years I had desperately lost my way, but I could not fathom where. My compass was spinning wildly around without direction, and I realised that I was facing a far greater trauma than simply concentrating on maintaining a charade of coping at work. I swung my sluggish body out of bed, slipped into my dressing-gown and immediately phoned my boss. It was quite simple. I told him I had had enough. After the call I felt profoundly released and refocused. I had taken the first step towards halting my internal torment. The world could go on without me for a while.

I packed a few belongings into my Karrimor rucksack and left. I had nowhere to live, no job, no money, no girlfriend, no car, no self-esteem. I felt nauseous and could not eat. From here I felt certain that the only way was up. Luckily, a friend going on holiday let me flat-sit. As she left, she told me that if I committed suicide while she was away, she'd kill me. Three weeks later I moved into a bedsit in West Reading.

Thursday 26 August 1993

Last night I went out to French's night-club. I spend time in the gay preserve downstairs at the moment, mainly due to the freedom of dress. I do not go out very much at all these days as the world is an intimidating place for an androgynous transsexual. When I do pluck up the courage to go out I normally choose a friendly gay pub where I can have a quiet pint of Fosters and be myself. But even an evening out in such a relatively harmless environment can be threatening for a pre-hormone-therapy transsexual. Last night, with alcohol coursing through my veins, I was feeling braver than usual so I decided to try hanging out in the straight part of the bar upstairs. Last time I tried this, when I was still living as Martine, a guy had offered to buy me a drink and had then insisted I was a man trying to be a woman.

I ventured upstairs, wanting to sample the atmosphere and to see if I passed as Paul. It is some years since I have felt at home in a heterosexual environment, not since my life masquerading as a woman. I climbed the stairs and sauntered across to the bar, where I leaned with my pint in a nonchalant fashion. I had been there two minutes when a young man sidled over to me. As he started chatting me up, I realised that my cover had been blown. He had seen right through the disguise to my physical gender. He thought I was a woman. I panicked, plonked down my glass and escaped to the Gents, only to encounter more problems. There was no lock on the single cubicle inside! This was not the most appealing place to drop my trousers, so I left in a big hurry and wondered if I could get away with using the Ladies. Once inside there, I came face to face with an angry woman of about forty. She glared at me, stony-faced and with hands on hips. 'These are the ladies' toilets,' she said with unnecessary emphasis. With my head bowed and my bladder bursting I turned tail and waited outside until she had finished.

Using the Gents after years in the warmth of the Ladies causes me all manner of distress. For a start, there is nearly always only one cubicle, and to reach it involves striding rapidly, with dry mouth, rapid heartbeat and averted eyes, past a whole row of real men leaning at the urinals.

I don't belong in either toilet. So I have to choose the one where I am less likely to cause a public affray.

Wednesday 1 September 1993

I continue to want so many things. A career, an identity, my health. I also yearn for the greatest love, the one that lasts forever and stays with you through rainy weather. I want back my winning feeling, the one I used to experience when I passed the finishing tape first, or blasted the football to the back of the net. But I will rise again, I'm just a phoenix waiting for the flames to die down.

Chapter Two

Saturday 4 September 1993
Every day I look in the mirror and I see him taking shape. In fact, I spend more time than is healthy mirror-gazing, trying to compose a visual image of how I will look as a man. Not surprising, really, that transsexuals are notoriously vain.

I am terrified of what the future holds for me, but I can feel a new power being intravenously fed into me as if I am attached to a drip feed, the precise content of which is unknown to me. Perhaps this sensation is the inner strength my mother often mentions in her religious citations.

Only now can I fully appreciate the charade I have played all my life. I have been empty, a soul denied the body it needs to survive. Now I must transform the body I have so it fits as closely as possible my image of myself. I have not yet had the benefit of male hormones, but already my transformation has begun. Paul the warrior, Paul the brave, Paul the daring, Paul the passion, Paul the power. I cannot tire of hearing my own name. Martine feels like a stranger now. Nothing I have been taught has prepared me for this unique path. I have only my gut instincts to rely upon. This is a journey into the unknown.

I miss playing football. Today I walked past Reading

Sports Club and gazed at the players through the wire fence. They were the ones fenced in, but I felt like the prisoner. My mother never liked me to play football. I can hear her words in my ears now: 'It seems like such a rough game for a girl.' I was eleven years old when I was first banned from the game I loved. I touted my talent all around the local football clubs but their universal response had been: 'You're very good, but, sorry, you can't play. You're a girl.' There was such a bitter sting in the last word and it made me curse my gender. At that age I didn't understand the significance of why being female should bar me from the sport I played with a passion. For the first time I was convinced the world had done me a serious injustice in making me female and not male.

Football had played a big part in my life, the leading role you could say. I had football, and the game had my heart. I remember my first-ever football strip bought for me by my father from the top shelf of toys in the newsagent's round the corner when I was seven. It was comical; my shorts were big, white and flapped in the breeze. The strip was in Arsenal colours. I didn't care, I still desperately wanted it.

The whole of my childhood was characterised by little sulks, basically because I wasn't allowed to be what I wanted to be. But I never sulked when playing or talking football. The resistance to my actually playing the game increased when we went to Little Heath Comprehensive School in Reading. The school was mixed, with a thousand pupils, and was a fifteen-minute bus-ride away from Underwood Road, where we were living in three-bedroomed, semi-detached suburbia.

I had spent the whole summer in quiet solitude, sulking because girls weren't allowed to play football at big school. Scoring goals had always provided compensation for my unhappiness. Yet the school was unenlightened. In 1978 games were strictly delineated. Girls were to play hockey and netball and were not, under any circumstances, to be allowed on to the football pitch during PE lessons. The world was altering my destiny, removing football from my heart and breaking it. I was an eleven-year-old child who trained with the boys in her own time after primary-school hours, who had her own size thirteen boots and who could be found every lunch-break without fail in the playground playing eleven-a-side with the lads.

I had coped with some stick to get this far, though. The boys had initially put up some resistance to me – I remember having my glasses kicked off on several occasions. They didn't like me playing with them because I was a girl, but eventually my gender was forgotten as we dashed around the playground kamikaze-style. In my final year at primary school I went to see the head of the PE department to explain that I had been playing football since I was three. My total sincerity was recognised and soon there was no question about the depth of my devotion to the game. Some of the girls wanted to play just to be a bit different and to wind up the teachers, but I had a genuine belief that I had been born to play. Soon my beloved boots were allowed out of their cupboard. But I'd had to fight to establish what I knew was right, and for the first time in my life I'd met resistance to my personality. From that moment on I became Martine the warrior. I prepared to do battle with the world.

It was at this time, aged nearly eleven and a half, that I distinctly remember thinking that I seemed more like a boy in a girl's body and that the world had done me a serious injustice. But I dismissed this thought as fantasy. After all, I had no idea that such a thing was possible. I was a victim of conditioning and felt obliged to conform, but deep inside I began bitterly to resent the body which confined me to a world of make-up and Sindy dolls.

Throughout secondary school, at Bath University and

back at home in Reading, I played football. In the first year the Reading All-Ladies was set up I scored twenty-five goals and was the players' player of the year. In the 1991–2 season I scored no fewer than fifty league and cup goals and was the top goalscorer for the Women's Southern League. Almost without exception I grabbed the sports headlines every week in our local paper. I lived for Fridays, the day the *Chronicle* was published. Out came the scissors and a new cutting would be glued into my scrapbook. Football was my religion. The game, and women, remain my two great passions. Maybe you can understand why I am now so miserable. My boots are gathering dust in the cupboard and heterosexual women don't give me a second look.

Sunday 5 September 1993
I look around and inspect my circumstances. A modest but cosy room in an eighteenth-century house in West Reading. A series of staircases climbs skywards and I inhabit an attic room on a level with the tops of the fir trees in the avenue outside. I have no job and I hover on the poverty-line waiting for my income support cheque to acquaint itself with my letterbox. I have lost everything but my pride, and my ego is trickling along at lowest ebb. But my soul is intact. I have to believe I am gold.

I don't know all the answers. I don't fully understand what is happening. I still ask, 'Why me?' I can't expect anyone to understand what it feels like to be born a woman, to succeed as a woman and then to have a man grow inside you like an alien, gradually taking over until one day he rules your world. Every day I cry to release the pain. I guess I'm not a big boy yet; big boys don't cry, do they?

My tears are a persistent rainfall, revealing a spectrum of emotion that has torn my heart in two. One half clinging desperately to the past, the other dreaming of a future which is like a mirage where I am whole and new. I let the tears fall because they help, and I will allow them to fall until the day when this underwater stream, hidden by my painted-on smile, dries up.

Wednesday 8 September 1993

I have made important decisions in my life today. Fear still weighs me down, but I have more balls than most. I have decided to take the steps to become the man I know I am. The time has come to stop moping and to make things happen. I have made an appointment to see a solicitor to change my name, a process which is free on income support. I have also been referred by my GP to an endocrinologist, a hormone doctor, in West Hampstead. His name is Dr Ellis Snitcher. It is he who will prescribe the hormones which will effect my transformation.

Now it is just a question of killing time.

Friday 10 September 1993

The state benefit system is a complete nightmare, a bigger endurance test than an appearance on *Gladiators*. I'm signed off sick by my doctor and today I tried to cash my cheque, but the benefits agency in Bracknell had failed to stamp it. This administration error cost me three hours waiting at the smoke-filled DSS. I suffered some embarrassment in the waiting-room as I stood in my Levi's and my trainers, chest bound flat. 'Miss Hewitt to cubicle five, please.'

I blushed redder than an out-of-condition jogger and was still fuming hours later, but was redeemed by the man at the post office counter. Attempting to identify myself as I cashed my giro, I handed him my passport, which I have yet to update. He took it in his palm and glanced down at the dark blue cover with my name, Miss M. Hewitt, written in the cartridge paper recess. Then he looked back up at me with a confused expression on his lined face.

'Shouldn't this be Mr?' he asked, puzzled.
'Soon will be,' I said.

Saturday 11 September 1993
I travelled to London to spend my twenty-sixth birthday with Karen. I find myself asking, 'Twenty-six years of what?' I feel as though my life has not even begun yet. But I can see Paul appearing right before my eyes, the man with breasts from hell in need of a miracle. I'm a scared little bear lost on Paddington station, miles from darkest Peru, and at times I feel as though I am dying. Where has my life gone? Where is that multi-talented girl who seemed to have everything? Now I'm dwindling away in a dark cavern, lost somewhere between my old life and my new one. I watch with envy as my friends live their lives while mine stands still.

All our friends turned up to celebrate our birthday and everyone called me Paul with no slip-ups. Each time I was addressed as Paul I could feel my identity swelling and taking shape, but all this good work was swiftly dashed to pieces at the night-club. Standing at the mirror-coated doorway, the throb of acid jazz filling the street, I watched as the bouncers searched the men in full view of everyone while beckoning the women to one side. In my mind the word 'inevitable' whirred round and round like a roulette wheel. When I reached the front of the queue I felt a cold chill as the bouncer eyed me up and down and took in my dark suit and white polo shirt before booming: 'Over there, madam.'

Once inside, I sat listlessly at the side of the dance-floor, feeling lower than a squashed worm. I gazed at the luminous tiles covered with pounding feet, watching men and women enjoying themselves. I wondered where I fitted in. But with a few screaming orgasms inside me, I buried my insecurities and bopped 'til my boots fell off.

I have developed a sneaking attraction for one of Karen's best friends. Unfortunately, she has only ever known me as a woman and it will be some time before I am able to convince her otherwise. Everyone decided to fight for floor space at Karen's after the night-club, as usual, and when Diane wouldn't share a bed with me 'now you're a man', I initially felt insulted. Then I realised that this was in fact a compliment, if back-handed.

My interest in women is now firmly revolving in heterosexual circles. I spent eighteen months on the gay scene as I was definitely attracted to the softness of female skin. But now I am a sportsman in search of the ultimate trophy, a heterosexual woman who will love me because I am a man. My lack of a penis will, I expect, be more my hang-up than hers. In my experience it is less important to lovemaking for a woman than an understanding of the sensitivity of female skin.

Sunday 12 September 1993

I am surveying this year's crop of highly significant, gender-specific birthday presents. A man's gold earring from Debbie, a purple silk shirt from Knightsbridge given to me by my best sister, and a new tie. You can reach into the heart of a man by looking at his tie. This one feels good. A multi-patterned Marks & Spencer special from the girls. Karen and I went for lunch at the Star and Garter in Putney and stood in the rain for twenty minutes trying to see the dinosaurs in a Magic Eye poster in a shop window. On my way home from London, I heard a car engine splutter behind me and then a shout: 'Excuse me, mate, could you give us a push?' He had called *me* mate, so how could I possibly refuse? I ran over, ignoring the rain, macho ego to the fore. Twenty minutes later we were still trying to persuade his tatty Escort to roll and I wished I hadn't felt obliged to prove my manhood.

I had an extremely pleasant birthday; the past two have been miserable. I am feeling much more upbeat, my internal motivator is giving me the courage to see a way out of this tunnel. It has taken anger to commit myself completely to the male role, the role in which I truly belong. I was beginning to wonder if I would ever have the guts to begin my battle for physical changes. I have come a long way in a short time. In November 1990 I had my first affair with a woman. Now, exactly eight women and three years later, I am leaping over the gender divide to become a man. I am hanging out for hormones.

The force of this decision is awesome. I have been a prisoner around my skeleton for too long. My eyes filled up with emotion-soaked tears as I opened my birthday card from my mother yesterday.

It said, 'Happy Birthday, Son.'

Emotional tightrope I can gaze at you from the chair where I sit and mope. I can hear the breeze flirting with your strands while I contemplate, how I can reach you? Have I left it too late? Emotional tightrope I think you are foe, but if I use your height I can reach my dreams, I know. For above your strength I can see my cloud, from a silver-lined scroll my angel reads my dreams out loud. Is she beckoning me through the gates of heaven or hell? I cannot be sure, but there is only one way to tell. Emotional tightrope, courage rising to the fore, I will take my first steps, sit in the lap of apathy no more. Now my feet are walking where for years I have only gazed, I can see my dreams more clearly peeping like the sun through the morning haze. Emotional tightrope, my arms are outstretched, I can taste all the glory my inner self has produced. My rope slips from beneath me and I lose touch with the world below, but not before my hand grasps the ladder which will take me to my dreams and to my heart, I know.

Tuesday 14 September 1993
I have a new girlfriend, Wendy. We bumped into each other in the aisle in Waitrose last week, both labouring under heavy shopping baskets. Aged thirty-two, she is office manager for a printing company. I can pinpoint the precise moment I realised Wendy and I were going to get on. The fire was roaring as we sat in a darkened lounge and I was playing biff-nose with her mongrel Marvyn. She said: 'Marvyn can tell the difference between men and women, and he definitely thinks you're a man. He thinks you're his daddy.'

She has this uncanny knack of always saying the right things. I cannot exactly say what it was that attracted me to her, maybe it was the *Watership Down* eyes but she was the first woman to make me feel like a real man. And that spoke volumes. That, and our complementary sense of humour brought us together very quickly.

The bedroom bandit was a force to be reckoned with last night. I am becoming more and more like an insatiable animal. But I am craving unconditional love and attention and hate sleeping on my own. I wonder if I must carry this pain around with me forever, or whether it will disappear slowly as my gender dysphoria is resolved. I have always been highly sexed, but since I made the commitment to become Paul I have become more horny than ever. For so long I was just my sister's clone. Now I am developing a sexual identity of my own.

As I had matured into puberty, the pressure to conform meant I could no longer engage in the rough-and-tumble of my childhood. Social pressures telling me who to be seemed stronger than ever. I certainly didn't feel I was following an internal, innate template of how I should behave. None of my feelings seemed easy or automatic. I awoke one morning when I was seventeen and with horror sensed that I was sharing my bed with someone, or something, else. The day before I had no breasts to speak of, but I had awoken with a huge pair from hell which seemed to have appeared overnight. I remember thinking I must have fallen victim to some bizarre genetic experiment. I am sure this is not what normal girls think, but how was I to know?

When my periods started I was seventeen. I did not really have any feelings towards this monthly ritual, except the relief that I could miss several months at a time if I was training hard. I coped with the disparate feelings inside myself by becoming increasingly remote and uncommunicative. I think by then that my mother was aware I was 'different' but was rather afraid to scrutinise what that might mean. The seventeen-year-old me would wear only jeans and trainers, while my sister's wardrobe was filling up with mini-skirts and feminine blouses. It was always Karen who resolutely pestered our mum for shopping trips into town, while I would keep a low profile, going out bird-watching and creeping around the bushes searching for rare species.

Karen would hug Mum, but I can remember not hugging her for months at a stretch. I began to avoid my mother's touch, briskly shrugging off any evidence of cloying maternalism. I am sure this hurt my mother deeply, particularly as she could see how close and easy I was with Dad. Things in their marriage had deteriorated and there were now enormous cracks in the eighteen-year-old masonry. Between them there was little communication and little love. Deprived of my father's gentle touch, I am not surprised my mother gave up trying to reach me in emotional terms and concentrated on Karen, who welcomed her touch and her love.

I was completely at sea in a female world. Even when I was given money to buy clothes I would spend hours shopping and come home with nothing. This was not for want of trying. I would leave the house with a clear-cut objective: I would buy myself something feminine. But my resolve would vanish as I wandered around the high street feeling a total lack of interest in skirts and pretty tops.

On the rare occasions I did return with a carrier-bag, it would usually contain generously cut trousers from a chain store such as Chelsea Girl or Etam. On such occasions I had been chaperoned by Karen.

As we grew older, Karen began putting on make-up and dyeing her hair, with the specific intention of going out with men. I tried to do the same, but I was trying to compete in an area where I had no hope of success. I was on unfamiliar territory, competing on female terms with Karen, so I resorted to the easy game of copying her relentlessly. I asked her to show me how to put on make-up, but even after I had been taught I couldn't do it half as well as she did. When Karen had her blonde hair highlighted I automatically decided to have my hair done as well.

I was quite good at being a puppet. I let the world pull my strings. At a time when you might have expected I would have been attracted to women, I was showing no such pattern at all. I was having normal teenage relationships with men, making me no different to the other girls in my class. But one fact did mark me out: I clung to my virginity with venom. I did not want to be penetrated. That was not to say I didn't fall in love, because I did. But while my female hormones were instructing me to surrender, something in my head was telling me otherwise. The writing was of course on the wall, but I was living in blissful adolescent ignorance, completely unaware of the emotional chaos that awaited me.

During my first summer vacation from Bath University, when I was at home in Reading, I met a tree surgeon and we had a pleasant, if sexually celibate, three months together. The first things I stumbled over, on my return to my room at Bath in September, were a dozen red roses. I counted myself lucky they weren't a dozen small oak trees. I had to write and put him straight immediately; suddenly I didn't fancy him any more. In my relationships with men I always had the controlling hand; very rarely could any man find his way inside my cold heart. I treated them as vital fashion accessories. A man on my arm? Yes, please, I'll have one of those. That made me a real woman, didn't it? That's what real women do, don't they? In reality, my heart was lonely, patiently waiting to be melted by the soft hands of my first ice maiden. Unfortunately, I didn't know that at the time or I could have saved myself a lot of aggro and a lot of broken hearts.

I was soon well into my third year at university and feeling fairly unhappy and unfulfilled. I had a brief fling with a male student from Cardiff, who in rare moments of passion did make my knees wobble, but he got stroppy when I refused to have sex with him. He couldn't understand how I could possibly resist his masculine advances. I now understand this feeling as the irrepressible male ego. I heard rumours that he told his friends I was either frigid or a lesbian. Wrong on both counts!

I was aware that something was wrong with my libido; I couldn't seem to achieve any emotional closeness with any of my male partners. Looking back, I'm surprised I had no idea at that time that men were not for me, but I really didn't. I just thought I had yet to find the right man. Despite my irrational sexual behaviour I had absolutely no feelings towards women at that point. The thought I might be attracted to females had never crossed my mind. I didn't consider the fairer sex an avenue of exploration that was even on my map. My middle-class background was so deeply ingrained, I had been conditioned so effectively, that I wasn't even aware of the fact I felt male. I just felt an emotional failure and an academic success. All my childhood sensations of masculinity had been alarmingly repressed. Nothing I did could detract from the vast cavern of emptiness which lurked in my underworld. I was still searching for answers.

When I was first attracted to a woman it was like being felled by a tree. But it brought me mixed blessings. The emotions flowed like the first black burst from an oilfield. I had discovered female skin.

The initial attraction was in her face. It was open, soft, expressive and warm. I watched her as she led by example, encouraging the less talented team members. She was a born leader and inspired everyone else. She was Nicky, the goalie in my local ladies' football team.

My sister and I had arrived back in Reading following our respective graduation ceremonies. I was bitterly disappointed to have achieved only a 2:2 in biochemistry. It is usual in the case of late-onset transsexuals for there to be a trigger which brings about the emergence of one's real identity, and my life began to change from the moment I began to play serious football for the Ladies. I was able to express my masculinity on the green turf, running with the ball obedient at my feet. I wanted to play football at the highest level and wanted it so badly it physically hurt. Soon my head was in a spin and my heart was doing a loop-the-loop.

Did I imagine it or did she take a special interest in me? We played an important team role together. She kept the ball out at one end, while I ensured it kept meeting the net at the other. We seemed destined to find each other. The signs were small at first, but none the less significant. I bought her a Tottenham match programme; she gave me a Pernod miniature. If I fell she would be the first to pick me up.

Our love was born in a bar over a drink following a game of squash. We were laughing with an unfamiliar freedom, and soon I was living for our meetings, twitching the curtains and waiting excitedly for her to pick me up in her burgundy Metro. Such feelings were entirely unfamiliar to me – no man had ever provoked me into such a state of super-tension. No curtain twitching, no stolen kisses, no urgent longing. The following day at football training I turned round on the pitch after some particularly nifty footwork. The sky was leaden grey, and little drops of rain were spitting down into the mud and dishevelled turf. Goosebumps stood out on my legs. She was standing by the greying goal-posts, straightening her dark blue football shirt, the words Umbro stretched across her breasts.

I looked at her for a long time, ignoring the shouts of the others about to resume play. I was in love. In love with Nicky. IN LOVE WITH ANOTHER WOMAN.

My game fell to pieces. I fluffed every move. My body acted as if both my legs, not just my feet, were embalmed in thick clay mud.

I didn't want to say goodbye to her at the end of the evening. I didn't want to say goodbye ever. I didn't want just friendship. Suddenly, I wanted a whole lot more. My head was filled with sensual images. I wanted to see her naked. I flushed. My legs stopped working altogether. Then my face drained of colour.

She came over at the end of the training session 'What's wrong?' she questioned me. 'Problems at home?' I nodded. I didn't know what to say. How could I possibly tell her that she was my problem? Then she made everything worse by putting her arm round my shoulder and telling me she was my friend and would always be there for me.

I felt that beneath all the camaraderie she was giving me sexual signals. Two days later she invited me round to babysit for her brother while her parents were out. She produced a tiny cuddly gorilla as a present to cheer me up. Then I knew. This wasn't just a friendly gift; it was loaded. I began to cry and she pressed me for answers. Under pressure, I blurted out the words, 'I am having problems dealing with the way I feel about you.' Relief. Release. But what now? My tears dried up with the shock of it. Was I really a lesbian? What did this mean? These feelings had appeared as quickly as a flash flood. Would they disappear just as quickly? In the absence of any other explanation for my escalating attraction, I fought desperately to come to terms with the only conclusion my logic could draw. I must be a lesbian.

We did no more than hold hands that night. It was as much as we felt able to cope with. But her hug felt so good. We were embarking on something entirely unfamiliar, the first female affair for both of us.

I spent the next week trying to back off, fighting with my feelings. I tried to kid myself this wasn't happening to me. Likewise, Nicky did the same. I remember one awful night spent sitting in her car, just looking at each other, bodies aching for one another. But we were both paralysed by social conditioning, which would not permit us to act. We were facing a huge insurmountable barrier and, oh, wouldn't boy meets girl have been so much simpler?

Within a week our feelings had consumed us. It took only a few drinks to loosen me up, to uproot my conscience. Alcohol knocked out cold the voice in my head telling me constantly that this was wrong and let my heart lead the way. Once the car had stopped we were in each other's arms in moments. 'I thought you were never going to kiss me,' she said to me that night.

From then on we were lovers. Everything I had struggled to do with men came so easily with Nicky. Social conditioning meant it felt wrong, yet it felt so fucking wonderful. Liberated, free. I remember thinking, if this is wrong I don't want to be right. Love had found me and I had found love. All my previous years felt like wasted ones, little more than long-winded dress rehearsals for the real thing. This was perfect love, conducted in secret and mostly in cold cars in dark lanes. We had nowhere to go; both of us were still living with our parents.

The intensity of our love was heightened by its illicit nature. Policemen knocking on the car windows, our parents rattling the keys in the front-door locks thirty minutes early. One hairy night we were downstairs in my mother's house, supposedly watching television. Then we heard the soft rhythmic padding of slippers on the stairs. Nicky rushed for her clothes, but I was so frightened I couldn't move. My naked body sat and awaited the worst confrontation possible. The longest sixty seconds ticked past and the slippers moved around at the foot of the stairs. Then they slowly started to ascend. I could imagine my mother's reaction on finding me naked with a man, but I thought she'd be a dead cert for a coronary on finding me naked with another woman.

The next evening Nicky turned up on my doorstep while I was in the bath preparing to go night-clubbing with Karen. I knew at once that something was wrong; she never turned up unannounced. Dressed only in a towel, I slipped out on to the porch. She couldn't see me again. Their television downstairs had blown up. Her father had gone up to her room to borrow hers. He had found one of my love-letters wedged underneath it. He had freaked out big time.

I couldn't believe this was the end. How could she say all the wonderful things she whispered in my ears last night, and dump me less than twenty-four hours later? It was so unfair. But I knew I wasn't giving up this love for anyone.

I was right. Within two days we were together again.

I couldn't deny I was in love with this woman, but all the while I had been going out with men on free nights in a desperate bid to keep up appearances and to preserve my own sanity. Of course, this did not go down too well with Nicky. She interpreted these misdemeanours as gross acts of infidelity. She said I could never decide who or what I really was. She was right. A titanic struggle was raging inside me. I spent most of my time strung up like a clock spring, a human grenade with the pin pulled out. To my horror, my interest in women was escalating, not dying the natural death I was secretly hoping for. Men just left me cold.

My increasing interest in women was confirmed to me in less than subtle ways. One day I was filling my car with £5-worth of unleaded petrol, but was so busy clocking a woman wandering across the forecourt with blonde hair and legs that went all the way up that I failed to notice the petrol counter zooming up to £6.50. I had to bow, scrape and grovel to the male petrol attendant, and I couldn't use any of my feminine allure either. My hair was short and I looked too butch to flirt.

These were months of intense discovery. I had discovered myself as a sexual person. It came as quite a surprise to find how passionate I was. Enter the bedroom bandit ... the quilt is my cape.

But Karen had set an agenda, and as her eternal copycat I felt compelled to follow it. Our six-month round-the-world trip, planned since we were little girls, was looming. Now I was not at all sure I wanted to go. Did I really need to follow Karen any more? More importantly, could I risk leaving Nicky and sacrifice the only real happiness I had ever known?

The seventh of April 1991 arrived far too quickly. First I wasn't going. Then I was. I didn't want to be at the receiving end of postcards from exotic places, I wanted to be sending them.

After five weeks of travelling I gave in. I was missing Nicky. I wanted her warm arms to wrap my frail body tight once more. I was sick. Sick of marching from city to city with my house on my back. I had discovered what it is like to be a tortoise and why they move so slowly.

When I phoned my mother to tell her I was coming home, she totally over-reacted. She had found herself a new boyfriend and was frightened my return would spoil things. Luckily, a guardian angel lay waiting in the wings, my nan. She offered to put me up for a few days and I ended up staying six months. She nicknamed me the pink panther because I was so quiet coming through the front door.

Things were not the same between Nicky and me upon my return. Our fairy tale was returned to its rightful owner . . . Hans Christian Andersen. I don't think she ever forgave me for leaving her. By September 1991 we had gone down separate tracks. I was devastated. I have never been good at handling rejection, but the loss of Nicky was all the more acute. She was the first woman I had ever loved. I felt that by leaving she had stolen a part of me.

I embarked on a period of self-destruction. I let people drag me down and convince me I was nothing. Nicky and I had to be kept apart by friends, we were so volatile together. We had a fight at a party once, the only time I have ever resorted to physical violence. She stuck her chin forwards and pointed to it, goading me to hit her. So I punched her and felt heaps better. Until she slapped me round the face. I burst into tears. I was full of bitterness, believing she had abandoned me just when I needed her most. My health suffered again, and so did my football. I was on the verge of being selected for the regional team but was unable to complete the last day of trials due to sudden and unexplained pains in my legs. On the evening of my twenty-fourth birthday I found out I had not been selected. I cried until I was exhausted.

But I picked myself up, dusted myself off, inspected my pride for superficial damage and prepared my torso for the next body-blow. I told myself I had to learn to keep my gloves up in front of my face.

Significantly, I had discovered that I was attracted to

women, not men. But it wasn't for another six months that I realised the full truth – that my relationship with Nicky had not been lesbian; it had been heterosexual. I had the mind of a man; I related to women as a male. This realisation was a massive relief. Suddenly I was free to be me. The seeds had begun to germinate.

Thursday 16 September 1993
For months now I have been a man with one foot cemented in the ground, turning round and round in circles, busy going nowhere. Trying to row a boat with only one oar. But I am believing in myself and in my future.

This is good because I saw Lisa in the pub last night and felt physically sick. Why do people always leave you when you need them most? Lisa was my fourth most significant relationship and the woman I was with when my transsexuality eventually bubbled up and emerged. In retrospect I realise that I had no right to expect her to stick by me – she had not known me long enough.

Last night I could hear her laughing all evening as though she didn't have a care in the world, as if our mad, passionate love-affair was a figment of my over-active imagination. Mind you, she always was a good actress. I wish I didn't love her so much. Life without her is lonely. I miss her warmth and our chemistry together. She was the one who looked warmly into my eyes and told me: 'It doesn't matter what you are. You are you, and I love you for it.' But being me just wasn't enough in the end.

I met Lisa, manager at a local plastics company, aged twenty-seven, six months ago. I had spent a week sunk deep in depression, and I was trying to cope with the realisation of my new-found identity as a female-to-male transsexual. It was a Thursday evening, and I had used all my strength of character to pull myself out of yet another all-time low. I was selling insurance at the time, and I issued short, sharp, motivating instructions to my brain. 'Go out and sell a policy,' I told myself.

I did and I went home pleased with myself, having tipped my emotional see-saw from down to up in a few short hours. In illicit celebration I opened the wardrobe door and fished it out: my man's suit. It hung on two interlocking hangers full of masculine promise. I slipped off my tight woollen skirt and tights, popped on some black socks and slid into its comforting creases. Then I surveyed myself in the mirror; it hurt me to see my real self. The suit had come from a Littlewoods catalogue because I was too scared to shop for it. It was shiny blue with wide lapels. Confident inside its comfortable woollen fabric with creases in all the right places, I decided to drive down to the pub for a drink, to be myself for the first time that day. I was really tired, but any excuse to get dressed up in male clothes was a good one.

I flung back the wooden door and noticed a friend, Jax, laughing at me as I struggled with my hand caught in the door handle. It was then that I noticed the unfamiliar young woman sitting next to her. She had short, spiky brown hair and sparkly green-brown eyes. She wore only touches of make-up and had a natural, earthy look about her. Not my type at all, but something about her spoke to me. I stood there in my suit, unsure how I should introduce myself. As woman? Or as man?

She broke the ice. 'Hi, I'm Lisa.' She was warm and friendly and all of this threw me off-guard. 'Pleased to meet you. I'm Martine.' In an instant I had lost my chance to introduce myself as Paul, but I sat down beside her in the space she made for me on the wooden bench and soon we were deep in conversation, which flowed easily, like the beer.

Lisa did not strike me instantly as drop-dead gorgeous, but there was something about her which appealed deeply to me. I had no idea whether she was gay or not. I didn't care. I fancied her. I noticed feminine touches like the gold ring on a chain around her neck, and the soft texture of her black silk blouse. Her eyes drew me in, and I wanted to know what was behind them. This was lust of an eerie kind. Then the bar bell rang. 'Last orders, please.' My hands felt clammy. People began to drink up and to leave. I wanted to see this girl again. I wanted to ask her out, but how? My ego was not the mountain it used to be when I was acting the part of a feminine woman; it was more like a speck of sand upon the floor. The bell rang again and she picked up her black leather bag and got up. 'Give me a call!' she shouted non-committally over her shoulder. 'I haven't got your phone number,' I replied.

Out in the street, as Lisa dug around in the glove compartment of her silver-blue Proton looking for a pen to give me her phone number, she seemed to have a change of heart. 'Fancy a coffee?' she questioned, looking directly into my eyes.

'Why not,' I said, chuckling to myself and recalling how I had come out for only one drink. I hate coffee, but it wasn't the coffee I was interested in.

I left, at the second attempt, at around four in the morning. Never before had I met someone who had excited so much instant passion inside me. This was the girl who introduced me to dewberry oil as our passion hit the burner, and whose kiss was always on my list – as we listened to Hall and Oates together – of the best things in life. And so began our furnace-hot love-affair. I had not planned to fall in love, but within weeks I found myself unable to imagine a time when I would not be able to hold her in my arms. Within six weeks I had moved in with her.

The first night we slept together I told Lisa I was a transsexual. I whispered it in her ear as we sat on a sofa holding each other close. As I uttered the words I half-expected her to react, slap me, jump up, threaten never to see me again. Instead, she nuzzled me and didn't flinch. 'Darling, I would fancy you if you were dressed in sack-cloth,' she murmured.

Bravely, she took my transsexualism on board. She called me Paul when we were alone together (being called Paul in bed made me feel ten feet tall). But in many respects I was still masquerading as Martine in public, at least for work. A job is a job, after all, and I was not yet feeling brave enough to make the decision that I knew to be inevitable.

Looking back, I realise this love-affair, wonderful as it was, served to distract me from my life plan, although Lisa tried so hard and even came with me to a meeting of the female-to-male transsexual group in Emmer Green. I had read about this meeting in a copy of the magazine *Boys Own*, which I began receiving when I became a member of the FTM Network. Initially, we didn't talk to anyone as we were dead nervous. Everyone was looking at everyone else. But eventually the ice was broken. It was difficult to come away feeling anything but positive, having met so many success stories. Many of the men there had made such convincing transitions to the male that it was hard to believe their biological origins. They had beards, firm handshakes, male mannerisms and stocky, muscular bodies. Most were hirsute. After the meeting, at which we listened to talks and met new friends, we arranged to go to a night-club. As we drove through town Lisa was ominously quiet. When I quizzed her she became defensive. 'I just want to go home,' she said quietly. I thought back to the plastics management ball three weeks earlier and began to notice a saddening pattern. I had wanted her to take me, but her words had been: 'You'll never get away with it.' I felt then that I was fighting for myself but she would not fight with me.

I realised I was masking lots of my problems. I was worried that Lisa would fall out of love with a depressive, so I played the happy fool, hiding my misery as well as I could.

But as the weeks passed by I was finding it increasingly difficult to keep up the façade; the gloss was fading on my clown's face. I knew that I had to become a man, but I was terrified that Lisa wouldn't love me any more. She thought she was with a woman and that was the way she wanted it. She liked me like that.

But the good times rolled on. One morning I sent her downstairs in her dressing-gown to get the post. Feeling mischievous, I locked her out and wouldn't let her back in until she shouted 'I love you' through the letterbox. A week later she gave me a gold wedding-ring. 'Your single days are over,' she told me.

But by August I had returned the gold band as a symbol of the end of our relationship, finished with the same fireworks with which it had begun. We had a blazing row and made up in a hotbed of passion, but decided it would be best if I looked for somewhere else to live. I thought I had found in Lisa everything I have ever wanted in a relationship. But Lisa was out of her depth in knowing what to do with me. She said she couldn't cope any more. She was too busy in her own demanding job to help me through my crisis, or maybe she just didn't love me enough. Who knows? I remember her as my dream lover to date; she will be a difficult act to follow. As I write this there are tears in my eyes.

Saturday 18 September 1993

I was trying to read my paper in an Earl's Court café this morning. An elderly man was intent on interrupting me. I thought nothing of him at first and then the penny dropped. 'Did I always wear make-up?' 'Did I have my hair cut at a female barber's?' Naive I must have been. I hadn't realised that Earl's Court is a hotbed of homosexual activity, literally. I left so fast I tripped over my legs on the way out. I am fairly open-minded; I am used to being a woman chatted up by straight men; I am used to being a woman chatted up by gay women. But being chatted up by a gay man who thought I too was a gay man was a whole new experience. Flattered? No. Just bloody confused. Well, wouldn't you be?

Monday 20 September 1993

I caught the train to London today for my first appointment with Dr Ellis Snitcher, the endocrinologist who has been recommended to me by a fellow female-to-male transsexual. This journey is bringing my dreams a step closer to reality. I had to use my birthday money to get up there, as the DSS again failed to provide me with a cheque on time this week.

I wore my best – my only – suit. The second I met Ellis my ego was boosted: here was a man even smaller than me. I'm five feet two, so he must have been only five feet tall. He had ginger hair and a warm, caring manner which immediately put me at ease. The consultation took place in his vast, airy sitting-room, which has a deep, green carpet and a selection of armchairs and sofas. He has a clinical room downstairs but avoids using it because he says it is easier for clients to relax and relate in a more domestic environment. I gripped my mug of tea tightly for comfort as I told him of my feelings and intentions.

When I had finished he explained that female-to-male transsexuals are far commoner than people believe. 'You are not alone,' he said, beaming a generous smile in my direction. He asked me to make one more visit to be sure in my own mind of the giant steps I will be taking, and then he would be willing to recommend the introduction of masculinising hormones. He explained what these would do.

'The body produces two types of steroids. The sex steroids, or anabolics, which build the body up. And the catabolics, which work with the metabolism to break things down. Testosterone is an anabolic steroid. Not only does it increase male characteristics, such as encouraging hair to grow and enlarging the voice-box so the voice deepens, but it also builds up muscles.'

He explained that testosterone given to a child will rapidly accelerate the onset of his puberty and sexual development, while giving it to a biological woman will masculinise her. But, he cautioned me, it has a number of potential drawbacks and side-effects. It can affect the level of fat in the blood, which can lead to increased cholesterol, furring up of the arteries and eventually heart disease. It is therefore very important to monitor the blood lipids using blood tests every six months.

'Introducing testosterone also negates the positive effect of oestrogens on heart disease. We would need to monitor you to check you are not at risk. Hormones can also affect liver function, so we'll measure your enzymes every six months to check they are stable. There's also the possibility of water retention.'

It was an avalanche of information, but nothing I did not know already. I have a degree in biochemistry and had done my research prior to coming to a decision about my life.

Then he spoke about all the exciting, magical, liberating things that will happen to me within the first year of fortnightly injections.

'Your voice will drop in pitch. You will experience profound changes in libido. You will grow hair on your face and chest. The hair you already grow, on your arms and legs, will thicken.'

Let the music play. This is melody to my ears. A new rhythm for my soul.

He said that it is very difficult to work out how much testosterone each client needs. The blunderbuss approach is employed initially; a starting dose of 250mg of Sustanon, the brand name for artificial testosterone, every fortnight is standard. This dose will be maintained for about two years until my changes have taken place, and will then be dropped to around 100mg every two weeks. This should be sufficient to prevent breakthrough bleeding.

Ellis reiterated that I was not alone, and not just because there are more transsexuals in the community than people believe, but because crises of gender are far more widespread than that. In campaigning mode, he finished like a lawyer with the impassioned statement: 'I would challenge anyone to put their hand on their heart and say, "I have not had some form of sexual confusion at some point in my life." Children often experience homosexual bonding, even if it is only through playing doctors and nurses or examining and comparing their developing bodies. Although most people show overtly heterosexual characteristics, we are all at different points in a state of flux.

'Gays and lesbians have a stronger same-sex interest. They want to know why they can't explore other people of their own gender.

'Transsexuals have a mind versus body dislocation; their own body undermines their own sexual image. Their biological gender is determined by chromosomes, but their brain doesn't accept this gender. The hypothalamus, that area of the brain which functions as a sexual switch, has a different perspective. This may be due to an imbalance of male/female hormones when the person was still a foetus.'

I left Ellis's surgery feeling like a boy rabbit who had just discovered girl rabbits.

Monday 27 September 1993

I spent the afternoon being poked and prodded like a lab rat in the various departments of the Royal Berkshire Hospital. I was subjected to an MOT; X-ray, ECG and blood tests, then a medical examination by one of the consultants. I felt like an impostor when I had to take my male clothes off to reveal the vulnerable female body which I despise. I am very embarrassed about it; it undermines my confidence and, for obvious reasons, I prefer to keep it covered up whenever possible. Without clothes I appear as an awkward female. I would not be taking this action if there were an alternative. I am not making a choice, I am simply taking the only course open to me. But I have tried desperately hard in the past to accept my female body, even resorting to super-femininity in an effort to convince myself I was female.

I used to take my clothes off for money. I was a full-time stripagram, probably not the occupation that springs to mind for a biological woman who goes on to seek gender reassignment to the male role. I started out doing a few strips to prove my femininity and ended up doing over three hundred bookings. It was quite a fun way of earning a living ... most of the time. Life was many things, but it was certainly not dull. I have memories of being pulled over by the police three times in one week. Each time I was wearing a different costume. On one occasion the conversation ran something like this: 'You're probably not going to believe this, officer.' Officer addresses kangaroo sitting behind wheel of a blue five series BMW, handcuffs in pouch: 'Hmm, somehow I don't think I am!' I was a man masquerading as a woman of many guises . . . policewoman, French maid, naughty nurse, jilted bride and many others. Oh, yes, I made a variety of fantasies come true.

At this stage, two years ago I would have described myself as a feminine lesbian. I was expending all my energy trying to prove I was something I wasn't. I played the part superbly and had most people fooled, even myself. I even did some modelling for a while, but while my breasts seemed to have a life force of their own – I've lost count how many times men exclaimed 'You don't get many of them to the pound' – I began to hate myself more and more. Perhaps that's why I behaved like this. My female body just felt like a mask; it certainly wasn't part of me, so I wasn't ashamed to flaunt it.

Fifty bookings down the line I wrote a piece of prose one night when my sensation of crisis was at fever-pitch.

The eye perceives this body as a single form, but each day a fragment of a new and conflicting personality is being born. How can I be so many people all at the same time? Intense yet carefree. A shy extrovert. A child-like grown-up making mud pies in the dirt. Under a thousand guises I am me. A lesbian lover in search of the right man. I am a footballer and a stripper, a youngster whose screams can be heard on the big dipper. As I cavort on the stage, a nymphomaniac nun, of one fact I am sure; I shall run until my feet are sore. I will not rest or abandon my quest until my dreams come true and these murky waters turn blue.

On shopping expeditions at this time I was always inexplicably drawn to the raunchiest outfit in the shop. I made sure I turned heads wherever I went, but it is only now I am able to analyse the reasons for this rather extreme behaviour. I was trapped. I wanted to be as successful as my twin sister but had no genuine programmed motivation. It was shit or bust. Trying to compete would often reduce me to tears in the privacy of my own room. I wanted to be the best me I could. I had always been a success, both academically and in sport, but being the best me really meant being a success as a woman. I had the boobs from hell, and wanted to be streamlined. There were no alternatives apart from a suicide leap from Clifton suspension bridge. I was empty inside, although when wearing my spray-on velvet hot-pants I had to beat off my suitors with a stick.

No, the problem was that I was dressing my body, not me. Deep inside I felt no better than that awful sticky stuff you scrape off your shoe. I felt hollow and doomed. I was feeding off the compliments as a tapeworm feeds off its hosts, greedily, desperately and parasitically. I kept my red lipstick carefully outlined, worn as my painted-on smile. I had made myself, my body, into a diversion. While I flounced around, masquerading as a walking, talking, flirting feminine icon, no one would guess my real identity. Would they?

Christmas 1991 came. And went. Over the next six months I continued working as a stripagram. Not a choice occupation for one of my educational background, but I knew what I was doing and I liked it. In this situation I could have the men eating out of my hands and this made me feel powerful. I couldn't join them so I would beat them. In my eyes I was the one doing the exploiting; men go weak when they see black stockings and suspenders. But once the act was over I would leave the pub or hall to the sound of cheers ringing in my ears, and the loneliness would return. I would grab my clothes and my wages – £50 for fifteen minutes of exhibitionism – and run.

But after eighteen months I began to feel uncomfortable with eager eyes caressing my half-naked body. It wasn't the scrutiny I minded, just that I was feeling more uncomfortable than ever before about my own body. My hair was now cropped very short, and one day someone hit a raw nerve with a comment I overheard as I darted off-stage: 'You can tell it's a bloke by the way it walks. Get yourself a woman's haircut. It's a bloke in drag.' My sense of internal confusion was day by day growing stronger. My maleness was now impossible to hide and was popping out all over the place, like Dolly Parton's boobs in a trainer bra. It began to get tedious tearing my clothes off just to prove – to the lecherous crowds and to me – that I was a woman. I was having as much difficulty posing as a woman as the average man would. I had pushed my body too far. I had tried to do something super-feminine and had ended up confirming my worst fears. I was turning into a man. I even overheard a leering, beer-bellied punter snort to his friend: 'That's half-man, half-woman, that is.' I was indebted to him. He had perfectly described me. I was a feminine body encasing a masculine mind.

It was the middle of summer and I was sat at the wheel wearing a ski-suit. I began to feel as though I would suffocate as the mercury line moved close to 30°C. I unzipped the padded suit and drove with it draped around my waist, the arms falling across the handbrake. You get some strange requests as a stripagram. The lady at the social club had specifically requested a girl in a ski-suit for the ski-instructor's fortieth birthday. I found myself cursing the idiot who had asked me to dress up like this in the middle of July.

I was sitting at the traffic-lights praying that they would change quickly to green. A man had pulled up next to me in his metallic green Audi, and his eyes were out on stalks. It is not every day you see a woman driving in her underwear.

When I arrived at the social club in rural Berkshire, I parked my skis outside. I made my entrance and removed my tinted goggles and thick gloves. I felt a bead of perspiration form on my forehead and the usual rush of adrenalin as I approached my unsuspecting victim. He was grinning from ear to ear as my titillating undergarments were revealed. It was difficult to make myself heard above the laughter, but the background noise took nothing away from the visual effects.

As I sat on Clive's lap, my red lipstick glistening on each of his cheeks, I began to read my poem. This was my favourite part, the time where I could show off my poetic prowess . . .

'I've written you a poem, Clive, now that you've turned forty. And I've been sent here to confirm that you are still quite naughty . . .'

The men were impressed. Clive's wife was less impressed,

as he scooped me up in his gorilla-like arms and carried me out of the hall, to the delight of the audience. If I remember rightly, she complained afterwards. Apparently it was 'not what she had expected at all'. What she really meant was that she had not expected him to enjoy it quite so much.

I had to do a booking on a river-boat once, at Boulter's Lock, Maidenhead. I had been booked to blend in as a waitress, in my shiny blue French maid's outfit, serving champagne to a party of middle-aged businessmen on a trip to Windsor races. I was the prize in a raffle, which was fixed, since I had the winning ticket poking out of the top of my left stocking.

When I had completed my act, I climbed off the boat with my clothes dishevelled. I opened the white envelope containing my money and realised that instead of a £50 note I had been given two tickets to Windsor races. I had to run up the river after the boat, my black stilettos sticking in the towpath, to point out the mistake. The organiser was so pissed he had given me the wrong envelope, and apologised profusely.

The most uncomfortable booking I ever did was for the head lad at a racing yard. I stood on the cobbles one cold November afternoon in my black G-string, surrounded by stable lads and jockeys, with hay strewn around, and the racehorses whinnying impatiently for their evening feed. My nipples stood out like the Egyptian pyramids, which no doubt added to the attraction. It took me three hours to get warm afterwards.

On another occasion I was booked to turn up in a business suit for a job interview. As I bluffed my way through the questions posed by my unsuspecting interviewer, I tried to keep a huge smirk in check. I could see out of the corner of my left eye the other employees filing into the office, through the glass window behind him. 'Have you any questions?' Mr Andrews asked me, peering through his misted spectacles. 'Yes,' I replied assertively. 'Have you ever been completely stitched up?' I would have loved to have been able to frame the expression on his face as the reality of his predicament dawned.

The largest audience I have ever performed in front of was at Lakeside Cabaret Club in Camberley. Employees of Magnet and Southern had travelled from as far afield as Bristol. Derek met me outside and kept bringing me out neat vodkas as I waited for the speeches to end. By the time I was due to go on stage I did not feel one hundred per cent sober, and I could not see the audience at all as huge spotlights were dazzling me and shining in my eyes. It was like performing in front of Gestapo searchbeams. Still, I can't have done too badly, as Derek thrust a £10 note into my hand as he escorted me to my car. This was quite something ... tips are practically unheard of in the cheap-skate world of the professional stripagram.

Chapter Three

Tuesday 28 September 1993
I paid a visit to the HMV music store in Oxford Street just to see the singer/songwriter Beverly Craven this morning. She did a live performance of songs from her new 'Love Scenes' album. Beverly was truly wonderful. Tall and beautiful and so sexy. One day I am going to have a woman just like that. I had my photo taken with her but could only manage a coy smile. I went weak in the presence of her beauty.

Thursday 30 September 1993
My new girlfriend, Sarah, called round to see me this evening. She told me she had had a row with her mum and stepdad last night. I knew by the look of disquiet on her face that it was about me. I have spent only an hour in their company yet they think they know me. Drawing upon their vast knowledge of gender dysphoria they have pronounced me as nothing more than a frustrated lesbian. Oh, ignorance, be still and get out of my way!

I was really upset. I don't know why, I should be getting used to it by now. I had to go out for a drink to prevent myself breaking furniture.

Monday 4 October 1993
I told myself in my sleep last night that every day in every

way I am getting better and better. I'm having to draw on all my powers of positive thinking these days.

I braved the wind and the rain to visit the Register Office to obtain a copy of my birth certificate for my pending name change. I skipped all the way home, like Skippy the bush kangaroo.

When I look back over my life I can see at least ten years of thick, choking fog. The emptiness and loneliness still break me up inside. I have single-handedly hacked my way through a jungle of confusion, finding answers only as I stumble upon them. Trying to keep pace with my development has required great emotional agility, and the physical effort involved has been like trying to keep up with Linford Christie on a training run.

But I have stumbled into a clearing, a clearing in which I can stand back and take stock. For the first time I can see a future for myself. I have had to go through all of this just to obtain what most people take for granted as their birthright. Even without realising it, most people are euphoric about their own sex. My twin sister loves being a woman and truly knows how to use her femininity to her best advantage. She is horrified at the thought of me losing my breasts. But that is the reaction of a woman.

I am a heterosexual male. The term heterosexual refers to my sexuality. The term male I use to describe my gender identity. I have no doubts about either of them. The bands that make up the spectra of gender and sexuality are as diverse as the colours of the rainbow or variations in eye colour. Sometimes there is blue and brown, but more often shades in between. I have done time in various imprisoning categories in my personal evolution and have met people of many varied sexual persuasions. I have respect for all of them, and I will not tolerate prejudice in any form. We do not live in a perfect world and that's what makes it so interesting.

I will probably never own a male organ, and that is a huge disappointment to me. In my mind I have one, but it's a shame Big Jack is invisible. I have traded his flesh and blood for insight, however. Having lived as a woman for so long I know so much about them and that insight is precious to me.

Wednesday 6 October 1993
I am worrying myself stupid at the moment as I prepare to leap into the unknown. I pray it will not be a case of out of the frying-pan and into the fire. In only a few weeks I will have my first injection of oily testosterone derivatives. I am hoping that before too long all the pain I feel inside will be just a bitter memory. Being a scientist, I feel compelled to use myself as the subject of a scientific study. I will keep a log of all changes and photographs of myself at various stages. I am something of a guinea-pig. Sex changes have not been around long enough for the medical profession to know in full the long-term effects of such hormone treatment.

Anyone can be born transsexual. The support organisation for British transsexuals, Gender Identity Consultancy Services, reports that on its books are doctors, nurses, dentists, civil servants, manual and military workers, lawyers and company directors. There is even a male-to-female bursar at an Oxford college. The trust estimates that there are twenty-five thousand transsexuals within the UK, and approximately 5,000 have undergone gender reassignment surgery.

Clearly, as a group they are as diverse as any other section of society; what they have in common is their compelling need to alter their bodies and bring them into line with their minds. Research has shown that transsexuals have slightly higher intelligence than the average, and they tend to be creative or artistic types.

Approximately four hundred people undergo gender reassignment operations in Britain every year; three physical men for every physical woman seek the therapy. Only twenty-five per cent of the actual operations are performed on women becoming men, which implies that it is easier for women to live as pseudo-men in our society without feeling that surgery and hormone treatment are vital. To use a crude analogy, a woman who dons trousers, a tie and a button-down shirt, cuts her hair short and butch is more socially acceptable than a man who wears a dress, puts his long hair in curlers, wears make-up and calls himself Tracey.

The number of people seeking to change their sex has grown by more than a third in less than a decade. Dr Don Montgomery, director of the gender identity clinic at Charing Cross Hospital, says that the number of new patients grew from 180 in 1985 to 250 in 1993. Surveys in the UK and The Netherlands also suggest that the number of transsexuals has tripled since the 1970s.

Tuesday 19 October 1993

I have made huge strides since my last diary entry two weeks ago. Small steps for mankind, but giant steps for me. I floated home following the signing of my Statutory Declaration feeling like a new man. Once all my documents have been changed I will no longer have to suffer the embarrassment of being called by my female name or being referred to as Miss.

Prepared by a solicitor, a Statutory Declaration is cheaper than the more expensive Deed Poll. Nowadays there is little difference. An SD is accepted by the passport office, etc. when presented along with a doctor's letter:

> *To whom it may concern. This is to confirm that my patient Miss Martine Hewitt is currently undergoing gender*

reassignment to the male role, and as part of this process has changed her name by Statutory Declaration to Mr Paul Hewitt. Your assistance in making the relevant changes in your records and in preserving full confidentiality would be appreciated.

At the moment, before surgery, I am likely to be able to have only the name on my passport changed, not my gender, despite the fact that these entries will be blatantly inconsistent. After surgery my sex can be updated. I can also change my National Insurance record to Paul, but the record of my gender is unalterable either now or after surgery. This means that my future pension entitlement will be based on my birth gender. I will be forced to retire as a woman at sixty unless there is a change in the law.

My income tax records and driving licence can be updated with the name Paul, as can bank statements and credit cards. My NHS medical card can be reissued, but the code number will always label me by including a symbol indicating 'sex change'. I can obtain new O- and A-level examination certificates and can write to request that records be amended to cover future enquiries by a third party.

But I will never truly escape my birth gender. In one crucial respect I will remain a woman. The most crucial evidence of identity – my birth certificate – is utterly unalterable. On this document someone born a woman remains a woman to the grave. This means, ironically, that I can spend my whole life fighting against my original gender only to have it written on my death certificate. This is the ultimate insult. I, Paul, will always be Martine, and my death will swell the statistics for female mortality. Complete escape from the constraints of my birth is impossible.

Equally damning is the fact that transsexuals do not have the same rights under the law as other members of society. As the law stands at the moment I will never be able to marry in Great Britain. I can fall in love, but should I wish to enter into a lifelong legal partnership with a woman I will be barred from having it legally recognised. By marrying the woman I adore I will be seen to be marrying someone of my own sex, despite the fact that it would be patently ridiculous for me to marry a man. Sex-change operations break no law and are endorsed by the establishment by being available on the NHS. The problem is the bewildering lack of legal follow-through.

Even more damning, a post-operative transsexual who marries someone of the same gender (i.e. if I married a man) can have his or her marriage made void if he or she cannot or does not consummate it. Yet in most of Europe, the USA, Eastern-bloc countries and Australia transsexuals are granted the same civil rights and responsibilities as others of their post-operative gender.

The British attitude is appallingly backward. I also have no protection under the Sex Discrimination Act; I can be dismissed from my job on the grounds of my transsexualism if I do not tell my employer my situation, despite it not being relevant, and he later finds out. By telling him or her at a job interview inevitably I risk prejudicial treatment. We're damned if we tell and we're damned if we don't.

I am a law-abiding citizen and have no intention of ending up in jail, but there is a further irony should I be convicted of a crime and face prison. Despite my new gender I would go to a women's jail. I guess I could live with that, being locked up with a bunch of women, but, with my beard and my muscles, would it not be rather inappropriate?

In February 1991 a male-to-female transsexual, Deborah Hart, who had lived as a woman for four years was sent to a male prison by a female judge. Deborah had had a sex-change operation to remove her penis and testicles four years earlier when she was twenty-four. Her lawyer, Felicity Hammerton, made an emotional plea to the judge to spare her from 'the nightmare' inside London's Brixton jail. She pointed out that Deborah, with her long strawberry-blonde hair, would be treated as a freak. She said that while awaiting trial her client had already been beaten up, and alluded to 'other things she doesn't wish to talk about'. But Southwark Crown Court judge Mary Arden QC ignored the request. Deborah was jailed for obtaining property by deception. A heroin addict, she admitted cheating her Brighton landlord out of £2,000 after promising to have sex with him. Clearly, she deserved some measure of punishment, but certainly did not deserve the humiliation of having her new gender ignored in the process of that punishment being administered. The judge showed no understanding, compassion or respect for her psychological welfare, yet it was another government system, the NHS, which actively supported and encouraged Deborah to undergo gender reassignment. Where is the back-up?

Similar cases of unfair treatment highlight the legal problems that transsexuals face over entrenched attitudes which make it illegal for them to update their gender on their birth certificates following surgery. Not only can we not be convicted of a crime in our new gender, but we are not seen as victims in our new gender. A post-operative male-to-female, the opposite change to me, cannot be charged with prostitution. Instead, she would be found guilty of soliciting, which carries a two-year maximum sentence rather than a £500 fine. If a male-to-female transsexual is raped, her attacker will be charged with indecent assault, for which the maximum sentence is just ten years and not life, as is the case for rape.

Wendy Clifton, a male-to-female transsexual, was sexually

harassed by two workmates in 1992. They prodded her new silicone breasts – product of a £6,000 sex-change operation a year before – and lifted up her skirt. But because Wendy was born Raymond the culprits were charged with indecently assaulting a *man*. Wendy planned to launch an historic legal battle at the European Court of Human Rights to have their crime recorded as indecent assault against a *woman*. Wendy, then aged forty-one, said: 'The surgeon who carried out my sex change is prepared to say I'm female. I pay my tax and National Insurance as a single woman, but when it comes to justice I'm discriminated against. The Crown Prosecution Service would only bring charges for indecent assault against a man even though I'll be listed on the charge sheets as Wendy Ann Clifton. I lived as a woman for eighteen months before my operation and I lead a normal sex life as a woman.'

Wendy was not the first to think of the European Court of Human Rights. The famous model and former Bond girl Caroline 'Tula' Cossey was born a boy, Barry, in 1956. She underwent surgery aged twenty-seven after an unhappy childhood in which she never fitted into the male role. After gender reassignment she became a professional model, adorned the pages of *Playboy* and had a string of boy-friends and admirers. In two autobiographies and numerous awareness-raising television and radio appearances she stated her femininity. Yet under British law she could not legally marry. Her first marriage, to Elias Fattel, broke down when her husband's parents discovered the truth about their daughter-in-law and he was sucked away from her and back into the bosom of the Jewish community. When Caroline met and fell in love with Canadian David Finch in 1991 they married at a Presbyterian church in the USA. Disillusioned with life in Britain, the couple emigrated there, but should Tula ever return to Britain her marriage to David will be null and void.

At home, December 1994 (*Rebecca Meagher*)

My parents' wedding, 1966

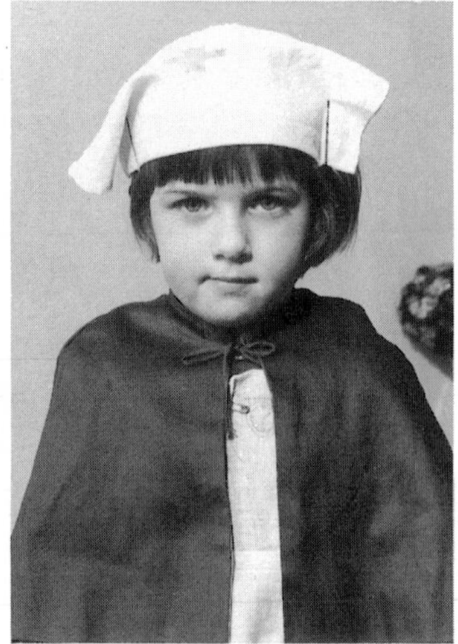

Aged eight, I didn't take kindly to being dressed up as a nurse

School photograph 1975 with Karen, left

I was already acting the role of the protective brother

Penis envy from an early age!

Running home to third place in the Berkshire cross-country championships, 1983 (*Mike Nicholson*)

Cross country at Englefield Park on Easter Lady, aged seventeen (*T. Wilder*)

At the MAFF sports day, 1988, I was voted Best All-Round Female Athlete

Twenty-first birthday in Corfu with Karen, left

'Sorry mate, no speak Swedish', Stockholm ferry, 1989

Cutting a dash on the dance floor with Crocodile Dundee, Helsinki, 1989

Cheers! Leaving Finland after a work placement there in 1989

With my dad on graduation day, Bath University, June 1990

Fortunately, there is a faction of MPs who want transsexuals to be given equal rights. Press For Change is an organisation chaired by Alex Carlile QC MP dedicated to pushing for legal reform. Earlier this month *The Times* published a letter from Mr Carlile and two other MPs campaigning for recognition for the rights of transsexuals. They wrote:

Sir,
We write out of concern for the individual liberties of transsexuals. We believe that they are a misunderstood and maligned minority. Most live responsible and law-abiding lives, have lasting and stable relationships, and make a strong contribution to the community.

Daily, however, they face the problem of not being allowed by the present state of British law to live in their acquired gender. The law requires them to be labelled as freaks throughout their remaining lifetime, despite the fact that there is now clear and respected medical evidence that transsexualism arises from biological and physiological causes.

In the cases of Rees (1986) and Cossey (1990) the European Court of Human Rights recommended the need for appropriate legal measures to be kept under review, having regard particularly to scientific and societal developments. In September 1989 the European Parliament passed a resolution which called on member states to grant legal recognition to transsexuals. In April 1993 calls for more humane laws were made at a Council of Europe colloquy, 'Transsexualism, Medicine and the Law'.

Some countries within and outside Europe have already made changes. Germany has a successful model for scrutinising the transsexual process, individual cases, and allowing full individual liberties where appropriate. Within the common law jurisdiction, South Australia has enlightened laws upon the subject.

After the Cossey judgment your then religious affairs correspondent suggested (September 29, 1990) that neither the Church nor the Government should be satisfied to leave things as they then were. That well justified statement has gone unheeded for far too long.
Yours faithfully,
Alex Carlile (Lib Dem)
Jerry Hayes (Con)
Lynne Jones (Lab)
House of Commons, October 1, 1993

I hope to see these changes in my lifetime. It may be only a couple of years before we are accorded the rights we deserve. But if the situation is bad in Britain, consider France. It was only in December 1992 that French legislation even recognised sex-change operations when France's highest appeal court ruled that transsexuals have the right to state their new gender on government documents! *C'est incroyable!* Other measures must feel to French transsexuals like an even more distant dream.

My next big step forward was to pay a second visit to see Ellis in London on 15 October. He has now written to my doctor recommending that I commence hormone therapy. I feel that the time is ready to begin my crusade for transsexuals everywhere. The motivating strength of this is in direct proportion to the intensity of the emotional pain I have suffered. I have decided to do an article for the *Daily Express*. The money will help me buy a word processor so I can launch my writing career, but I also want to stand up for what I am. I want to show that while I am unashamed, the situation with regard to transsexuals' legal rights is shameful. I dream of a world where we are not castigated and subjected to prejudice, but where we will be viewed as individuals who are genuinely suffering through no fault of our own from gender dysphoria.

I was interviewed over lunch by Jane Warren of the *Daily Express*. She had my attention, as she had soft eyes and legs that went all the way up. I felt my masculinity threatened by her sheer size; she stood head and shoulders above me. In just two days' time I will have gone national tabloid. Will I be held up to the world as a hero or a freak? Am I being either incredibly brave or incredibly stupid? Naive is a word that springs to mind. But I know that while transsexuals continue to cower in the shadows we will remain as freaks worthy of national headlines. I strongly believe in the power of the individual to change things.

Wednesday 27 October 1993

It is six days since I made it on to the front and centre pages of the *Daily Express* on my mother's birthday. Waiting for the article to be published – I had not seen the content – was like awaiting my execution. I was down at the newsagent's at 8 a.m. on the twenty-first and was initially horrified to see my photograph on the front-page blurb. I paid my thirty-two pence and took my chances. Thankfully, it was sympathetic and insightful. Within hours the communal payphone downstairs at home had become my own personal hotline. I also had the *News of the World* on my doorstep three times. The reporter appeared at my door like an apparition. Panic had set in and my imagination was veering away in a supernatural dimension. She had a ghost-like quality and reminded me of the woman in the horror film *Carrie*, with her long black hair and long winter coat. Her face was beseeching and seemed to be beckoning me into the danger zone. I shut the door in her face, wondering how on earth the *News of the World* had found out my address; the *Daily Express* had not given it to anyone. I felt frightened, and my heart was beating like a tom-tom drum.

I had two television offers, from *The Big Breakfast* and *UK*

Living. I declined the offer of sitting on the bed with Paula Yates. I could not imagine why *The Big Breakfast* would want me on their show, except to ridicule me in front of millions of viewers. But I accepted *UK Living*. I also agreed to do an interview for *Bella* magazine. More importantly, I was contacted by a literary agent with a view to publishing my autobiography.

I have always had stars in my eyes but never dreamed I would achieve notoriety for such bizarre reasons. This was not my game-plan, but as Jan Morris says in her seminal work about her transsexual journey, 'If life hands you a lemon, make lemonade', or words to that effect.

My head is a whirlpool of jumbled-up emotions. I am trying to keep pace with the events of the past few days, but although I haven't yet had my first injection I can already feel my new life beginning.

I visited my GP this afternoon. He has agreed to prescribe hormones indefinitely, and as I left his office I wanted to shout at all the empty sniffling faces in the surgery: 'I'm going to be a real man!' I'm on a repeat prescription, and once every two months I will be supplied with four injectable capsules of Sustanon.

Next stop was the chemist for my exciting prescription. I handed over this precious, life-transforming piece of paper, and while I waited for the chemist to dispense my precious vials I was irresistibly drawn to the counter displaying shaving-foam and Gillette razors. I had to get a grip on myself as a tear threatened to journey down my left cheek.

My post came bearing good tidings. I received a letter from Jane Warren of the *Daily Express* telling me of her support. Also enclosed was a letter from a reader, June Cowley of Portslade. She touched my heart with her words of encouragement: 'Good luck to you, my boy!' I nearly cried again. I have waited a long time to hear such words.

Thursday 28 October 1993
Today was a super-deep depression. The accumulated grief of the last three years could not be suppressed. I let the tears spring easily from my face as I felt my soul cleaving. As they slid down my cheeks I felt they were carrying away all the pain from deep inside.

Monday 1 November 1993
Today is the day. Day One of my gender reassignment treatment. I walked to the surgery, a twenty-five-minute stroll down through a small housing estate on the outskirts of Reading. My appointment was for 4.45 and I had to hold myself back; my feet kept wanting to break into a run. The sky was a rich velvet blue and wispy white clouds scudded along at high altitude. A crisp wind made me shiver, and I pulled my black bomber jacket tighter around me. I swung open the double doors of the surgery and was told I would have to wait thirty minutes. I could feel the tension mounting in my chest, compressing me. I don't enjoy injections and this fear was mingling with the significance of the contents of the chemist's paper bag in my hands and inducing a state of panic. My boots squeaked on the plastic floor as I shuffled my feet around, agitated, as if an army of ants was marching in my underpants.

A light went on outside the treatment room. It was my turn. Sister Ellen Lord gave me a sympathetic smile and I followed her into her room. She is about thirty and deft with a needle. Not a woman to be trifled with, I felt. On the floor was a cushion shaped like a pink liquorice allsort with a black middle. 'I regularly give intramuscular injections but not for the reason you're here,' she said with a twinkle. I leaned against the paper-covered bed and dropped my trousers, trying to relax. It was over in a second. I felt a deep, throbbing, good sensation as the cold fluid spread into my flesh. There were no regrets, no turning back, just pure, unadulterated testosterone.

I arose from the bed a calm and collected man and thanked Ellen for her time. It was then I realised that my buttock was killing me. My elation slipped a notch and I hobbled out of the consulting room. Sarah had come to meet me and was immediately by my side. She drove me back to her house in her van, considerately trying to avoid the bumps in the road, and as I'm writing this I am leaning on the opposite cheek, feeling stressed out, weak and rather pathetic.

Tuesday 2 November 1993

I cried my eyes out last night in a moment of exquisite sexual release. I am becoming more and more male between the sheets. I felt as though I really did have a penis. For the first time ever I felt completely sexually fulfilled and satiated. This is attributed largely to my involvement with Sarah, a woman who treats me completely as a male, not as the woman I have left behind.

When I first discovered myself as a sexual person it frightened me – big time! Whenever I had been in the company of men, being treated as a woman, I was as cold and unresponsive as a pound of cod at a fish market. So imagine my surprise at discovering this wild, roaring animal who is difficult to contain. I am so passionate that at times I feel quite haunted, knowing I do not have the normal outlet for my very male sex drive. A song which springs to mind is 'I Can't Get No Satisfaction'.

I am always the dominant, aggressive force in bed. I like to enjoy total control. Most men keep their brains in their underpants, but it is not their fault. I blame it on the testosterone. The brain has little control over the magnetic forces of nature. Sarah makes me feel good at a time when I really hate everything about myself. No one hates themselves more than transsexuals. Sarah says all the right things. I don't know what I would have done if she hadn't been there for me.

It is true that having a penis does not make you a man, but it is bollocks to disregard its significance or importance to self-esteem. My heart is permanently broken because I haven't got one. The pain, if I stop to think about it, is worse than a knife twisting inside me. It will not stop me from seeking happiness, from leading a normal life, but I cannot put my hand on my heart and say it does not matter to me. Men have suffered deep depression through feelings of inadequacy because they have a small one. But having a small one is infinitely better than none at all. I sank into a blissful state and expected a night of deep, satisfying rest. It was not to be.

I was back in the surgery and could see the plastic-covered medical posters lining the partition walls. Ellen emerged from her cell dressed in stark Victorian nurses' apparel. When she mouthed my name she stared at me and I felt immediately self-conscious. Then I realised why. All around my shoulders were long, fragrant strands of blonde hair. I scrambled to contain the flaxen growth and piled it back on top of my head, securing it with an assortment of pins, but it fell down again, longer than ever, swirling around my breasts, luxurious and long. I tried again to hide the hair behind my head, but it was growing thicker and longer and faster, like a runaway spaghetti-making machine. I looked up and saw that I was on my own, the surgery was deserted and I was standing naked, more feminine than ever, hair like a mane reaching down my back.

Thursday 4 November 1993

I must be patient, for it will be a few months yet before I am able to observe significant physical changes, but I feel that the emotional changes are already apparent. I have far greater confidence simply because I am moving forwards now rather than backwards. I crave my next injection in a fortnight. Eventually, I will expect my body hair to increase, my muscles to thicken, my periods to stop and an Adam's apple, and a correspondingly deeper voice, to develop. After a year of hormones I plan a mastectomy, which is often followed by a hysterectomy. I'm not even thinking about lower surgery. My head has quite enough to deal with at present.

I could have metaidoplasty, where my own bits are rearranged to look a bit more male. Or the cutting-edge phalloplasty, which is something of an imprecise art in Britain. Many female-to-males opt for a prosthetic penis and await advances in technology. In the USA, Switzerland and Holland phalloplasty is more advanced but prohibitively expensive. The result is a phallus which looks natural, is sensitive and can achieve an erection. The biggest problem is creating and attaching a new urethra, the tube along which urine passes down the length of the penis. For some female-to-male transsexuals being able to pee like a man is crucial. Others are more concerned with sexual function alone, which can make the surgery simpler.

Now for the nitty gritty, which revolts me. A radial section of skin is taken from the forearm, and rib cartilage or a piece of bone is used as a stiffener. In some cases a vacuum pump is placed inside which allows the phallus to be flaccid or erect. The forearm skin which is used already has its own network of nerves and blood vessels, and micro-surgery grafts these on to the existing vessels and nerves in the groin. The shape of the glans at the head of the penis can be constructed by grafting a small piece of the vaginal wall on to the tip. The penis has good sensation because the forearm nerves are intact and the clitoris is incorporated into the base of the penis. A scrotum can be made by cutting and stitching the labia majora after each side has been filled with a prosthetic testis made of silicone.

The Six Million Dollar Man or Frankenstein's Monster?

My friends the male-to-female transsexuals go down a slightly different route. Although they take hormones before opting for surgery, no amount of hormone therapy can alter the pitch of the male voice, as the voice-box cannot shrink. Instead, voice coaching is vital, especially for talking on the phone where there are no secondary sexual characteristics to prove that their voice belongs to a woman. Neither can hormones prevent beard growth. This can be achieved only through expensive electrolysis, a long and usually painful process.

Genital surgery for male-to-females is of two types and private treatment can cost £5,500–£8,000. Non-interactive surgery removes the penis and testes and forms the labia. But full gender reassignment is achieved by vaginoplasty. This state-of-the-art surgery creates a vagina in a biological male so that heterosexual intercourse is possible. The penile skin is formed into a tube and a cavity is made between the rectum and the bladder. Into this space the skin tube is inverted, forming a vagina. The urethra is shortened and repositioned slightly above the vaginal entrance – as it would be in a genetic female. A clitoris is created by using the tip of the glans penis and transplanting it together with all its nerve endings and placing it just inside the top of the vaginal lips – again where it would be in a genetic female. Most of these procedures are very successful and the results are virtually indistinguishable from biological females.

Before a transsexual undertakes gender reassignment it is vital that he or she considers whether he or she will pass successfully in the new gender in close, everyday contact with people. This involves scrutinising one's vocabulary, mannerisms and personality. To make an unconvincing change and never to be fully accepted in the new gender would be deeply distressing and disorientating. A brawny, muscular man over six feet tall will find it harder to pass as a woman than a man of five feet six inches who has a small bone structure. I have very small hands, which are my giveaway, and I will probably never recover from being a dwarf of five feet two inches. My parents are both small, so I never had a chance really. But I content myself with the fact that there are plenty of men of my diminutive stature. I keep noticing them on the London Underground and elsewhere.

There have been various theories about why transsexualism occurs, but there is still no definitive answer. Conditioning in childhood is now widely discredited as a plausible explanation; having a parent who wishes you were a child of the opposite gender and therefore treats you as such is not sufficient stimulus to create a gender dysphoric. There is also no gene for transsexualism and no evidence that transsexuality runs in families. The most favoured theory is connected to an incorrect hormonal stimulation which the foetus receives *in vitro*, but no one knows exactly how the process of being wired up into male or female is muddled and why certain hormone messages are not received at critical periods of development.

Male sperm may be X or Y but the female egg is always X. An X sperm mating with an egg will always produce a girl (XX); a Y sperm mating will always produce a boy (XY). Yet although normal embryos are either male or female, they all begin to develop as biological females for the first three months. If the embryo is XY (male) the ovaries will then move down in the embryo and become testes, and the clitoris will begin to grow into a penis. The male brain is basically a female brain modified by boosts of male hormone which effect these changes at crucial developmental periods, i.e. three months. But if something goes wrong in this developmental process, an XY baby boy may not receive sufficient male hormone to place his mind in line with his body; he may be left with a female mind. Quite how female-to-male transsexuals like me are affected by hormone imbalance in the womb is even less clear.

But despite the highly technical surgery, the term 'sex change' is a misnomer. Biological sex is unalterable, although some transsexuals do have chromosomal abnormalities. Caroline Cossey claims to have both XY and XX chromosomes. I have not been tested.

The fact that my predicament can be explained in biological terms makes me feel less of a freak, but I still feel grossly misunderstood by people who don't want to understand. I have my own little theory, as follows:

The elves were busy working, industrious along their production line in the sky. Little boys in blue boxes, little girls in pink. What elf could go wrong? On this particular day, however, we find that God the supervisor had knocked off early. And with their supervisor away the elves were getting careless and chattering among themselves. Enter the head elf, Inky. This day he was feeling particularly stressed. As the baby factory clock fast approached 1700 hours, Inky picked up the next baby, a little boy, from the line and without thinking inadvertently popped him inside a pink box. His mistake went unnoticed until the day of reckoning twenty-five years later.

Thinking about this, I started to shed tears of injustice. Tears of what might have been. I shed tears for the schoolboy, tears for the groom, tears for the father and tears for the Liverpool centre-forward scoring the winning goal at the Cup Final at Wembley.

Transsexualism raises all sorts of questions about the nature of gender. I find that people expect me to have profound insights. Although I do have a different and unusual perspective, it is not as detailed as people imagine. Although I have a female body, my mind has always been male. I therefore can't compare the inner workings of the mind of man with the mind of woman. I am able only to compare the societal differences in the way that men and woman are *treated.* My female form attracts a social response quite different from what feels natural to me, and once my metamorphosis is effected I am sure I will be able to comment on the very different way that men are treated.

We may indeed be born as physical specimens of one biological sex, but it is social conditioning to a large extent which impresses upon us the expectations of that gender. Culturally, individuals with male genitals are treated quite differently to individuals with female genitals. I am lucky not to have been born sooner than I was, as these boundaries are weakening.

When the female-to-male transsexual Michael Dillon was growing up as a girl, in a 1920s upper-middle-class household, the maiden aunts who raised him felt a duty to encourage him to be demure, self-sacrificing and essentially passive. As a girl, he did not receive any formalised education. Thankfully, the extremes of this scenario have changed today, and with every successive generation equality is becoming realised. Now the similarities between men and women vastly outweigh the differences. But strong subconscious gender differences do remain. Even without realising it, parents create stereotypically 'male' and 'female' behaviour in their children by the way they treat them. A famous study at Sussex University confirmed this.

One group of babies was dressed in pink and another group was dressed in blue. Volunteer parents were asked to treat the blue babies as boys, the pink babies as girls. In fact, some girls were dressed in blue and some boys in pink. But the 'parents' treated the babies they thought were girls very differently. They let them crawl away from them less far before picking them up, they were more gentle with them, they cuddled them more, they let them cry less before soothing them. The boys were handled more roughly, spoken to more and allowed to crawl away further before being gathered up.

Yet the volunteer parents reported that they were treating both male and female babies the same. The fact that children are treated subconsciously in such different ways is a clear indication that their social environment influences their behaviour to some extent. Yet despite this strong gender programming used by parents to guide their children into developing acceptable gender characteristics, transsexualism still develops.

And I am living evidence of this fact.

Wednesday 10 November 1993

Nine days have passed since my first hormone injection but still no sign of hairs on my chest. Each morning I scrutinise my feminine flesh. Nothing I have learned in my life so far can prepare me for the changes that lie ahead, as testosterone begins to metamorphose my body into that of a man.

However, some changes have occurred even at this early stage of my new body's development. Small changes they may be, but they are none the less significant despite their subtlety. I seem to be eating far more than normal and my weight has responded by increasing a few pounds to eight stone exactly. I also seem to be getting broader and occupying more space generally, but part of this is no doubt due to the surge in confidence I have felt since I made the commitment to start hormones.

As I write, the hairs on my legs are getting longer and curlier. I have abandoned my Epilady – it never worked anyway – and the ritual of leg shaving. The hormones can now take their course. Each day seems longer now I have no need to spend time patiently ridding my body of excess hair.

I want to be as 'bear-like' as possible. Let this secondary sexual characteristic – which says very profoundly 'I am masculine' – grow.

But I must be patient; it will be a few months yet before I am able to observe the best changes of all. The thrill accompanying this thought means that each injection is an exciting prospect. Each injection is a goal in the game-plan of my life. I am falling in love with testosterone, as I watch it free me from the chains of the body I have tolerated but never liked. Its oily serum is liberation from the grease-monkey life of being a man with someone else's body. I do not know who this body belongs to, but it is not mine. I have started a fitness programme in order to speed up the process and I have set my heart on having pecs like Arnold Schwarzenegger's. I have also taken some measurements:

Shoulders	16 inches
Waist	26½ inches
Thigh	22 inches
Inside leg	33 inches
Weight	8 stone
Height	157 centimetres

I am spending almost every night at Sarah's at the moment. I can't bear to be alone at night; I need her arms around me. This business of gender reassignment is the most frightening experience of my whole life, more than A-levels or finals. I just want someone to hold me and to tell me that everything is going to be all right. The only way I can express how I am feeling through all these changes is to keep writing resolutely; in effect, I am counselling myself. Sometimes I feel that if I confide in someone then I will fall apart, as I find this situation at times too painful to talk about. I am an emotional decorator, who has papered over the painful cracks in his past. Being brave is not all it's cracked up to be. I feel as though I have already spent an eternity being brave, and the worst is yet to come. Still, I am looking forward to being able to go out to the shops to ask for a loaf of bread with a deep voice. For now, I am a mouse, timid and squeaking. And what's more, still being mistaken for a woman. At the moment I prefer to let the rest of the world go on without me.

Saturday 13 November 1993
Friday night is traditionally party night, so I ignored my currently sluggish, reclusive tendencies and forced myself to go out to the pub. I love having a few pints of the 'amber nectar' on a Friday night and a chat with the lads. While I was chatting to an old school friend a guy came over and told me that the young lady perched on a bar stool fancied me. Lucky me – she just happened to be the tasty brunette I had been lusting over the week before, so I seized my chance to do some serious chatting up! Since she fancied me it was clear she wasn't gay so I made it my business to talk to her. Extracting her phone number was not a difficult manoeuvre, but I have felt guilty ever since as I am involved with Sarah. Unfortunately, not guilty enough to stop me phoning her today from Karen's flat in Putney.

I waited until the evening as I didn't want to appear too keen. I refuse to get too excited as she is no doubt unaware of what she's letting herself in for with me! Nevertheless, hot date Thursday.

Sunday 14 November 1993
I had a good night at the Slug and Lettuce in Fulham yesterday. I was in my element surrounded by Karen's female friends. But I had had a crisis of confidence before we left the flat, wondering if I could cut it. I was swiftly reassured, however, when everyone called me Paul all evening without a single slip back into addressing me as

'Marts'. This felt like a big breakthrough as it shows I am passing perfectly. Even people I had not met before did not suspect I was really a woman in men's clothing. When Karen bumped into two men who were once her neighbours she introduced me and they instantaneously shook my hand, as men do. But the biggest compliment of all came just before closing time. Karen was accosted by an Australian at the bar who started to chat her up with a vengeance. She played him along for ten minutes and when she came back to the table said: 'Paul, do you know what he said when he realised he wasn't getting anywhere? I wish I looked as young as your twin brother ... he's well away.'

Sarah came to Putney to pick me up, but I felt very miserable because I have decided it's all over but don't know how to tell her. I feel I have a lot more experimenting to do yet. How is it that I have got myself in such a pickle? I promised myself I'd stop playing around when I reached double figures. The woman I have a date with on Thursday is woman number ten, so perhaps this one is going to be my kind of chick!

Monday 15 November 1993

The significance of today is that it is Day Fifteen of my gender reassignment programme. This evening at 5 p.m. I will have injection number two, but I am growing impatient waiting for the physical changes to take place. There are times when I feel on top of what I am tackling, but at other times I am struggling to hold the pieces of my shattered life together. I wish at times that life did not feel like just surviving. I am finding that being in a physical relationship is sapping all my energy. The demands are both physical and mental. I get very frightened at the prospect of being on my own and the future scares me. Although I know that what I am doing is one hundred per cent the right thing, nevertheless sometimes I wonder what lies in store for me.

Last night I had a nightmare and the image of what I dreamed has been burned into my brain. It is following me around, sitting just to the side of my consciousness and chilling me.

I was in my room and I walked over to the white-painted wooden mirror which sits next to the sink. I looked into it and searched for my reflection but all I saw was the mirror image of the ceiling and the bookshelves. Frantic, I scrutinised the mirror, my face just inches from the cold, sleek glass, and slowly an image began to form. I concentrated hard, willing it to materialise, and gradually I saw my chin, then my nose, then my eyebrows appear on the glass. Next I saw my lips, painted with red Rimmel tartstick and I froze, but the image now had a momentum of its own and the rest of my reflected features quickly came into sharp focus. My palms started sweating as I stared at the vision in front of me. There was long blonde hair swinging around my shoulders, my neck was delicate and slender and my eyes were made up with mascara and eye-liner. I looked more feminine than ever before. Slowly, I smiled at myself.

I awoke and sat bolt upright, my heart threatening to jump right out of my body, then reassured myself by reaching my hands down to comb the hairs upon my legs before falling back into fitful sleep.

But today the dream, and the sleepless night that ensued, has left me feeling I have been dragged through the past few chapters of my life by my hair.

I told my landlord this morning that I am changing sex. I thought it was only polite to let him know. He was cool about it and said: 'Good on ya, mate.'

I still have a sore bottom following the last injection, and I am having to turn the other cheek, so to speak, in bed. As I lay there I realised I was missing Sarah. I have suggested a trial separation, but although I feel like a shitbag it was for the best. I know I have hurt her, but she is also an expert at papering over her own emotions. We are still best friends – I cannot believe she is being so understanding.

Jumping Jehovah's Witnesses! I've just looked at my chest and noticed a lone, long hair growing there! It is pale brown, fine and with a slight curl. He looks like a single ear of corn on a fallow field. I have named him Bob, my one hair. He is an early pioneer on barren female skin and has great sentimental value.

Tuesday 16 November 1993

Day Sixteen of my hormone treatment. Bob is looking good. He is now a few millimetres longer and has himself the beginnings of a brother and sister just poking out from the surface. Is it wishful thinking or have my breasts shrunk ever so slightly? And is that bum fluff growing on my face or is it just the light?

I have a numb left buttock following last night's injection but I limp with pride. I draw great comfort from the knowledge that every painful step I tread is a step on the road to my becoming a real man. I did not anticipate physical changes this soon. I had been briefed to be patient and told that I would have to wait months. I gave myself the once-over this morning and found I had a little collection of dark hairs on my bottom. I am starting to see the appearance of a male body shaping up in the mirror. Shame about the huge tits!

England play their last World Cup qualifier against San Marino tonight so the world is looking like a brighter place. Can't wait to take this gorgeous woman out on Thursday.

Wednesday 17 November 1993

I have finished with Sarah for good. I left her a note. I know I have a long way to go towards finding myself and that other beautiful women will soon be arresting my attention. I feel like a complete bastard, but know I am better off single at the moment. I care about Sarah too much to drag her through the maelstrom, and I don't want to be responsible for hurting anyone's feelings at the moment. In my own way it is because I love her that I have to let her go.

I am excited by how quickly the hormones are taking effect with no apparent side-effects. I did suffer a dodgy chest for a few days after the first injection but have decided it was probably due to binding my chest too tightly. I was a little over-enthusiastic with my new bandage!

I have had only two injections to date, but at this rate I could be a gorilla by Christmas.

I watched an original episode of *Dr Who* this evening – the Daleks used to terrify me and cause me to hide behind the sofa – and I listened to the doctor's definition of courage. If his definition is true, I have decided that I am more courageous than I have been giving myself credit for. He says that having courage does not mean that you are unafraid. It means you *are* afraid but do what you feel you have to do anyway. Well, I am terrified. Beneath this cool, calm, coping exterior lurks a small and petrified me who just keeps battling on, trying to separate the warring factions; a mind and a body which don't tally.

I have just checked my face in the mirror and I really, really have got bum fluff on my chin, honest. I am all choked up with emotion, and it is all I can do to hold back the tears. Looks like I'll be shaving soon, guys.

UK Living mailed me a cassette of my recent TV performance. The interview had been pre-recorded but went out on satellite, and I do not have a dish, so I had not seen it before. As I watched I was absolutely staggered. Staggered to see every eye movement, every verbal expression, every movement of the head and nuance of body language as completely male. There was a man on screen dressed in my one and only navy suit and, what's more, that man was me. Suddenly, I have been supplied with a new resolve. I have the evidence of my masculinity on videotape and no one can refute it now. All my fears were dispelled in a few short minutes, and seeing the easy manner I have with myself I find myself posing the inevitable question: 'Just who exactly have I been these past twenty-six years? What and where have I been?'

I went to bed feeling very emotional and needing a big hug. If I could invent something really useful, it would be a giant teddy bear that hugs back. One with soft fur you could lose your face in and which would soak up the tears, and with huge, protective bear arms that wrap around you. I am currently reliving the pain of twenty-six years in the wrong body.

Thursday 18 November 1993

England are out of the World Cup. No surprise, really, since they had the virtually impossible task of beating San Marino by seven clear goals in order to qualify for the finals.

I checked myself in the mirror this morning. The texture of my hair is altering. It feels thicker, and my skin looks different somehow . . . more greasy. I will be shaving soon, I'm sure of it. Either I have laryngitis or my voice is beginning to start its descent. It sounds as though it has dropped a few notes.

Hot date tonight. Why do spots always save their appearance for days like this?

Monday 22 November 1993

My hot date four days ago turned out to be scorching. I was quite prepared to be a gentleman but the woman in question kept me up all night. On Friday morning she was still with me, so we wandered around town together in a daze after two hours' sleep. I shopped for my first pair of men's Levi 501s but I needed encouragement from Sally to risk the changing-rooms in Top Man. Luckily, it was late in the afternoon and real men were short on the ground, so I sauntered into the empty changing-room with a veneer of confidence. I can't get used to the way that men's 501s hang on my body, which does not quite have a completely male shape to it yet.

I also splurged on a television with the proceeds of the *Daily Express* interview. The Granada salesman asked me to write my name and address on the back of the warranty, and with a flourish I took the pen and wrote down Paul Hewitt. He processed the warranty and tapped away for a bit on his keyboard and then handed me back a printed till receipt which read Ms P. Hewitt. I felt livid when I saw it. For God's sake, I feel so completely male now that I can't understand how anyone else fails to see my masculinity, especially as my arms were entwined around Sally on this occasion. I nearly informed the salesman of his mistake, and his unintended threat to my masculinity, but decided it wasn't worth the aggravation. Besides, it won't be long now before these sorts of mistakes will be ancient history.

Friday night at the pub with Sally turned out to be a complete nightmare. She acted all possessive and gave me hassle I really don't need now. Come back, Sarah, all is forgiven.

Chapter Four

Tuesday 23 November 1993
I have bought a Hitachi electric shaver, but the choice was almost too much for me. I hadn't a clue what I was looking for, but in the end I settled on a model which was mid-price-range and mid-quality. Now it sits in pride of place on my bedroom table. I felt all the excitement of a pubescent boy longing for his first shave just like Dad. After I had taken it out of its box, I was too scared to use it, frightened of cutting my soft skin. So I enlisted two female friends who shaved my face for me while I sat attentively in a chair in the front room.

Deciding to shave was rather a dilemma. I wanted to encourage the hair to grow but at the same time I was desperate to shave in order to experience the unique sensation for the first time. But I've been reassured that the more you shave, the thicker and faster it grows, so the incentive was there and I didn't feel too much loss as my precious bristles swirled down the plug-hole.

10.05 p.m.
I am devastated. My father has just left, walking out into the crisp night. I am having a good cry, staring into the mirror through smeared optics at a man in so much pain. My Christmas is not going to be much fun because he has just

told me it's best if I don't go up to Norfolk to visit him and his family for the festivities as I had planned. I think he is afraid to tell my nine-year-old half-brother about me. This is breaking my heart. It makes me want to smash a chair over someone's head. Luckily, there is no one around.

The support of family, including extended family, is not crucial to my progress, but it would certainly help. I'm also worried that Simon will grow up not knowing I exist. What will my father tell him when he asks why his sister does not visit him or buy him presents any more? I find myself remembering the time my sister and I first found out we had a brother, not long after our parents' separation. It was a shock to find out this well-kept secret after so long, but our devotion to our father wasn't challenged. He could commit murder and our love for him would remain, such is the strength of the bond between the three of us.

We welcomed his fiancée with open arms, knowing she was the woman responsible for our father's happiness. Now I had hoped to receive the same generosity of spirit, but it seems that my transsexuality has thrown the family into confusion. I do not wish to apportion blame, but they will never appreciate just how much it hurts to be excluded from certain activities just for being myself. We have met our brother Simon only a few times, but the acceptance was instant. He is a well-adjusted little boy who reminds me too much for comfort of myself at that age. Last time I was visiting them in Norfolk I was still called Martine and living as a woman. Simon asked me to take him to the park to play football. 'OK,' I said. 'No problem.' Next thing I knew there were about six of his friends outside the gate waiting for me to take them out. I was his brother long before hormones, but I think I was the only one fully to realise it.

I feel that the problem about Christmas has also illustrated my father's lack of understanding. I can feel his division of loyalty, torn between his new family and his old one, but I feel very sad that he does not support me enough to persuade Jill of my convictions. I approach the writing of this book with renewed determination. I want to tell people how lonely it is to be stuck in a body which isn't yours.

But as far as bodily changes go I can report that I am definitely broadening out. My shoulders are increasing in muscularity and my waist is gradually disappearing.

Friday 26 November 1993

Another blow to my self-esteem today. I went to see an old university friend at her flat in London's East End. On my arrival she mistakenly referred to me as 'she'. She blushed and quickly corrected herself, but the damage had already been done. It wasn't her mistake itself which bothered me so much as the realisation that she was still thinking of me as a woman. She also shook my hand in greeting, which seemed a little formal. Maybe she did it to make me feel as if she was treating me as a man? More likely, I think she was not sure how to behave with me, and once again I am reminded of people's discomfort when faced with someone not sitting fairly and squarely on one side or other of the gender divide. I cannot bear being mistaken for a woman or being referred to as Martine when I am trying so hard to leave my past where it belongs, in the past. I will have to leave behind old friends who are not behind me one hundred per cent. The company I keep right now is crucial.

Midnight

I am tired with having to fight so fiercely for what I am. I'm gonna be one hell of a guy, then the world will just have to sit up and take notice of my maleness as it fills up the whole room, like some powerful narcotic substance.

Saturday 27 November 1993
Today I was searching the fourth floor of Debenhams in Bond Street for the gents' toilets. A middle-aged man bustled over in the crowded store of Christmas shoppers to ask: 'Do you know where the gents' toilets are, mate?' A nondescript question to anyone else, but to me a massive ego boost. This simple enquiry lifted my spirits in the morning damp. After a further search I found the toilets and for the first time felt quite comfortable entering the door with the two-legged symbol on it. I felt I could have chatted to the men inside without being outed as an impostor. Entering the Gents is the most frightening thing about changing sex; men's toilets are notoriously foul. Women's toilets are a comfort zone, a place where you go to gossip. Years of conditioning mean that I will probably always feel more comfortable in the ladies' toilets. I have to force myself to go into the Gents because I know I don't fit in the Ladies. Yet I don't enter the Gents a whole man. Putting it crudely, I can't flop it out at the urinal and do my business.

I met up with the solicitor who is representing me as I haggle over royalties for this book. She said to me afterwards: 'You're not a woman.' I found her outspokenness immensely reassuring.

I seem to be having fewer problems passing as a man as my appearance gradually metamorphoses. I had my eyes tested this afternoon and no one at the optician's seemed to be aware of my secret.

Sally came round tonight looking stunning in a flowing, butter-yellow dress. She is big-time gorgeous, with curves in all the right places. I am your typical 'phroarr, get a load of that, Kev', hot-blooded sort of guy, totally at home sleeping with a woman as company, her mammaries as soft pillows. It tends to be tall women who arrest my attention, which some would say is bitterly ironic. Sally is important to me, not just because she has captured my heart but because her curvy femininity serves to enhance my feelings of masculinity. I suppose she is a heterosexual trophy. I have just done my 'manly bit' by walking her home, despite the fact that she is two inches taller than me. She is probably more dangerous wielding the pointed end of a stiletto and her handbag than I ever could be in my trainers.

Monday 29 November 1993

I shaved again this morning. Today is Day Twenty-nine of my hormone treatment and INJECTION NUMBER THREE. I look forward to each injection. They mark the small-term goals in my life which will eventually lead to me getting where I want to be.

I had that funny feeling in my chest again this morning, like birds tweeting in my ribcage. I'm not sure if it is stress or the bandages, then I wondered if the hormones are having an effect on my blood pressure. The nurse checked it after my jab in the bum but it was quite normal.

Feeling uplifted by the jab, which for the first time was completely painless, I expected the world to treat me well, but it didn't. I spent the whole morning in the DSS waiting for a replacement income support cheque as mine has failed to arrive. Is someone pinching my mail? I made the long walk to London Road, striding against the biting wind and freezing temperatures without a penny in my pocket and suddenly feeling very degraded that my life has been reduced to this base level . . . dependent on the state for food. I cannot wait to be back in the rat race again. I don't miss the early starts but I certainly miss the money and the independence.

At the DSS I also had to suffer the indignity of explaining my name change, despite the fact I had supplied them with a copy of my Statutory Declaration and medical note last month.

Sarah and I have drifted back into firm friendship plus something more. Today she took me for my injection and I am sitting up in her bed writing this, as she has gone to work. I am fulfilling my endocrinologist's predictions and experiencing an upward rise – good choice of words – in my sex drive. I am certainly a bit of a handful at the moment, but since I always have been, at least as long as I have discovered women, I do not blame this entirely on hormones. I guess when you are seriously horny anyway, there is little margin for improvement.

Tuesday 30 November 1993
Looked for my waist in the mirror today but could not find it. It appears to have disappeared.

Wednesday 1 December 1993
Staying with my sister in Putney, I listened to the tube trains rattling overhead within yards of the window. It was late, and I became aware of a strange sensation. I suddenly had the feeling that I was physically a much bigger person than the reality of my small body. More like six feet three rather than five feet two. I lay motionless as the sensation washed over me. I felt as though I were experiencing my own rebirth, like a huge man was being born inside me while I rested. Crazy as this may sound, I am certain I was conscious and not dreaming at the time. As the days pass, I become more and more in touch with my real self.

I got up the next morning, but did not get far. I dropped into a sweating heap on the bathroom floor. The colour had drained from my face and I had to lie still for a while. Could this collapse be due to hormones? I feel wretched, like I am going through the menopause early.

Sarah arrived on my doorstep. I was very pleased as I needed her today. Within minutes, she made an astute diagnosis. 'Your body is in a state of confusion,' she said.

'Isn't it time for your period? And yet it's being suppressed as testosterone accumulates in your system.'

Sometimes I think Sarah is the only person I can really talk to. She knows that I am not coping with my predicament as well as I pretend. I feel stranded in a whole new world full of social codes that my in-built gender has not had time to learn.

We went out for a drink, to a straight pub. I perked up a bit and never once got the feeling that anyone there thought I was anything other than a man. Mind you, I was making a bit of a bold statement as I had my trusty red rugby sock stuck down my trousers! I am feeling permanently horny and wish it was more than just a cosmetic touch. What I wouldn't give to be like other men and have my brains stuck there too.

Monday 6 December 1993

More problems with the DSS. I told the woman scowling at me behind the counter: 'Changing sex is a piece of cake compared with getting money out of you lot.'

I went home and my mood plummeted without warning. The fact that I can cry to release my pain and rage does not, in my eyes, make me any less of a man. It is just a facility I have developed, having been brought up as a woman. I was never exposed to the pressures on males to suppress the tears as a child.

I took a train to London to meet Karen. By coincidence I met an acquaintance called Andrew, a female-to-male who underwent gender reassignment five years ago. It was not a meeting I particularly welcomed. He talked my ears off all the way to Richmond, having followed me into a carriage and sat down opposite me. He talks so loudly that the whole train must have guessed we were both on male hormones. I would prefer not to discuss the personal details of my life within earshot of a carriage full of commuters. With two people sitting opposite us, and not knowing where to look, I would have preferred to talk about the weather. I hope I will have a more positive outlook than him in five years' time. He still considers himself disabled. I prefer to think of the positive aspects of being transsexual, such as the comprehensive perspective of both genders it gives me. Men always say they can't understand women, but because of my past, to a certain extent I can. My experience has given me a unique dimension into personality which I am proud of.

I am now convinced I am growing a willy. The anatomy of my female genitalia is changing. As the clitoris becomes enlarged it seems to have shaped itself into a mini-penis. It makes me wonder if the difference between the two sexes is really so dramatic.

Tuesday 7 December 1993

So what of changes on Day Thirty-seven of my hormone treatment? I had another shave this morning and now look like a 'clean-shaven little cutie' – Sarah's words, not mine! The hairs on my legs are getting thicker and curlier, though not enough for a carpet yet, and I continue to get curiously bigger in the 'girlie bits' department. Watch this space!

I took Sally to the pub last night and lots of people were jealous of the pretty woman on my arm. I know because I intercepted and deflected their lustful gazes.

I think Sally was pleased to see me. She flung her arms around me when I came to pick her up. She had bought me a big soppy Christmas card with 'For My Boyfriend' on the front. Sally told me she didn't care what sex I was, she still fancied me. She finds me an attractive person, never mind my gender problems, and she believes 'there is sexual attraction minus bits'. Her past history is a predominantly heterosexual one.

This is, however, destined to be a stormy relationship.

We cannot keep our hands off each other, but we argue too much, and I feel unable to offer her anything at the moment. I must not let my feelings of lust make me forget exactly where I am going. If I did have a dick, I'd be in serious danger of thinking with it.

Wednesday 8 December 1993

Oh, God, I awoke to blood spots. I can't believe I am suffering from breakthrough bleeding at a time when I thought I'd purchased my last box of tampons. This feminine part of my physiology makes me want to stick my head down the toilet and read Armitage Shanks at close range. My mind is totally disconnected from my female genitalia, and dealing with the blood I feel as if I am dealing with someone else's body. At times, even at this early stage of transition, I am prone to forget my origins as a physiological female, but a tampon resting in the inside pocket of a man's suit is a bit of an easy giveaway. I *must* be a typical male. I even hate the word 'tampon', and any mention of periods makes me go cold, especially when I'm eating! It has killed me to write it down here.

I bought my *Daily Express* at the news counter in Sainsbury's and was served by a woman with more facial hair than I have. Watched the European football on television this afternoon. Not being able to play is agony, but I am determined that I will play again.

Saturday 11 December 1993

On the bodily changes front, I am getting chunkier than a Yorkie bar. I now weigh eight stone four pounds . . . I was seven stone twelve pounds at the outset of hormone treatment on Friday 29 October. Initially, I thought it was Sarah's banoffi pie, but, no, my weight is holding.

Only fourteen days until Christmas, and this could turn

out to be the best ever, simply on the strength of my new-found identity. I am looking forward to my fourth injection on Monday. My voice is gradually deepening; at times it is an effort to talk. I will not be at all surprised if it has actually broken by Christmas Day. This would be the best present I could hope for, with the possible exception of a date for my mastectomy.

I had my first heterosexual night out in a long time last night ... it was a friend's annual company Christmas party. I am finding that I am now passing very well as a male and am at last attracting the attention of straight females, although unfortunately it seems to be teenage women who are unable to keep their hands off me. There is clearly something adolescent about my male appearance so far. I was called 'sir' by the waitress last night and went weak at the knees, while one particular girl kept grabbing me on the dance-floor and calling me 'sweetie'. Her boyfriend was less impressed by the attention she was giving me.

Got back that winning feeling again this morning when I played squash for the first time in ages. My legs were half-hairy and I looked rather androgynous, so I was glad no one was watching me. I really feel as if I am making progress now, but also feel totally unable to suffer fools, people who refer to me as she or call me Martine. I am becoming increasingly vocal and more determined about what I want and how I am going to get it.

Mr Blobby is at Number One – God help us.

Tuesday 14 December 1993

I am trying not to get too depressed on skid row, but I think it is harder on the male ego than the female one to be unable to earn money and provide for oneself. This may be an old-fashioned attitude, but basically I am an old-fashioned guy, and I hate not being able to go out and spend my money on women. I have more chance of being made Pope than my family have of getting a Christmas present from me this year, and that hurts.

I had injection number four last night. I am getting used to having a sore bottom for one week in every two. My voice is still threatening to break. I am quietly ecstatic about the changes but know I will have to search for a job in the new year as having no money basically means you have no life, and I can't wait to get on with mine.

Wednesday 15 December 1993

My article came out in *Bella* magazine today with the headline 'Please call me Paul'. I was fairly pleased with the treatment. There was little deviation from the facts and I don't feel it invited any ridicule. I was glad to see I was not on the front page, but I shall be even more pleased when a cheque drops on to my mat. The *People* want to interview me, but I have to stop somewhere.

I am now eight stone five pounds and my voice is croaking and squeaking like a frog in the mating season. I can't sing a note – no change there! I have just treated myself to a haircut and have decided to cultivate some sideburns. I am growing hungrier with each day that passes, both physically and sexually. My appetite for life is increasing.

When I look in the mirror now, a new person looks back at me. The reflection is beginning to show distinct changes: a thicker neck, a torso which is bulking up, increasing jowls and hair on my face. Yet the person inside is still the same. I am worrying that life will be an anti-climax after the sex change is over so I have given myself three goals: to model for a men's catalogue, to play for a men's football team and, in my dreams at least, to become a male stripper. The second one is probable, the first and last mere fantasies played out in my head.

My *Daily Express* interview by Jane Warren was reviewed

by Tomasz X, from Catford, in this month's issue of *Dyscourse*, the Gender Dysphoria Trust publication. Tomasz is a female-to-male transsexual who works part time as an adviser for the Gender Dysphoria Trust and is also an accountant in Surbiton. He praised the article, his only criticism being the one observation that I myself disliked. I quote:

> *The author had a rather damming physical assessment of Paul, as she states that to look at him, she finds it hard to perceive him as a male (he has not yet received hormones) and that she 'feels no chemistry or physical threat' just finding herself 'getting close in a way only women can'. I feel this was an unnecessary observation as it is her subjective opinion. Transsexuals are only too aware of their physical shortcomings and dragging up such issues only serves to imply that such differences make them lesser men or women.*

Saturday 18 December 1993
I have had a fairly depressing week, as again my income support cheque failed to arrive. I spent Thursday and Friday morning at the DSS, but in the end I have now got them to give me an order book, so I can easily cash my money at the post office every week. This is a great weight off my mind.

I rang Stuart, a fellow female-to-male transsexual, on Wednesday night as a few things were worrying me health-wise and I have been unable to contact my endocrinologist, Dr Ellis Snitcher. I am troubled by three medical factors and need his advice. The tight feelings in my chest continue, but continuing to wear the chest binder is vital to my state of mental well-being. I need to know whom I should contact about my mastectomy; getting a date fixed up would go a long way to relieving my stressed-out state.

Stuart took me with him to see our mutual friends Alan

and Sandra in Guildford on Friday afternoon. Alan, another female-to-male transsexual, aged twenty-nine, has just come out of hospital following his hysterectomy. I first met him and Stuart at the FTM Network female-to-male get-together in June 1993. Alan is small in stature but with very male features; he is quietly spoken, but every inch a man. Although sound in spirit, he is shuffling around like an invalid.

We ended up staying well into Friday night, as Sandra, a twenty-eight-year-old secretary from Ealing, who has been engaged to Alan for four years, cooked us a wonderful meal and we had a good chat about life and our situations in general. There is no substitute for first-hand experiences of transsexualism, as told by guys who are five years ahead of me.

Alan and Sandra – who is and has always been a totally heterosexual female – met in 1986 through mutual friends. At the time Alan, who was still biologically female, was going out with another girl, but Alan and Sandra soon became close. At the beginning it was not an easy road. Sandra was attracted to Alan, but initially had difficulty understanding her feelings as she knew she was not a lesbian and had never found a woman attractive before. Basically, she was falling in love with Alan's personality.

Today they consider that they have normal sex and find it no different to normal heterosexual intimacy. Foreplay is no different and the final sex act can be simulated, or a prosthetic used if this is absolutely desired. Orgasms can be achieved by a variety of methods. From my own experience I know that in many ways sex is more fun, satisfying and varied as there is no risk of a penis forcing an unwanted and premature conclusion to lovemaking. Having lived as a woman, I believe that penetration – and sexual satisfaction – are not penis-dependent. Of course, biological men cannot understand this. They are socially and sexually educated to believe a penis is as vital to the woman they are with as it is to them. They don't realise that they actually deal in status symbols when they worry about the significance of size.

I was more than a bit interested to learn that Stuart has the most up-to-date prosthetic penis called a Herb. It is semi-functional and made by an American company charmingly entitled Creative Growth Enterprises. It was designed by an American female-to-male transsexual who recognised a gap in the market, as it were. Introduced into Britain in 1993, it looks and feels real and is available in three different sizes. It retains heat, is waterproof and you can pee through it by way of a medical catheter bowl which pools the urine at source and conveys it through a tube to the end of the prosthetic. It can therefore be used to urinate while standing up – this is a fundamental difference between the sexes. Sitting down can be a chilly reminder of one's genetic origins. Not only can you use it to urinate but, most importantly, it will pass the urinal test with its realistic veining. What's more, this willy won't shrink to nothing in cold weather! However, Stuart, who bought his last year, says it takes some getting used to. If you are desperate to go, you end up wetting yourself – the force is too much for the catheter and sends the urine down your leg. Conversely, if you are not in great need, the pressure is insufficient to propel it into the tube in the penis and all you do is fill the catheter bowl.

As for sex, the Herb comes with a manual erection device which is inserted when the desire takes you. A tiny vibrator is an optional extra to stimulate the wearer's clitoris. The drawback is the cost – £450, and it's not available on the NHS. That feels like an unjustifiable amount of money to spend on a willy! At the moment I am not desperate for one, which is a good thing as sexual pleasure of this nature is well out of my price-range.

I am fast forming the opinion that the partners of

transsexuals are in many ways more special than the transsexuals themselves. They certainly suffer just as much. I have nothing but admiration for Alan's partner Sandra, with her down-to-earth qualities. She had an understanding, uncomplicated acceptance of Alan's condition before his reassignment and continues to be supportive, revelling I think in the fact that her life is a little different to the normal. She thinks the world of Alan and has taken two weeks off work to help him during his convalescence.

The little old lady who runs the launderette along the Oxford Road near the cinema totally crucified me yesterday while I watched my Top Man boxer shorts race round and round. She was speaking to a young couple in their twenties who were hogging the driers. She looked from them to me and asked if this 'young lady' could use one of the machines. I looked around and did a double take when I realised she was talking about me.

I was upset and insulted because she knows my situation. I have been using the launderette for six months and only last Friday opened my heart to her about the reasons I am not working. I told her about the sex change and she said she 'liked the sound of my determination to follow my own path in life'. She had said that she did wonder if I was a girl or a boy when she first saw me.

The couple, however, did look very confused and no doubt assumed that her eyesight was failing her. I certainly do not look female any more, and on reflection I realise I may have to find myself another launderette as I am still finding these misunderstandings very upsetting. It is like having a flesh wound which keeps being reopened.

Monday 20 December 1993

The wind is howling, and the rain is rhythmic on my clouded window-panes, but it cannot dampen my conviction that Sustanon 250mg has saved my life. Today is Day

Fifty of the hormone therapy. I no longer have any nagging doubts about the wisdom of gender reassignment. When I analyse my doubts, and those of other people, I see they consisted of three main issues:

(i) Am I just gay, and simply changing myself in order to become socially acceptable? No. There is nothing remotely socially acceptable about self-mutilation in the name of conformity.

(ii) Will I die young due to the effects of the hormones – and what other effects will they have on my life? Will I go bald? Will I develop spots? Will my male body be scarred? Will it be as good as the female body I am trading in? These factors are unimportant. My conviction that I must bring my body into line with my mind is absolute, to the extent that I would even opt for cosmetic and functional imperfections in that body.

(iii) Fear of the unknown. The nagging feeling that better the devil you know and that I have no right to go against nature and mess with my body. I have no option. Undergoing this change is the only route to sanity and happiness.

Now I've answered these fears the issue looks remarkably unclouded. The physical transition from female to male is simply that. It's a mechanical process and one that for me cannot happen fast enough. The sooner I get my body in line with my mind, the sooner I can get on with my life.

I spent the day with Sally yesterday and she let me open my Christmas presents early. I experienced an intense emotional high from a couple of pairs of men's underpants, albeit extremely sexy ones. I posed for over an hour in front of the mirror in my new black G-string, a pair of socks in the pouch. How can the girlies resist me? I questioned myself. I cannot recall ever getting this excited over women's underwear ... not on my body at least.

Friday 24 December 1993
I met up with my dad three days ago. We went for a drink in the Cunning Man, a Reading pub popular with families; it has a children's room and a garden with a play area. Dad used to take us there as youngsters for Sunday lunches. Minutes after we walked in he met one of his old football mates, Willy Smith, whom he used to play with in 1965 when he was playing for Rabson's Rovers, a local Reading team. 'Hello, Jim, how are you, mate? This your boy?' asked this stout chap with a prominent beer belly. My dad nodded the affirmative and a string of lights lit up around my heart.

I have always considered myself extremely close to Dad, yet he seems unable to broach the subject of what is happening to me. Likewise, I feel hardly able to tell him. He displays the typical male trait of being unable to talk about his feelings, and I now know why I have grown up in denial, keeping my unease to myself – my role model was emotionally reticent. Yet I know he loves me – in a rare moment of candour, after three or four beers, he gave me a hug and told me that he does. Yet despite the alcoholic lubrication I found myself unable to answer back.

Sally and I visited Alan and Sandra in Guildford on Tuesday evening. We make up a symmetrical foursome of two female-to-male transsexuals plus partners, so I feel very much at ease. It was a thoroughly enjoyable evening. We ate Sandra's special spicy pasta, played music and chatted. There was an added *frisson* of intrigue when I noticed Sandra observing me on a couple of occasions, yet when I caught her eye she quickly looked away. I felt a fleeting attraction and wondered whether she had felt it too. Sandra is much taller than Alan, but then that is not difficult, about five feet nine inches with a warm personality. I am typically attracted, at first sight and personality aside, to extremely feminine and beautiful women. I like height, long legs, long dark hair and expressive eyes like those belonging to the rabbits in *Watership Down*. But if I am overwhelmed by a person's personality, looks just fade into the background. Of course, sometimes I feel an electric attraction which cannot be explained by any of the above.

When Sally was not in the room Alan seized the opportunity to tell me how lovely she was. 'You always get nice women; you must have something,' he said with a chuckle. People are constantly telling me how nice Sally is, wherever we go! But clearly there is more to sex appeal than pure physical appearance. The magic went out of my life when Lisa left in August. As I drove Sally's car, a W-registration battered blue Ford Escort, I felt my male ego lift a little. I miss having my own car and the freedom it provides.

I got a surprise visit from Karen on Thursday. She looked like a native after a week in the Canaries and as always it was great to see her. We went back to Mum's as we had arranged, but within ten minutes we had had a row and my mum was in tears. She greeted me as Martine and instantly I wanted to up sticks and go home. In these situations I become verbally aggressive, defending my own personality like a deeply prized possession that someone is trying to take away from me. I tried to reason with her, as I wanted her to recognise that I am truly a man and have a right to be called by my male name. I don't need any support other than this recognition, but when it was not forthcoming I wanted my legs to take me where no one could find me.

Sometimes I even fantasise about faking my own death and coming back with a new identity altogether, like Reggie Perrin; it seems like a far more attractive option than the burden of fighting for my own identity with these detractors. Yet it is always Karen who saves me from such dramatic reveries, acting as diplomatic mediator and helping me systematically to correct my mother's mistakes. I was left bitter by the experience. My mother was not even attempting supportive rationality and was putting her upset ahead of my need.

I picked Sally up by taxi, but my heavy state of mind made me utterly convinced that we are not compatible. The minicab driver drove like a lunatic in his battered Ford Cortina, wheeling across the road and jumping red lights. I was sitting in the front, with Sally in the back leaning over and stroking my hair while the taxi driver made vain attempts to chat her up. I found myself feeling jealous for an unusual reason . . . Once upon a time it would have been *me* sitting there in sexy clothes getting chatted up and being the centre of attention. Instead, I was on the sidelines, but I can't have it all ways.

When he dropped us off he said to me, *sotto voce*: 'You have a very pretty girlfriend.' I felt myself swell with pride; he had taken me as a man. These little triumphs are the advantages of having a pretty woman dangling as a heterosexual bangle on my arm.

Incidentally, I went back to the launderette three days ago and left the little old lady there a note and a copy of the *Bella* article all about my condition. Today I walked past the launderette and she called out to me: 'Hi, Paul, how are you today?' In her hand was a Christmas card with an apology for referring to me as a 'young lady' last week! Looks like I won't be looking for a new launderette after all. I have an ally.

Saturday 25 December 1993, Christmas Day

At almost ten o'clock at night I found myself walking alone in the darkness on Christmas Day evening. It's a long four miles from my mother's house to my own and this was an act of defiant stupidity. The allure of the park and the trees in the crisp daylight had vanished at night. I was the only soul on foot and there were few cars around. I pictured families surrounded by decorations and pine needles, debauched by sherry and wine and stationed contentedly in front of the television. In contrast, I felt very much alone, as I always do, even when surrounded by people.

I lingered for a few moments on the corner of Liebenrood Road, staring at the Roman Catholic church. I darted down Honey End Lane, deciding it was lit best. My training as a woman means that self-protective instincts still emerge when I am in a dangerous situation. I can still be raped as a woman, but physically, and practically, this is a virtual impossibility. No one has ever been able to penetrate me, and no man (unless he's gay) is going to try to rape someone who looks like a man. My biggest fear is of being robbed and beaten up, as I am now an independent male of rather inferior physical presence. I always feel obliged to walk Sally home protectively, now I am a man, but then sprint all the way back to my place, just in case. I could give Mr L. Christie a run for his money in this regular late-night training run.

What a relief it was to be home safe by nearly eleven. Top Cat, the ginger cat belonging to the young couple who live in number thirteen, was waiting. We played rub face for a few moments on the stairs, and then I went upstairs with cat in hot pursuit. I caught my reflection in the long mirror at the bottom and was cheered to observe my pert, manly bum in the mirror.

I was supposed to have stayed with Mum tonight, and yet I feel entirely suffocated when I am around her, as though I surrender my identity like a passport when I cross over the threshold of her front door. So I did what I always do when I cannot cope: I walk away from it. I am facing the fact that my mum will probably always call me by my female name and, although I do understand that my dysphoria must also be deeply traumatic for her, nonetheless I do need her support. If she doesn't try to accommodate my needs, she will lose a son as well as a daughter. It's a tough old sweet to chew on, but she makes me feel deeply entrenched and trapped in the past while instilling a sense of confusion in me about my identity.

To make matters worse, after Christmas dinner with my mum and Karen was over I spent the whole of the day slumped on her green velour sofa reading the autobiography of Caroline Cossey, the model known as Tula, who underwent a gender reassignment from male to female in the 1980s. I was unaware of *Only Fools and Horses* and *Birds of a Feather* flitting across the television screen as I read of her struggle to find a man who would accept her for who she was. And of her disastrous marriage to Elias Fattel, whose strait-laced Jewish family was unable to accept who their son had married, despite the fact she had converted to Judaism in accordance with their wishes. When the tabloids seized upon the marriage, Elias's domineering mother sucked him back into the community. Caroline had also taken a motion to the European Court trying to get action passed that would enable transsexuals to have their marriages accepted legally. The motion had been unsuccessful.

The book depressed and distressed me. I was reminded of the prejudice – both personal and political – that transsexuals face. The government which allows the surgery to be performed legally will not protect you in your new role. It has no regard for giving transsexuals equal rights, abandoning them in legal no man's land.

But I do have some great friends. I am dazzled by the Christmas presents I received this year. New boots from the boys' department in Saxone from Sarah. Socks; I must be the only man in England actually flattered to receive socks this Christmas! I also received a complete range of Givenchy products – I am spoiled for choice for aftershave now. I have Paco Rabanne, given to me by Karen, which has a cool icy smell, and Incense, which smells enticing.

I had no money to buy Christmas presents but in a flash of inspiration decided to give away my best female clothes as presents. Strangely, it was a reluctant parting, they were so much a part of the feminine identity I tried desperately hard to forge. I gave Karen my little blue office suit which she has had her eye on for ages, and Sally received my favourite sexy black jacket. I knew it would look great on her and it did. Her flatmate looked at me, astonished that I knew exactly what size to get. Sally and I exchanged knowing glances and I said quietly: 'It used to be mine!' I checked with Karen to see if I was free to give away the 'entwined serpents' ring she had given me on our eighteenth birthday. I have no use for it now – it was Jan Barden, the acting woman's editor of the *Daily Express*, who pointed out that it was far too feminine. At that moment I could have kicked myself for not having disposed of it earlier. I wanted to give Sarah something really special as she has been so supportive of me, so she received the ring, wrapped up in tissue paper, her face riven by a look of half-smile, half-sadness. Now my hands are bare, waiting for new additions.

The rest of my female clothes continue to gather dust in my wardrobe. I never owned vast quantities of make-up, but still it sits, stagnant in my make-up bag.

It's past midnight and Christmas Day is officially over. What is it about Christmas and birthdays that is so depressing when you're having a crisis? One feels under intense pressure to be having a good time at this period of the year, even if you're horribly depressed.

Monday 27 December 1993, Boxing Day

A woman with long dark hair and velvet eyes came up to me in the supermarket this morning. 'I just want to say, I saw your article in *Bella* magazine, and I really admire what you're doing.' I wanted to pick her up and put her into my shopping-basket.

It's Boxing Day and my boobs have definitely shrunk. My size 34D is now a 38B. As for my weight, well it has soared to an all-time high of eight stone seven pounds. And it's not flab, it's muscle. My closest friends tell me that I look better for it.

Although for months I have thought that I had the support of my parents I realise now that they are indifferent to the mechanics of my plight. There is nothing active or constructive about their attitude. They are simply ignoring my condition and are in a state of denial. My father won't broach the subject; my mother calls me Martine. I feel that I have no choice, and for the sake of my serenity must cut myself off from them until they can accept who I am. I shall keep in contact by letter only, signing myself Paul and explaining in detail my feelings of liberation. This way there will be no room for unsupportive and unconstructive debate.

Wednesday 29 December 1993

Today was a good day, simply by virtue of its being time for injection number five. I got all the way to the doctor's surgery before I realised that I had forgotten my Sustanon. However, I wouldn't be Paul if I wasn't having these bouts of 'scatty-itis'. It has been sixteen days, rather than fourteen, since the last injection because of Christmas, and this time I hardly know I've had a jab as there was no soreness, no pain. My room looks like home now and I'm proud of it. I've always wanted to sleep on just a mattress on the floor, so I am now using the bottom part of the bed as a purpose-built zoo for my cuddly toys.

I have now been on hormones for eight weeks, but physical changes have happened much more quickly than I had been led to believe they would; my voice is significantly deeper today than it was yesterday.

I feel so much more content and relaxed now. But I am impatient for a date for my mastectomy, as I view my now-flattened breasts with contempt. I feel violent if anyone tries to touch them. I simply cannot and do not want to relate to them as part of me. They make me feel like a freak.

Looks like I am going to be a single man again, as Sally and I are looking likely to go our separate ways. The heterosexual world presents a challenge for me now, and I am desperate to prove myself within it. According to the book *Bodyshock* by Liz Hodgkinson, most transsexuals either have low sex drives or are uninterested in sex. Unfortunately, I am not one of them and would now give anything to have a natural penis and to be able to engage in normal heterosexual sex. I watch sex scenes on television with increasing envy, and feel bitter that I have been cheated of my manhood. I have not yet had any complaints, but although I don't feel exactly less of a man without one I still don't feel exactly complete. Breakthrough bleeding again. Ugh.

Thursday 30 December 1993

Usually the night following an injection is a painful one, but last night I didn't feel a thing. I was still restless, though, and I'd give anything for a decent night's sleep. I feel all lethargic today, but I stubbornly refuse to give up my press-ups and sit-ups. I have also composed a letter to my mother.

> *Flat 17, Reading*
> *Dear Mum*
> *I wanted to say thanks for the Christmas dinner . . . it was really nice! Unfortunately, I do have another reason for writing to you, as there are some things I feel I must explain.*

It hurts to say this, but I cannot see anything positive coming from us seeing each other at the moment. It always ends in tears! I know you've had it tough – we all have one way or another. I know it is difficult for you to come to terms with me as a son rather than a daughter. But for all my understanding of that, I am finding spending a few hours in your company very threatening to my own serenity. You can continue to refer to me as 'Martine' and 'she' all you like, but I simply cannot be around to hear it. I have made my decision, and it was a tough one, and the only people I can have around me are ones who are 100% behind me, who help me to reinforce my own identity rather than wash it away with ill-considered references.

I love you, and it hurts me that I cannot be around to help you through your *troubles, but for survival's sake, this is the way it has to be. If you want to keep in touch by letter, I will be glad to, but I have decided to keep out of your way until you have come to terms with me as I am, however long it takes.*

Take care of yourself chooch,
Your son Paul xx

New Year's Day 1994
It is 1994, but I cannot admit to being utterly thrilled. Right now I am too tired – and hung over – to appreciate the dawning of what I hope will be my perfect year. I went out with a group of my sister's twenty-something friends from Swansea University. It's an annual party held every year, this year at the White Hart in Frimley Green, near Camberley. But I had to get seriously drunk to enjoy myself, firstly because I have no energy and secondly because I still feel extremely insecure in the company of 'real' men, those lucky individuals born with fully functioning male bodies. I long for such personal, physical union but am currently much more comfortable in the company of women as I find

them easy to understand and less of a threat to my masculinity. I believe that most women think I am a male, but I am haunted by the fear that men will spot some residual evidence of the woman in me, perhaps from the years of conditioning I experienced.

Being in a busy, heaving, straight pub on Hogmanay was quite a stiff test of my passability. I was nervous going in and out of the Gents all night as there was no lock on the cubicle door, but the more Fosters and Southern Comfort I downed the less I worried and the more I realised that no one looked askance at me anyway. The highlight of the evening was the clock striking twelve and a voluptuous blonde woman of about twenty-five coming over to give all the men in our group a New Year's kiss. She came over to me twice, saying: 'He can have two because he's so cute!'

I also seem to be bringing out the mothering instincts in little old ladies. Karen was chuckling at me on the number seventeen bus from the Three Tuns to the Bear Inn this afternoon as a white-haired lady of about seventy invited me to sit next to her, 'So you can watch your luggage,' she told me. I struggled to keep my feet as the bus lurched and she grabbed hold of me from behind, curling her hand with its crinkled skin around my belt and yanking. I do not feel like a young boy, except when I'm watching *The Lone Ranger*, but that is how I am being treated at the moment. Girls fancy me, women simply think I'm cute, and grannies want to protect me. I guess I can live with that.

Sunday 2 January 1994

Karen has just left to go back to London, and I'm lonely now that she's gone. Sally is in Austria (skiing) for two weeks and so I have plenty of time for peaceful reflection. Karen and I are closer now than we have ever been. After her initial devastation at my decision, she now totally accepts it and is being consistently and intensely supportive. She is my shining light, there for me when I need her. We are twins – brother and sister spirits entwined. I can share my pain and fears and she does not judge. Because of her strength I decided to meet my father and his family last night. Karen and I took a bus to the Reading Forte Posthouse Hotel. I was reluctant to go because I knew what to expect, but with Karen beside me decided to give them a chance. Simon was still calling me Martine. He is, after all, only a child of nine and understands nothing of the circumstances, which makes me view my father as a coward and yet hate myself for it. My father does not appear to have the balls to take his son to one side and say: 'Look, son, your sister Martine is now your brother Paul.'

Jill's sister and husband also seemed ignorant of my plight, for, despite my being introduced as Paul, they constantly referred to me as 'she', and to Karen and me collectively as 'Jim's daughters'. And there was I, into my third month of hormone treatment, looking dead butch and using the men's toilets, and being called 'she' continuously; it was desperate stuff. I felt my stomach churn as Simon came steaming around the corner as I sat facing the bar. He looked at me and said: 'Hello, Martine.'

Jill chatted to Karen all night about her life. No one seemed interested in mine, and I felt like the invisible man, cast as the social outcast and family misfit. It is now clear to me; I am having a sex change, but as a family we ignore it. Instead, we cover the imperfect cracks of our collective existence with small talk. Once again I was forced into the position of the second-rate sister and it made me squirm. I thought I had left all that inferiority behind, but I see now that my hopes were premature. Dad bought Karen and me drinks and gave us money for a taxi back home, but I don't want his money, I simply want him to acknowledge my identity and not sweep me under the carpet in the presence of others. I have a right to be me, and to be accepted for that. I know I can't handle this unsupportive attitude, so I'm not going to contact either my mum or my dad until after my operations. I am determined that when we next meet they will be the ones who will look daft if they insist on feminising me, as I will grow a big beard – so bushy that squirrels can build their dreys in it! I hate beards, but if that's what it takes then a beard it will be.

I have little dark hairs growing on the back of each hand. Testosterone, do your stuff. My love-life is very quiet at the moment, but it is hard to lead the life of a playboy without a penny to my name. For once in my life neither sex nor cash is a high priority.

Wednesday 5 January 1994
New Year's resolution: I shall eliminate alcohol, caffeine and chocolate from my diet. Hopefully, I shall exclude whatever it is which is making me feel so awful. Wot, no Fosters? This could be tougher than changing sex.

I had a nasty experience last night. I awoke feeling nauseous and spent an hour rolling around on my bathroom floor. I looked in the mirror. My face had gone a horrible yellow colour, my hands were shaking and I was sweating like mad. This is the second time I have gone through this horror since starting hormones. Sarah cheered me up by cooking me lunch. She said I was getting so big she could hardly fit her arms around me any more. She's now calling me Popeye because I've got big muscles.

Friday 7 January 1994
Today I noticed a small amount of serious stubble.

I got a call from *Bella* magazine after lunch. The editor of the *People* is determined to run my story with or without my cooperation, so I figured I may as well make some money out of it. I phoned Linda McKay of the *People* and told her to contact my agent. He phoned me later on to confirm an interview for Monday 10 January.

Saturday 8 January 1994
Thoughts of the interview have got my subconscious working overtime. I have had a spate of nightmares which remain with me when I awake, stunningly clear images in my head.

Last night I walked into a classroom in my old secondary school. As I entered I heard a tidal wave of laughter and saw fingers pointed at my legs. I looked down slowly and saw that my legs were bare and covered in thick hair. Then with horror I noticed that I was wearing white open-toed strappy sandals on my feet.

Moments later I was trying to balance on top of a tiny two-foot-wide clifftop surrounded by raging waterfalls. I struggled to keep my footing in the wet, swirling sand. One false move and I knew I would slip to my death.

Sunday 9 January 1994
Last night I went to a gay pub, and although not a drop of alcohol passed my lips no fewer than three people tried to get off with me – one male, two female. It's ironic, really. I used to get so upset that I couldn't compete with Karen, and at times I doubted that changing sex would make any difference. I felt certain that she would always be more attractive than me. But now I realise I needn't have worried. Women don't seem to be able to keep their hands off me. My personality is shining through because my physical and social shortcomings as a constructed male are totally outweighed by my new peace of mind. One woman who grabbed me for a smooch even stood head and shoulders

above me. Perhaps even being vertically challenged won't turn out to be such a horror after all.

Monday 10 January 1994
Rain and more rain. It seems ironic that while Chichester fire brigade pumps water out to sea from the flooded high street, bush fires are claiming lives in Sydney.

The first hurdle in preparation for my trip to London to be interviewed by the *People* was getting dressed. I haven't worn my best white shirt since November and it doesn't fit. I put my arms into the sleeves and tried to do the buttons up but it was pulling under my arms and there was no way I could persuade the collar button into the hole. Instead I wore a pale green shirt which is not my favourite and didn't do a lot for my street cred. It was one I ordered from a catalogue; they always look so good on the models (unfortunately, I ain't no model!).

At my agent's office I awaited the arrival of the journalist who was to be my lunch date and meal ticket for the day. She was jolly nice; another good-looking female writer, but she came bearing a new deal. The *People* had decided to pay me £500 now and make it up to £2,000 for the final story in a year's time once I'd had my operations. I felt cheated. In the end I settled for £750 after some discussion with my agent.

Friday 14 January 1994
Thursday morning and I was bristling among the commuters swarming like insects on the 9.43 a.m. to London Paddington. Pristine in my suit, my first stop was Chancery Lane for a photo shoot with Mirror Group Newspapers. I was met by Paula, yet another tall brunette, who whisked me by taxi to a studio round the corner, firing questions at me all the while. By the end of the road I had scored eleven points with no passes. I can foresee a time not too far away

when I will become thoroughly sick of talking about myself as an object of freaky fascination.

I had make-up slapped on my face, which was a disconcerting feeling. I haven't been near make-up for a good eight months. The lady responsible said she had made up all the stars ... Arnold Schwarzenegger and Sylvester Stallone as well as Tula, alias Caroline Cossey, the former Bond girl and male-to-female transsexual. She told me that Tula and I were similar in our down-to-earth attitudes.

Once home, I flicked through information which had arrived in the post about the various penile prosthetics on the market. I have now definitely set my heart on buying myself a Herb from Creative Growth Enterprises in the States.

Saturday 15 January 1994
Sarah and I had a fit of giggles in bed last night discussing the Herb and wondering if the supplier would take a cheque so we could buy as soon as possible. We can hardly wait!

Linda Udell of the *People* rang to say they were going to run the story straight away. She was meticulous in checking details, so I put her mind at rest by saying: 'If you write as good as you look we have nothing to worry about.' I can't resist the chance to chat up a good-looking woman.

Sunday 16 January 1994
A sharp intake of breath was required when Sarah came round clutching a copy of the *People* at 9 a.m. There I was on the front page in basque and suspenders. I hadn't remembered giving them the photo of me posing in modelling test shots and I felt sick inside. The article at one point made me out to be some sort of tart, which I certainly was not, but I put that down to their misinterpretation of my words. I was immensely relieved; the article was not nearly as tacky as I had feared and showed sensitivity to transsexuals. It also

said I was courageous, which went down well with me. The new photos were great. I didn't realise I scrubbed up so well.

My face feels like sandpaper. Sarah was threatening to tip me upside-down and sweep the yard with my stubble.

Today I wore dark glasses in case anyone should recognise me.

Tuesday 18 January 1994

All my photos were returned from the *People* this morning. There was also a note included with them from Paula, the picture editor. I called her as requested and she told me about a friend of hers studying psychology who is keen to interview me for a project. I agreed. She might be good looking! Never one to miss a chat-up opportunity, me.

My body still seems to be welcoming the introduction of testosterone. He is a male ambassador in my body. The more male my appearance is now, the more desperate I am becoming for a mastectomy. Having boobs really is very depressing, not to mention de-masculinising. My shoulders and arms are now thick and muscle-bound, but I am so unhappy with the top part of my body and consequently I have had some more nightmares.

I awoke in a hospital bed cocooned in clinical sheets in a room on my own. Karen and Sarah stood over me as I removed blood-stained bandages from my swollen chest. I was horrified with the result. The surgeon had made a real pig's ear of it. My right side was bigger than my left and the nipples had been reconstructed artificially from plastic which resembled eye-droppers. Gingerly I tried to stand, and threw up in a sink by the bed. Eventually I stood without assistance and looked at my gaunt features in the mirror. I was horrified to see hollowed, sunken eyes and skeletal hands and feet. I looked like the surviving victim of a nuclear holocaust. Then Sarah's mother arrived and handed me a huge card inside an envelope. I tore off the paper and turned the card over. The message on the front was 'to wish you luck with your new life'. My eyes widened as I opened up the card to reveal five pictures of naked, beautiful women with long auburn hair. Each one of them was wearing a phallic, plastic, strap-on penis. I blacked out.

Chapter Five

Thursday 20 January 1994

Publicity is both liberating and overwhelming me. Each interview confirms my convictions, but I certainly have no wish to become a professional transsexual, trapped in a limbo land where I exist only for the fact I am newsworthy. Gender is a characteristic that divides the population into two categories, but a person's gender does not fully describe him or her. Society delights in labelling me but forgets I am more than just 'transsexual'. I am first and foremost a man, and it is for my achievements and for my qualities that I would prefer to be known.

Transsexualism does not define my personality in any way; it simply refers to a medical condition from which I and a small proportion of the population suffer. Haemophilia is also suffered by only a small percentage of people, yet we do not whisper, 'Look at him, he's a haemophiliac.' Unfortunately, victims of gender disorders are usually immediately judged and stigmatised.

I am a man who has had problems. I am not a freak, and the sooner I can leave space between me and my unfortunate start in life the happier I will be. While others live their lives with fast cars and nice houses with 2.4 children, I wait patiently to begin living mine. Eventual anonymity is my intention, but is perhaps a little unrealistic by virtue of the publicity I have attracted. I have chosen to tell my story to others despite the fact this is likely to make my life more difficult. I hope that my actions will help to smooth the rocky path for transsexuals in the future. Rather than having chosen this path in life, I feel that this path has chosen me. I consider that I have been selected as a spokesman, strange as this may sound, for female-to-male transsexuals. This has given my life direction and purpose. For so long I was a lost soul searching for a worthy cause to fight for; now the cause has found me.

Nevertheless, the requests from curious onlookers who smell a lucrative and intriguing story continue. Everyone wants a piece of me. Today I mailed off photographs of me at various stages of development to *Woman's World* magazine in New York in response to their phone call. Publicity abroad troubles me less than in this country, and the money is certainly useful at this very expensive time in my life. I am already growing out of clothes bought a few months ago. Publicity in Britain on the other hand has turned my weekly shop in Sainsbury's into something of a low-key ordeal, in my head at least. As I skulk around the aisles in search of chicken breasts and Uncle Ben's sweet and sour, I imagine I will be outed by hordes of middle-aged ladies who read the sort of publications – *Bella, Express Woman,* the *People* – in which I have appeared.

Paul Hewitt, jet-set transsexual extraordinaire. Have detachable penis, litter-trained, own skateboard, will travel. If only . . .

The second post brought me more 'fan mail', this time from the matron of a rest-home in Huddersfield. Samantha Cannon had just read the article in *Bella.* She had written a lovely letter of encouragement.

It is testimonies like hers which restore my faith in human nature. I immediately sat down and tapped out a reply, while her words were still fresh in my mind. It was the least I could do since she had taken the trouble to write during her coffee break.

One of the most unsuspected offshoots of the interviews I have done has been the mail they have elicited. Significantly, all have been from women, and have fallen into two types. In a minority are letters from God-squad evangelists who feel it is time I was enlisted, and feel it is Jesus alone who can heal me 'from the inside out rather than the outside in'. But the majority fortunately are letters of support from a broad cross-section of women. Some simply wish to say 'Well done, my boy, and good luck to you', while others are written by people who have some inkling of what I am going through, either because they are transsexual or because they are close to someone who seems to fit the profile. Some are even jealous, wishing they had the courage, or didn't have the ties of young children, to take the same bold step.

I decided to construct a reply to Mrs White, a God-squadette from hell, although she called it West Yorkshire. Mrs White is a lay preacher, a teacher at a secondary school and mother of three children. Although she was certainly not a loony, her letter was fervently evangelical – she seemed possessed by the idea that God was somehow instructing her to contact me. When she rang the *Daily Express* on a Sunday and was instantly put through to Jane, who had written the initial article, she was even keen to believe that this was divine intervention. I feel it was more connected to the fact that Jane works one Sunday in three!

Jane suggested Mrs Fire and Brimstone, as I have dubbed her, should write me a letter which she would forward. In it, Mrs F & B described her 'deep sense of urgency and concern' at my decision to embark on the process of gender reassignment. She felt it was Jesus alone who would offer the 'key to the deep distress within my being'. Having read her sermon in neat black italics on cream cartridge paper, I discussed privately with myself whether or not I should ignore it. I decided to reply. There was too much ignorance which needed to be put right. My reply was a ferocious one; it was not abusive but I made my point.

Dear Mrs White
I write in reply to your letter which I received via the Daily Express. *Unfortunately you succeeded in immediately alienating me by referring to me as 'she'. No doubt if you'd known my previous female name you would have used it.*

I have to begin by thanking you for expressing your concern. It obviously took time and effort to put pen to paper, and it is clear to me that you sincerely believe what you have written. What is also glaringly obvious to me is that you have little or no knowledge of gender dysphoria, the medical condition from which I suffer. I am now well into my gender reassignment programme, and I cannot describe the joy in my life now I have found my true self.

In answer to your questions. I have not been influenced by my father's desire for a boy . . . this is not something I desire. I quite simply am that boy. My mother has never had a miscarriage and I wouldn't even know what the occult was, let alone be able to dabble in it! You refer to my decision to embark on a programme of gender reassignment as if it were one of choice. It is not something I have thought up on a whim . . . I have been through years of hell before coming to these conclusions, and am merely making positive steps to deal with my condition in the only successful way possible.

I am well aware that mastectomy is a traumatic operation. My sister was upset at the thought of me losing my breasts. But this is a typical female reaction. You are talking about the reactions of real women. I am a man, and will feel nothing but liberation come next spring!

Finally, I feel it is possible to be a spiritual person, with very strong beliefs and morals, without worshipping a God. So, I thank you for your kind invitation, but no I will not be committing to God. Not this Christmas anyway!

I know you meant well, but I know what I am doing is right, and what I really don't need right now are people around me who are not with me one hundred per cent. I don't mean to be over-rude, but you have your opinions and I have mine. Please don't waste your energies worrying about me, because I am a survivor, and as such will be just fine. I am also quite stable, and am lucky enough to have a very logical head on my shoulders. May I be so bold as to suggest that a little research would be in order before preaching about conditions you quite obviously know nothing about.

Yours also very sincerely
Paul

In contrast, I felt warm and happy as I completed my reply to the supportive Huddersfield matron and ran my right-hand fingers through the stubble taking up residence on my chin. I resisted the urge to put my razor and foam to work. Much as it irritates, I decided to bask in this hirsute glory for another couple of days. Little physical changes like this uplift and exalt my masculinity. At moments such as these I feel that nothing can stop my march forward in search of my own destiny.

I came out of the bathroom feeling six feet tall and almost collided with Tracey, who lives in the second-floor flat. I covered my shortcomings with a smile, and scuttled back upstairs like an outed cockroach into a back alley.

Saturday 22 January 1994
Melancholy has kicked in. It is a constant battle to keep my spirits high. My bottom lip always hits the floor when there is nothing interesting in my letterbox. My progress seems to

lie in other people's hands, as I wait patiently for cheques and letters that are expected but never seem to arrive. A watched pot never boils. Most significantly, I am awaiting a date for my first operation, my double mastectomy. I can't wait indefinitely; it is draining my spirit and my resilience. I always crash into a low when my progress has reached a stalemate. I put my depression down in part, however, to exhaustion. I cannot resist doing weights when my body is not up to it, and I seem to have exhausted my muscles in my desperate bid to inflate them.

Positive action is the only way forward in such circumstances. I gained small comfort in filling out the passport form I had picked up from the post office yesterday. Without hesitation, I marked an M in the box reserved for the gender of the applicant. Would that I could alter my birth certificate with such ease. Actually, it was not quite that simple. In spite of the fact that I had enclosed a doctor's letter and declaration of name change with my application, I still received a letter back with the following enquiry:

Dear Mr Hewitt
Thank you for your completed application form. In order for us to process your application further, we require a letter from the medical specialist in charge of your case, stating whether in his opinion your male orientation is likely to be permanent. . . .

This letter annoyed me intensely. I had already enclosed the relevant documentation, and I took rather personally the suggestion that my male orientation could be anything but permanent. Some may go into gender reassignment looking over their shoulder – not me! It was a male life from the moment my name change became legal back in September. There has never been any suggestion of my returning to the hated female role. I wrote a rather forceful letter back providing the address and phone number of my endocrinologist, Dr Ellis Snitcher, suggesting they contact him if they required further confirmation.

Within days my new passport arrived, like a form of rebirth. I had included two fresh passport photos, and had waited to take them until my stubble was at its fullest, and wore my earring and my best suit.

I have set my heart on going to the Winter Olympics in Norway to see Torvill and Dean win gold. I doubt I will make it, being penniless, but I can dream, can't I? I just want to take off somewhere, spread my wings, free myself from this interminable waiting game. It would be nice, just for a few days, to forget I am transsexual.

Tonight I sped round to see Sarah, with my new passport joyfully in hand. I had feared my gender would be marked as female, since I am pre-op, but, no, there it was in black and white. Paul Hewitt, British subject, male. I had a much greater feeling of excitement than I did on receipt of all my other name-change documents, e.g. bank book, driving licence, medical card. To me it was far more than just a passport – more like a ticket to a new beginning. Sarah benefited from my elevated mood, and we went out to celebrate. I bought a bottle of Buck's Fizz from the corner shop, and we went to the next-door neighbour's house-warming party. I had the attention of the twenty-or-so Sloane Rangers who were sipping cocktails from the moment I nearly removed a light-fitting with the cork from my bottle.

As I walked into the kitchen, a slim woman in a nicely clinging charcoal-grey mini-skirt broke away from her conversation to stare at me. She had been chatting to Sarah in between the beer barrels. Her hair was dyed but she had a nice smile. 'Is that your brother, Sarah?' she asked in a slightly slurred voice. Sarah glanced around, leaned towards her and whispered: 'He's my toyboy, actually.' I was feeling wonderful and emptied glass after glass of anything I could get my hands on. Nothing could break my stride that night, and I was feeling lucky. Actions loosened by alcohol, I slid on to the dance-floor, which was cunningly disguised as a living-room carpet, and began to enjoy myself for the first time in ages. The hostess Mandy appeared from the other room. She was a secretary with a Sindy doll face and, with the element of surprise in my favour, I grabbed her from behind and pushed myself against her, dancing provocatively. She looked as a rabbit does when a car passes its field – startled! But soon I was back to klutz mode and doing my usual stupid things, like trying to open a screw-top wine bottle with a corkscrew. Nice one, Paul. By midnight I was holed up in a corner with Lynn, a squirrel-like brunette in her late thirties (she had fluffy hair and was driving me nuts).

'I would love to have children,' I said wistfully when she told me about the antics of her two under-fives.

'Easy to say!' she said. 'It's all right for you, you don't have to carry them for nine months.'

I smiled inwardly but felt a curious melange of emotion: gratitude at my new incarnation and the fact that I now pass convincingly, and despair at the fact my children will never carry my genes.

Sunday 23 January 1994

I am constantly amazed by the thwarted male who is resident inside me. As I mature and develop, he is regressing into the childhood he never had. I watch *The Lone Ranger* and *Planet of the Apes* on television in thrall. I am also finding myself becoming more driven sexually. My sex drive has matured as I have and is now increasingly male. Distinct feelings of lust overtake me at the most inopportune moments. If I had a willy it would be permanently erect! I am not compelled initially to look beyond the surface for the personality within, but these superficial inclinations are the male genes and hormones, not me. Paul wants to know everything about a woman he is drawn to. Old friends are still the best friends. When I met up with Awen, a girl I had studied with at university, having invited her round to dinner, I could have hugged her.

'You are so much broader,' she said as she looked up from her coffee. 'You are looking really good in your Levi's.' I gave her a grin, like the looks we used to exchange when out on the town in Helsinki during the summer of 1988. But it is my sister Karen who is my universal constant. I got a strange phone call from her after I had waved goodbye to Awen's little Fiat Panda. I picked up the receiver and heard silence. After a few moments Karen spoke. 'I just wanted to say that I love you and I miss you, and don't go going anywhere because I'm not sure I can live without you.' I was taken aback. I am not used to such displays of emotion from my sibling. The conversation ended there, and I sat staring into space, watching next door's ginger cat digging up the carpet. I was thinking of Karen, in her cosy London flat, swathed in new towelling dressing-gown with glass of Kahlua and milk in hand, and longed to be with her. With all the trauma and crises in our family of late, we seem to be growing closer than ever before. I felt inspired to write her a letter, noting down all the feelings we normally transmit by telepathy.

We have been aware of our unique gift for some time. At school we would get identical marks despite the fact we were sitting on opposite sides of the room. When one of us is in physical pain, the other feels it. If one cries, the other cries too.

In my letter I told Karen how much she means to me and how crucial it is to have her support. I worry about her too, because we are twins, and as such I know she feels my pain. I enclosed a photo of me looking totally unsexy the morning after the New Year's celebrations wearing a red Santa hat with a rebellious white bobble. In a state of contemplative joy, I wandered downstairs.

'What's up?' asked Sarah. 'Who was on the phone?'

'Karen. She phoned to give me her support. I didn't think it possible for us to get closer.'

I relayed brief details of our conversation. Sarah looked up from her coffee and her paperback. 'I think she is excited finally to have the brother that she always knew she had.'

In the soft light of my bed-sitting-room I went over and gave Sarah a big bear hug – she has an uncanny knack of always saying the right things – and then felt I had to go out for a while into the softly falling rain.

Wednesday 26 January 1994

I hunted high and low for my tape-measure yesterday. When I found it I confirmed I now have seventeen-inch shoulders with muscles which are still expanding. They are two inches bigger than when I began taking hormones almost three months ago. I glanced down at my hands; they looked like a real man's hands, playing host to a whole new set of thick, dark hairs. Injection number seven came and went in a blasé haze. What was initially an ordeal is now routine. I pressed Dr Dodson for details of my mastectomy and was devastated to learn that he had only this week sent off a letter to the plastic surgeon. I had been wasting my energy watching my letterbox.

I suffered another vivid nightmare last night.

The hospital waiting-room was cavernous. It smelled of stale antiseptic, and although the faces of the people perched on the seats were strangely out of focus they were staring intently at my fresh-looking face. I was the outsider. As I crossed my arms defensively, I looked down at my watch, which looked odd because there were no hands to tell me the time. I looked up, hackles raised, feeling like a rat backed into a corner, but I couldn't see a clock in the waiting-room. My heart started to pound and sweat beaded upon my brow. Where was the consultant? The walls of the waiting-room seemed to be contracting around me, then they began to pulsate, as if I was trapped inside a living body. Then he appeared, lurching round the corner, a tall, imperious figure with a malevolent scowl. He was dressed in a flowing floor-length white coat which looked more Messianic than clinical. He peered leeringly down at his clipboard through tortoiseshell-framed spectacles as if examining a rare specimen, then up at me. I saw the word form upon his lips before it came out and I thought my heart would stop beating. Then it happened. He shouted at the top of his shrill voice: M-A-R-T-I-N-E . . . The awful word, the label that once pertained to me, pierced my innards like glass shards and reverberated around the chamber.

I awoke in a sweat, sitting bolt upright, the terrible sound still resonating on my acoustic windows. The bed looked like a battleground and my alarm clock said 04.54.

Tuesday 1 February 1994
I seem to have done nothing but eat this weekend. My appetite on hormones is enormous. I have given up on my diet as it is far too depressing. Besides, life would be truly bleak without chocolate fudge cheesecake.

I have been on the phone this morning trying to find out what has happened to the cheques for the articles. I am becoming increasingly angry at the way I have been treated by the various publications. P.J. don't take no shit, man! I don't want sympathy for what I am going through; just a little respect. I realise that to my agent and potential publisher I am seen as a pound sign on legs. My personal tragedy is their business opportunity. I intend to turn the tables on this tragedy and make it my opportunity too. But I am not motivated by money. I am undergoing a titanic struggle to establish my true self, with fairly high odds stacked against me. I refuse to be taken as a fool, so it is vital that I watch my back and safeguard my own security. Never again will I be a yes man. For the first time in my life I believe in myself. I speak my mind even when it offends, and I can see hope and fortune darting along a distant horizon which moves by day ever closer.

Socially I am having no problems in passing as a normal young man. This I proved to great effect while out in London with Karen on both Friday and Saturday night. Plenty of girls, men trying to get past me to get to my sister and a drunk swaying and trying to spill a pint over me.

Nevertheless, I am going through an insecure phase. I am loth to admit this to anyone other than my closest friends, but I am now part of a whole new world which is intensely intimidating. I am no longer the object of male gallantry. Instead, there are certain acts of social etiquette which are expected from me. Confidence in my own masculinity has taken several months to acquire, and indeed I still occupy a position on a learning curve. No doubt this is the same for adolescent males going through puberty. Confidence in my ability to attract women as a male is also taking some time to acquire. In the night-clubs and pubs it is easy to watch without actually taking part, as taller men make a play for the woman I fancy. Though I pass perfectly, my feet are as tree roots, firmly implanted in the ground.

I feel as though I have been shoved into a massive arena of unknown quantities. I am no longer the centre of attention and have sacrificed attention by switching roles. I am now the attentive one rather than the one who draws attention, the 'hunter' not the 'hunted'. I pay the compliments rather than receive them. Although I am beginning to grow confidence at the same rate as I am growing hairs on my body, I remain grotesquely aware that I cannot compete with the physical stature of natural, genetic males. I am five feet two inches tall with a petite bone structure and no penis. I keep quizzing myself: 'What would a woman want with me when there is an abundance of real men on this planet?'

I must shake this attitude. Ninety-five per cent of success is mental. I will stick to my new exercise regime. Karen is a trained aerobics instructor, and she has developed a programme with me to build up my body. My muscles are still swelling like Popeye's and I haven't been near a tin of spinach, but my weight remains static at eight stone seven pounds. This is good news. When I was facing up to the trauma of my predicament last year I lost a stone in weight. My voice continues to deepen and strengthen. This is one of the advantages of being a female-to-male transsexual. The larynx can increase in size, which lowers the voice, while male-to-females have voices which cannot be 'unbroken'. They are trapped with an unnatural-sounding falsetto, as their larynx does not shrink on hormones and only training can alter pitch. I also believe it is easier for a female-to-male transsexual, of whatever height, to pass muster as a man and blend into the population virtually undetected. It is very sad to see male-to-females with heavyweight body-frames squeezing their six-feet bulk into frocks and high heels. They will always be more conspicuous.

I aim to be a Dinky toy version of Arnold Schwarzenegger, so don't push me! I have a strong compulsion to go to a gym and work out on their machines, but this is not possible yet. My chest binder inhibits movement and breathing when exercising. I am at the mercy of the NHS, and as such my future is in the hands of the person controlling the purse strings. My desperation increases as the days pass.

I have also temporarily lost interest in women, which is atypical. I suppose love and her cool hands will creep up on me when I am least expecting her arrival. Debbie, my once on/off girlfriend, is back in my life as a friend and has bet me a tenner I can't last three months without a new woman in my life!

Wednesday 2 February 1994

The world has been kind to me today! Good news, long overdue, and lots of it. Tracey from flat thirteen needed two hands to carry my post up to me! The *People* sent me payment for my interview and the cheque felt good between my hands. But better than that, I received a letter from Mount Vernon Hospital for Plastic Surgery in Middlesex with an appointment date to meet a consultant, Dr Morgan. At last I have one foot on the road to surgery. I felt about six feet tall as I walked into town this morning with imaginary air cushions uplifting my size four feet and propelling them along like mini-hovercraft. I think I could walk on water today if you asked me to. Finally, I am back on track. Some days I can see my destiny, other days it is almost invisible. I bathed my face in the sunshine as I strolled into town, appreciating fully the best weather we've seen this year. I was tempted to stop and share my mood of euphoria with strangers. The smile on my face was so wide it was embarrassing!

My father called round to see me last night. When he saw the candlelight he asked if I was conducting a prayer vigil. But my luck is changing. He has told my nine-year-old brother Simon that I have renamed myself Paul.

Standing by the aluminium sink unit illuminated by a shroud of inconsistent light, my dad looked at me in an appraising way. For the first time he showed a genuine interest in my gender reassignment. 'Your voice has definitely changed. It is much deeper now,' he said with conviction, and I felt my chest tighten as he spoke. 'Your shoulders are much bigger too, aren't they?'

I put the flags out in my heart to welcome him. I had waited a long time for my dad to acknowledge my transformation.

'They'll get much bigger yet,' I told him excitedly. 'And that's just my shoulders!' I speak about my changes in much the same way that kids tell their fathers about a trip to Alton Towers.

'Aren't you scared at the thought of the operations? I mean, a hormone injection is one thing, but major surgery ... You must be terrified.'

He didn't seem to know how to continue. I helped him out.

'Just between you and me, Dad, I *am* terrified,' I told him. 'But at the same time I'm excited. This operation is my passport to a new life and if I had it tomorrow it wouldn't be soon enough.'

'Well I'm just glad to see you looking and acting a whole lot happier. You had us quite worried at one stage, you know, when you wouldn't eat. Everyone is still a bit confused,' he added. 'It's a huge adjustment for us to make. Jill's sister took her aside after our get-together on New Year's Day to ask whether I had twin girls or a girl and a boy.'

I wasn't surprised to hear that. On that occasion I had been constantly referred to as Martine, but I knew I was clearly male and I had been using the Gents in full view of everyone.

When my father left, we hugged. It felt more like a father-to-son hug this time around. I'll never forget, in the early stages before hormones, when he kissed me in the pub and I nearly died of embarrassment. I said: 'Dad, you are going to have to stop doing that!' I took some solace from his gentle and accepting comments. Perhaps it will take less time for my parents to adjust to their new son than I had initially feared. Today I feel indestructible.

Friday 4 February 1994

I have spent the last two days at Sarah's house trying to recover from my cold. We had a blissful day of domestication yesterday, cooking up spaghetti bolognese and watching videos. Despite my cold I am feeling quite the action man at the moment. I battled through my fitness programme last night labouring under three-kilogramme weights. This also affected my libido. Rather than crash out, I found myself harassing Sarah for sexual favours every ten minutes. Sarah didn't seem to mind; we spent half the day in bed! There is something very erotic about seeing a woman at the sink doing the washing up. It certainly does things for me, anyway! I blame it on the hormones. Now that I have some money and a date to see a plastic surgeon I feel more goal-orientated. I have eight weeks until the appointment and I plan to have a very well-developed torso by then. I figure the flatter my chest, the less fat there will be to lop off!

My hair had begun to do its own thing, so I went to see George at the Italian barber's on the Oxford Road. Rows of chairs, razors being sharpened and different-coloured hair on the floor. No Ikea décor here, unlike the ladies' hairdressers I've attended all these years. I hopped up the steps propelled by my black pull-on boots to hear the hallowed words: 'Can I help you, sir?' It felt so good I had to resist the temptation to ask him to say it again. Sir, sir, sir . . . music to my ears. I wanted to punch the air in triumph. I have at last arrived. But tonight I am scratching the back of my neck, which is sore. George shaved my fluffy bits. I now seem to be sprouting hair in a variety of eccentric places. These hairs are boldly growing where no hair has ever grown before, not on the uncharted territory of my body at least! Now I know what to do with that piece of white tissue paper you are always given on leaving the barber's.

I am on a fascinating learning curve, discovering what it is like to inhabit a male body as it develops around me. This is infinitely more comfortable than female puberty. Growing hair on my face gives me a strong sense of satisfaction which has been long overdue, whereas my maturing breasts as I went through female puberty, and the monthly bloody hell, left me feeling detached from my body and isolated inside myself. I welcome my maturing male form with open arms. He is my long-lost son.

My conscious mind copes with confidence with the hormonal and social changes, but still my subconscious, free to wreak havoc while I sleep, is battling away on overload. The nightmares frighten me. They are evidence of the stress I face on a daily basis. I wrote a verse describing my latest nocturnal horror story when I awoke at three o'clock last night. I wrote it while it was clear in my head, but it looked strange the next morning.

There is a place where I can go
It's my place, a hiding-place
Where nobody knows
I hide at the top of my tree
I feel like a crocodile, with only
His bulging eyes showing over the water level
No one can see me
This is my tree
Where I can be free
I must not breathe too loudly
For I will be discovered
Because I am running away
Who am I running from?
Everyone?
The world?

I need an escape
And my tree is my escape
People sit and look at me for hours
Not knowing I'm there
I'm so quiet and still
I can see Judy Finnegan
From ITV
She looks up
But can't see me
I fancy her!

Saturday 5 February 1994

It is taking intense mental effort to keep believing in myself and to keep strong. The excitement of the past few days has caught up with me, as have excessive weight-training and sexual activity. I am burning with a new psychological energy that my body seems on limits to match.

I rang my dad today and my half-brother, Simon, answered.

'Can I speak to Jim, please?'

Simon, being a well-mannered nine-year-old, asked: 'Who's speaking, please?'

I replied simply, trying to keep any sense of self-consciousness from my voice: 'It's Paul.'

There was a short silence while the little boy disentangled the name from his memory, then he piped up with: 'Is that the one that used to be Martine?'

'Yes,' I said, elated. Simon bounded off, sounding excited, to fetch my dad. I just sat back and basked, relieved that at last he has explained me, at least in simple terms, to his son. This made me feel tremendously uplifted. My father was very relaxed on the phone and as we spoke I heard a little voice in the background shout, 'Hi, Paul.'

So much for the dissenters. Simon has taken to his new brother like falling off a log, just as I had predicted. Children adapt to new situations with such ease. So much of the protectiveness that adults exhibit towards them reflects more on their own adult inadequacies and shortcomings. Of course, Simon does not understand the sexual and gender issues that underpin my decision. I've decided to reserve him a copy of *A Self-Made Man* and present it to him on his sixteenth birthday. This will enable him to understand how it was for me and why his sister 'disappeared'.

I exchanged eye contact with an ex-boyfriend on the number seventeen bus yesterday. I saw recognition briefly cross his face. A long pause for scrutiny was followed by a look of shock and disbelief. I pretended I hadn't seen him. He's probably not aware that his relationship with me was homosexual and I didn't want to horrify him further.

I hit the town for a few beers. Sarah drove me to the Manor Arms, and after ten minutes in its mock-Tudor interior a familiar tall blonde figure entered the bar. Angela is a psychiatric nurse and was the first person to introduce me to the term 'transsexual' eighteen months ago. I remember our conversation as if it were yesterday, me struggling to elaborate on the growing unease inside of me, her listening, stony-cold.

Despite her training and her involvement with transsexuals, she seems to inhabit a narrow world, surprising in its rigidity. I know she is unsympathetic. She seems to view me as someone with deep-seated childhood problems rather than as a transsexual. Psychiatric nurses always seem keen to pin behavioural disorders on childhood problems – perhaps it makes them feel as though they are putting their training to good use. She makes me feel inadequate, but why should I care what she thinks? She sidled over as I caught her eye. She was not wearing a look of warmth, but there was no missing her curiosity.

'I saw the article in *Bella*,' she said without further elaboration, a fact which left me rather defensive.

'Yes, fame for all the wrong reasons,' I replied flippantly.

'You do seem to be fairly committed,' she said.

'I've got an appointment at Mount Vernon with the plastic surgeon.'

This was machine-gun-fire conversation, and I instantly regretted my honesty. She took a sip from her pint of lager, running her fingers around the glass and looking at me without smiling.

'Be prepared for them to recommend you have two years of counselling first.' This was her parting comment, and she spun around on her black boots to walk away. As if I didn't already know what I was up against. I didn't feel I needed the benefit of her wisdom – I certainly hadn't asked for it! I couldn't leave it alone, and as she turned away I launched a reply like a verbal missile in her direction. 'If I have to wait two years for surgery then I simply won't be around.'

I redirected my attention to my pint of Fosters and looked deep into its oily bronze for answers. Angela's insensitivity had left me shaken. I expect detractors. I expect to be jeered. I don't expect anyone to get me through this except me. I am prepared to tackle misconceptions about my dilemma. I will evangelise, proselytise in order to communicate what is happening to me and how it feels, but I am surprised that a psychiatric nurse should demonstrate such a profound lack of understanding. What hope is there for other people who do not have a basic grounding in the complexity of the human mind and its intricate workings? Angela showed no awareness of my convictions. I will do whatever it takes to get surgery. It is central to my existence. It is the only action which will liberate me.

Transsexuality divides people, as the Berlin Wall once divided Berlin, and I am victim of frequent misunderstandings. What surprises me even more is the lack of loyalty old friends can show. My ex-girlfriend Lisa was a nurse, another person you would expect to exhibit more compassion and understanding than most. But her behaviour towards me since we split has been a revelation. Where once we cuddled our kittens on the sofa and bravely faced up to my family together – at that time I thought nothing could divide us – she now treats me like something you wipe off your shoe. She is stonewalling me, and it is almost as if I never existed. It seems easier for her to erase my memory completely. For me it is not that simple. I guess I should stick with those who can provide an insulating, supportive cladding around me. But I don't blame her – it was always going to be love or hate between us; nothing in between.

Monday 7 February 1994
I fear I may have inflicted permanent damage to my shoulders by trying to lift weights that are too heavy for my small-boned frame. I have pains in the tops of my arms, and my shoulder sockets keep clicking. My mind keeps insisting I am Arnold Schwarzenegger, the Terminator, but my body is unable to keep up. Trying to 'pass' as a male is not a problem, but trying to fulfil my own expectations is proving to be an uphill battle. My body will not respond in the way I wish it to.

Worse, I was under the illusion that my voice was deep enough to pass over the phone by now, but when I tried to reconnect the phone line in my flat this morning – I finally had the money – the conversation did not go as planned.

I dialled Freephone 150 to arrange the reconnection. 'Good morning. This is British Telecom, Alan speaking. How can I help you?'

'I would like to have my phone reconnected, please.' I gave details of my address and previous addresses.

'Have you had a phone in your own name before?' the disembodied voice enquired.

I paused to think about the question. I said no, as I had not had a phone under my new name, only as Martine.

'What is your name, please?' came the swift reply. I could hear the tapping of computer keys at the other end of the line.

'Mr Paul Hewitt,' I said.

There was a horrible pause. I swallowed.

'I know you're not him,' came the caustic, cutting reply. 'You'll have to get Mr Hewitt to speak to me personally before I can allow reconnection.'

My mind raced. I felt bewildered. What exactly had his computer spat out at him? I didn't feel I had sufficient armaments to argue efficiently. Perhaps he had found some cross-reference to Martine Hewitt and was trying to connect the two appellations. Then my subjectivity kicked in. I couldn't believe this man was challenging my gender. I have been living under the illusion that although my voice has not actually broken it is deep enough to pass without fault as male. Suddenly my beliefs and my confidence were being eroded by the faceless Alan, a BT minion with no points to score.

I took a deep breath, acutely aware of the painful pause at my end.

'I *am* Mr Paul Hewitt,' I said calmly. I wondered whether it would be worth explaining my gender situation but did not want to give him the satisfaction of having a good laugh with the lads at my expense. I simply awaited his reply. Surely he would realise my credibility.

'I don't believe you,' came the reply. 'I can hear the voice of a woman, so don't try and tell me you're a man.'

I felt myself spinning, shrinking, dissolving in the unseen gaze of my invisible assailant. My breathing had quickened. Then anger took over. This man was branding me a liar. My voice was terse when I spoke: 'I will come into the BT shop to sort this out.'

When I put the phone down I was flushed and shaking, feeling as though I had committed some act of gross fraudulence. Me, a fraud, spotted through the invisible ether. Time dilated and suddenly I saw myself seven months before. Martine with her big breasts and her skin-tight hot-pants, hiding behind a Rimmel-red smile. Her dangly ear-rings and her permed, hairspray-starched, long brown hair. Martine the mimic, Karen's clone. Martine with the high-pitched voice and the eyes so sad. I had been convinced that I had left all that behind me. I had counted my ability to 'pass on the phone' as an early victory; now I slumped in Sarah's bed disconsolate, my illusions shattered and dispersed in the bedclothes around me.

I took time to compose myself, dragged on my Levi's and denim shirt, and marched off into town in the direction of the BT shop. If the mountain wouldn't come to Mohammed, then Mohammed would have to go to the mountain! I refused to let this solitary incident turn me into an insecure recluse. Once in the shop, my task could not have been simpler, and I ran through the same conversation with a middle-aged woman whose spectacles almost covered her whole face.

'My name is Paul Hewitt, and I would like to get my phone reconnected.' I looked 'big specs' straight between the eyes, refusing to acknowledge the aviary of canaries fluttering in my stomach.

'Certainly, sir. What is your telephone number?'

Minutes later I walked out on to the high street victorious and punched the air. P.J. one, rest of the world nil. I had not even been asked my age.

My cheques have cleared so I paid off my debts then took the momentous and thrilling decision to order my Herb. I have not been this excited since Mum bought me an Action Man helicopter! I have even cancelled my ski holiday in favour of a willy . . . it was no contest. I browsed through the detailed order form as one browses through a kitchen catalogue and briefly pondered which size – small, medium or large? It didn't take long! I think Creative Growth Enterprises should have taken a leaf out of the McDonald's school of marketing and relabelled them large, extra large and enormous. Yes, I'll have a large down my trousers, thank you very much for asking.

I need my artificial limb like an amputee needs his artificial leg. One just doesn't feel dressed without it! I posted off my cheque for £450 and primed Sarah as to what to expect when it arrives. 'If you ever come home from work to find a message from me on your answering machine saying come over quickly, it's urgent . . .'

I count Sarah as my best friend and also I guess my girlfriend. We share intimate domestic and sensual moments, but make no demands on each other. We lead very separate lives when we are not together, but I know I can always count on her, and hopefully she knows that she can always count on me. Certainly, she's always there if I need a spider extracted from the bathtub!

With money from the cleared cheques firmly wedged in my back pocket, I decided upon my first full-scale, serious shopping expedition as a man. I had no qualms about using the men's changing-rooms. My rebirth is well under way. I marched into the changing-rooms at River Island, carrying a pair of black Levi's under my left arm. In men's shops I always know exactly what I am looking for. My confidence sits fairly high, accompanying me with pleasure through Burtons and Next for Men. In Top Man I noticed with dread the weedy form of Richard Evans, a guy who used to live in my area during my childhood. He briefly went out with my sister. Now he was staring at me, with something approaching recognition on his baby face. I instructed myself to look and act confident – I had as much right to be there as he did – and continued to flick through the racks of grandad shirts. Richard is the sort of man who would inevitably take a vision of me back to his friends in order to mock me. On a jerk scale of one to ten, he was always high-scoring.

I collapsed in a heap when I got back to my flat, dropping bags as I fell. I was surrounded by the fruits of the afternoon's pickings, and I surveyed the scene with some pride. One pair of black Levi's, one pair of tan Caterpillar boots (boys' department), one thinly striped green sweat-shirt from Next, a thick manly belt in the smallest size, and more Top Man undies ... I mean underpants (tight-fitting jockey-style boxer shorts, in fact) – years of social condition-ing are difficult to erase suddenly! I keep calling my wallet my purse by mistake.

I dressed myself up in the Levi's, the sweatshirt, boots and belt. I was having my own personal coming-of-age party. I surveyed myself in the mirror, and I liked what I saw. I put wax through my fingers and on to my hair, and coated my stubble with some Givenchy aftershave. Tonight I took Sarah out for dinner, which swelled my male ego a little. Shortly after we were seated in a quiet corner of the Leathern Bottle in Wokingham. Sarah leaned forwards and whispered: 'P.J., you look really manly in your new clothes tonight.' I grinned, she grinned back, both of us knowing what I was feeling.

After eating I slipped into the Gents and caught sight of myself in the handbasin mirror when I emerged from the cubicle. I was pleasantly surprised to see how much of a man I looked now, with big shoulders and a more rugged profile.

You could be forgiven for thinking 'how vain!' But most transsexuals *are* to a certain extent. Transsexuals are always telling each other how good they look, passing comment on each other's appearance. Having missed out on a lifetime of looking into the mirror to see a man looking back, I am still making up for lost time. Now I can look and like what I see. I am motivated by my finally becoming whole, my exterior façade being the physical embodiment of my inner quest. We all want our image to reflect the person we feel we are inside. I liken myself to the svelte would-be athlete trapped in an overweight body, determined finally to shed the extra inches. I am like the office nerd who dares to step into glad rags and set the disco alight. I am like the bank clerk who leaves the city to play professional football. I have lived a good part of my life in a body which is alien to me. I have been treated as a woman and addressed as 'luv' or 'sweetheart' for twenty-six years. Finally, I am saying no to all this pretence. My body says to the world, this is who I am, a man. Is it any wonder that I attempt to comprehend the reality of my predicament by indulging in some vainglorious mirror-gazing?

Wednesday 9 February 1994
This morning I received the February edition of *Dyscourse*, the Gender Dysphoria Trust International newsletter, with a brief letter enclosed from the gender counsellor, Fran Springfield. 'How are you coping with all the publicity? Please give me a call and come and see me.'

I immediately rang her on my freshly connected phone line. 'I've been following your progress in the media. You are coping brilliantly with the press attention. I think it would be useful if we could meet up for a chat. I know you're short on funds, but I would rather you come and not pay than not come at all.'

'Thank you. You've made my day.'

Late morning, I caught the bus to my mum's house in an attempt to find some old school reports for this book. I walked to the bus stop via the Tradesman's House, where I called in to see Lisa at work. She took a break to talk to me. I had been nervous about seeing the woman who really took my heart, but as we sat together drinking coffee I felt as though I had begun to banish her ghost. She told me she was seeing someone else, a woman. I had expected to feel wildly jealous but I didn't because I'm a man and as such can't compete with that! We hugged as we left, and I looked at her and realised why we could not go on together. I was a heterosexual man, albeit in the wrong body, and had been having a relationship with a lesbian. I still fancy her, though.

Searching for my old school reports in my mother's loft, I discovered a dust-covered shrine to my childhood. Everything was in serious disarray, and I stumbled upon possessions without chronology. It was like taking a trip in a crazy time-warp machine. There were my well-thumbed books about birds, coarse fishing and natural science. Endless shoeboxes filled with football annuals and collector's cards. I even found a Pro-Shot golf game still in its yellowing cardboard box. My prized Liverpool Subbuteo football team was intact, the players' legs and heads still attached, but the most touching find was inside a battered suitcase with a rusty zip. Action Man. A piece of his fuzzy hair was missing but he was all man and still dressed in his frogman outfit. He looked more fragile than I remembered him, and his joints squeaked as I manipulated them. I put this embodiment of the young me in my pocket and washed my hands of dust.

When I got home I had a bath before injection number eight. I have now been on hormones for three and a half months and my voice has dropped again. Hair is rife on the tops of my legs as well as on my calves now. Soon I expect to be offered a walk-on part as a bear in *Grizzly Adams*.

Thursday 10 February 1994

I left at lunchtime to visit Calcot Primary School in an effort to assimilate myself with my past. The bottom entrance was closed, so I had to walk the long way round. The last time I had walked up Curtis Road was in 1979, and as I rounded the front gates the memories engulfed me. I saw small children in red jumpers lined up in the playground against the brick building. I remembered myself in a charcoal-grey skirt kicking a football with the lads at lunchtime, scoring a goal, oblivious to the ranks of little girls and their skipping-ropes and games of hopscotch.

I have had the same dentist since childhood, and I was rather apprehensive as I have changed sex since my last appointment. I had sent details of my gender change by post in December, and now I had to face the music.

'Mr Hewitt, would you wait for Mr Thompson. He's running a few minutes late,' the receptionist said in her brisk, professional manner. I felt intense relief. She handed me a medical questionnaire, and as I sat down ready to reveal the drugs I was taking – a virtual hormonal field-guide to my reassignment – I spotted the Christmas issue of *Bella* on the magazine table. Fortunately, I was alone in the waiting-room so I did not feel the need to shift nervously or don dark Ray-Bans.

Friday 11 February 1994

Sally and I went out for dinner. I did the ordering at the food counter at the Mansion House in Prospect Park and still felt a massive thrill at being called 'sir'. I think I will never lose that charge at the full acceptance of my gender role. There can be no substitute for all the years I have missed. We took a taxi to the Manor Arms. I must stop going in there as it is a gay pub. A middle-aged man kept trying to pick me up. He followed me into the toilets on three occasions and on the second trip whispered: 'You are a really hunky guy.' I was perversely flattered.

Chapter Six

Saturday 12 February 1994
I am tripping on a lesser-known narcotic called maleness. I cannot expect non-transsexuals to understand the thrill I experience each time I am called 'sir'. This new hormonal orientation is highly addictive. I now know that I couldn't cope without it, and there will be no weaning me off it. Karen cannot get used to my being called 'mate' wherever we go. She keeps erupting into bouts of uncontrollable giggles! It is a constant source of amusement to her after twenty-five years of having a sister.

All the physical changes which have so far taken place seem so natural. I have taken to maleness like the day-old duckling takes to water. The reactions of other people towards me have also been an excellent confirmation of my own observations, while the tenancy of testosterone in my bloodstream is accelerating the physical changes. In the bath this morning I peered down through the clearing water to see a furry blanket of body hair coating my whole body.

Sarah took me to meet her elderly parents last week in Blackpool, and yesterday evening she rang to tell me that her fifty-nine-year-old mother, Hilda, had said how nice it was to see her with 'that lovely young chap'. Hilda and Harold, a self-employed builder, know nothing of my condition, and Sarah knew her mother's comments would make my day. She was right, they did.

I scored last night! The first time I've ever had the nerve to ask a woman to dance, or should I say the first time I have been able to do so since appearing to the world as a man. Vocal cords lubricated with Fosters lager, I sauntered over in the darting strobe light, my heart pounding with a mixture of fear and the silk-sexy voice of Dina Carroll singing 'This Time'. My target was of medium height, with long dark hair and dressed in tightly fitting hot-pants, just like the ones I used to wear. We had been exchanging eye contact all night, and a slow dance seemed the natural progression. I caught her eye once more and beckoned to the middle of the floor. As we moved through the ranks of swaying bodies I felt my ego growing. The night is a bit of a blur, but I remember apologising for being so short and her replying: 'You make up for it in personality and you have a lovely face.' After a couple of slow dances, where I held her tight and hoped she wouldn't notice the feel of my chest binder, she whispered that she had to go. 'My husband is waiting for me back home.'

As I kissed her goodbye I wasn't unduly bothered – you never know what you've pulled until the lights go up! I was simply triumphant that I had proved the ultimate point: she thought I was a guy. Well, at least with my clothes on.

Sunday 13 February 1994

Sarah and I went shopping yesterday before our night on the town. Her presence made me feel braver as we walked together round the men's shops. I came home with a new black shirt and purple Wilson trousers. 'They're dead smart, they are,' the ruffle-haired salesman had told me. What's more I bought two five-kilogramme dumb-bells from Argos which Sarah had to carry home for me! I had planned on wearing my new clothes out to the disco, but when my post-operative female-to-male friend Stuart came to pick me up at eight I wasn't ready; things hadn't gone according to plan. First of all I'd put my new top on, but the grey panels down the sides seemed to highlight the bulk of my bound chest. Then I'd discovered that my new trousers, which had fitted so snugly in the shop, were suddenly two inches too long. I'd slung them off and stepped into a shirt, 501s and a blue-patterned tie.

Tonight I sit and ponder the disadvantages of being a man rather than a woman. I certainly don't get wolf-whistled at by big, hairy builders any more, with huge bottoms that hang out of their trousers! And I don't suppose anyone will buy me flowers either. I guess I can live with that. I remain preoccupied with my height at the moment. I am insanely jealous of genetic males with their stature, which is, virtually always, larger than mine. I feel very inadequate in this respect. Perhaps Gary Glitter would do me a deal on his platforms? But exercise helps, doing weights every other day and seeing horizontal, if not vertical, changes goes some way towards massaging my tender male ego.

All I need now is for my Herb to arrive and for my chest to be flat and I will be quite dangerous. I am also aware of significant temperamental changes since I began taking hormones fourteen weeks ago. Sarah says my fuse is getting shorter and I am definitely reacting to situations in a more aggressive way as once-hidden opinions find themselves a voice. I have become more confident and assertive, and at times my new outspoken nature has surprised me. Was that really me categorically refusing to buy Sarah a packet of cigarettes?

10 p.m.
In a few hours my mood has swung from one of motivation, joy and euphoria to suicidal despair triggered by one short phone call. Lisa phoned in a rage at seven o'clock. 'What are you doing telling people we used to live together?' she spat down the phone. 'Sam's just told me that she heard it from Lynn. Don't you understand I'm terrified that people at work will hear I am gay? I can't afford to have you going around and mouthing off.'

Initially I was too startled to defend myself. I could not deny her allegations, and as such was unarmed. After I'd apologised and put the phone down, I thought about what she had said. I had always considered my relationship with Lisa to be heterosexual. I am proud of our time together; at least I used to be. I am a man who lived with a woman – to me it was that simple. I'm incurably honest about my life and so the truth comes easily and is part of me making a stand for my male identity. But hearing Lisa's attitude made me want to claw my hair out in desperation. I feel angry with her – by disagreeing with my take on the relationship she is denying me my masculinity. The woman I once loved is ashamed of our relationship and ashamed of me. I maintain that I've told no lies, but I shall bow to her request to forget our love ever existed. I'm for a quiet life, me.

However, the phone call proved one thing in black and white. I do not have Lisa's support. I have been coping with my life and the publicity surrounding it with my head blissfully hidden in the sand, kidding myself that by speaking out I can gain acceptance and change people's opinions. But Lisa's phone call brought home to me the reality of what I am trying to do. I feel quite alone inside this woman's body, and I can't even expect support from my friends and ex-lovers. I have to stand up and fight for myself. I can attempt to defend myself until the sun stops shining, but at the end of the day people are going to make their own judgements, just like Lisa's friends, who by their comments intimated I was a gay woman. And how people love to judge!

For the first time in weeks I broke down. But once I'd brushed away the tears my resolve began to harden. I promised myself this story will be told. I will not rest until transsexuals have found a voice. At the moment I am denied football, the only thing that has ever been supremely important to me, and I am just hanging on, waiting to start living again. I am desperate to speed up my metamorphosis, aware that my time clock is ticking away. I have already missed twenty-six years as a male and my football-playing years are ebbing away. But the big question I am asking myself on the eve of 14 February is: do transsexuals get Valentine cards?

Monday 14 February 1994

They do. I got two this morning. One was sickly sweet – something about me being a 'special person' – while the other contained words too rude to print!

Tonight Sarah and I went down to the Manor Arms and boogied the night away. I had to be virtually dragged out on to the street, with the sound of the dance band, M-People, singing 'So Excited' still ringing in my ears. But my enjoyment of the evening was tarnished with a sense of disquiet. The MA is a gay pub which I have been visiting regularly for eighteen months, yet while there I became acutely aware that I now do not really belong. I'd watched two women exchanging a passionate kiss and couldn't relate to that at all. Strangely, it was more of a turn-on than a situation I could picture myself in. I can no longer approach the women there and they will no longer approach me; the final semblances of Martine have gone. Then I'd looked around at the men. The concept of sex with a man is totally abhorrent to me. So there I stood, a heterosexual man in a gay pub. It was not an atmosphere designed with me in mind.

On the way home I picked up a video of my stripagram days and sat down to watch. My feelings as I viewed this dip into my past are hard to explain. I cringed as I saw a man in a woman's body cavorting around wearing large mammaries and teasing the unfortunate male victim, a lecturer at an agricultural college. I use the word 'victim' loosely here, as the pained expression on *my* face made it difficult to determine just who was the victim. His eighteen-year-old students heckled as I stripped and laid the lecturer down on the floor. All I could feel at this moment was pain. I saw nothing more or less than a man in drag. I could see the discomfort in my own eyes, but only lusty curiosity in the eyes of my oblivious male audience. I realised just what a good 'actress' I had been.

Wednesday 16 February 1994

Sarah woke me yesterday morning with shrieks of 'Look at the snow'. A velveteen white carpet lay glistening on the ground outside. Waiting for me in the post-box were another two Valentines. *Oh populaire cette année!* One was from Susan, the *Bella* reader I have been writing to. The other remains a complete mystery, posted in Basingstoke, sealed in two envelopes and posted a day late. It said 'Hey Goodlookin'' on the front and 'Happy Valentine's Day you gorgeous creature' on the inside. If I didn't know better I would have thought it was from Lisa, as it was addressed to P.J. and only about three people call me by this name.

I am desperate to play football, so I decided today to get in touch with some of the players from the Ladies' Football Club. I am toying with the idea of training with them until I pass sufficiently in football kit to play in a men's team. But it will take guts to face these tough, outspoken women in my new gender role. I phoned Jo, the captain, this afternoon, but her attitude was difficult to assess. I had told her of my transsexualism some months ago. She is going to consult the team members and ring me back with their answer. I put down the phone and sat back feeling very stressed out. I went for a run to calm down but overdid it – even brushing my hair would be overdoing it these days – and now I feel like someone has made a smash-and-grab raid on my vital energy reserves.

It is only six weeks until my appointment with the plastic surgeon who can give the go-ahead. I long for the day I can ceremoniously dispose of my chest binder. I am considering looking for a part-time job. It will be enough to preserve my morale and keep me sane. Full-time work would be suicide in my current state of health.

Thursday 17 February 1994

Cheered myself up in the evening. I sought solace with Sarah, and a Chinese takeaway with chocolate fudge cheesecake to follow. Small comforts. I rang up for an application form for the job of trainee croupier at Reading Sporting Club. It could be right up my street: smart uniform, electric night-life, plenty of chicks. The perfect job for a sociable young male with a keen interest in the opposite sex!

Saturday 19 February 1994

Still no clues to my mystery Valentine!

Tuesday 22 February 1994

I am exhausted. I can assume only that this is the mental pressure I am under taking its physical toll. I was a recluse all weekend. Even admiring my new crop of hairs in the mirror was too much effort. In desperation I phoned the

Good Health Company in Marble Arch this morning. They operate private homoeopathic health screenings. I have made an appointment for Monday. I sat and thought about the wisdom of this for a while and then went down to the health shop, where I bought a bottle of Aloe Vera, a tub of garlic tablets and an extra-large jar of high-octane multi-vitamins. I have decided to ban alcohol, chocolate and sugar from my diet and to start pumping iron again. I have been the dictionary definition of lethargy of late, and my weights have been sitting gathering dust in their box.

Today Mr Tappenden from the Reading Sporting Club left a message on my machine. I have an interview for the croupier job on Thursday.

The headlines today say it all. They were robbed. I simply cannot believe that Torvill and Dean did not win gold last night in Norway. Were the judges asleep? What's more, gay men have failed in their bid to lower the age of consent to sixteen. Instead, it has dropped from twenty-one to eighteen. This isn't equality. Can't the right honourable gentlemen and ladies see that all that homosexuals want is equal rights? Nothing fancy. Just to be treated the same as the next man. Only the next man is heterosexual!

Today I attempted to research the role of croupier for my interview. The library was closed, the careers library got as far as books on nursing, and when, in desperation, I visited the Sporting Club, nobody had time to help me. I spoke to a woman with hair and make-up more at home in the *Rocky Horror Picture Show* than a posh sporting club. I hope she's not interviewing me on Thursday.

Back home, I filled in an application form for a one-year press photography course with the National Council for the Training of Journalists. By this time it was 4.30. Sarah picked me up and deposited me at the Circuit Lane Surgery for injection number nine. I have now been on hormones for exactly four months. My voice is stubbornly refusing to break and my stubble does not yet qualify as designer. But it will.

I lugged my new bedding up the hill from the shop today. I have taken the indulgent step of buying myself a double quilt. As I write I listen to the sounds of Alison Moyet singing 'All Cried Out' on the Love Zone, Radio 210. I know exactly how she feels. I am all cried out as well. But, single-minded, I continue.

It is lucky for me I am a determined little bastard.

Thursday 24 February 1994

The day of my interview. I set off early, dressed in my best suit – in fact my only suit – my new blue shirt and my favourite tie, pale blue with squiggly shapes. I always feel ten times more confident when dressed up. I swaggered along as far as the front reception, where my swagger quickly converted itself into a less assuming stance, and was immediately put at ease by the interviewer, Anne-Marie Marshall. She did not have the *Rocky Horror* haircut, and after twenty minutes of general discussion as to what the job entailed she intimated loosely that I would be offered a place on the trainee croupier course beginning on 7 March.

Then came an unexpected question. 'But there are a few things I will need from you in order to register you for a gaming licence. Your birth certificate and a couple of passport photographs.'

I felt the colour drain from my face as she mentioned these words. Passport photos I could do – no problem – but showing my birth certificate would prove a tricky dilemma. I felt like a secret agent. Being forced to hand over my birth certificate would tell my potential employer everything I was trying to hide. My cover would be blown. But I smiled, regained my composure, shook her hand and promised to send her what she required.

Sunday 27 February 1994
I am wound up like a clock spring at the moment. I cannot sleep. I have such an irresistible urge to push my life in positive directions. I am the world's most impatient man. Sarah says that when I sleep she can't decide whether I am making paper or crushing grapes. Come sunrise and my bed looks like a battleground.

I visited my mother yesterday. She spent the afternoon in a kind of schizophrenic limbo, randomly interchanging 'he' and 'she', and 'Martine' and 'Paul' with all possible permutations. But she does appear to be trying, bless her. Give birth to twin girls and you expect them to remain so. I can't fathom what a shock this must have been to her, but I have not the emotional energy to expend wondering. At the moment my own problems are about all I can cope with.

While at my mother's large, detached and recently underpinned house, I picked up some more of my childhood belongings from the loft, including my school exam certificates. My interests leaned towards the scientific subjects, but my grades were consistently high throughout. I also discovered my collection of birds' eggs from the days when plucking these from nests was not illegal. All twelve of them were intact, wrapped up in handfuls of decaying cotton wool and stored in an old roller-skate case. I have decided to buy a glass case for them when I can afford it, and preserve them forever as a memory of hours spent in the grounds of Fairmile Hospital as a youngster, peering up into tree foliage while balanced on my father's broad and well-muscled shoulders. My mum and my uncle would spend a couple of hours visiting my aunt, while Karen and I would spend the afternoon bird-watching with Dad. Mum would often tell my sister and me off for singing in the back of the car, but Uncle Colin would say, 'Leave them alone, June, they're singing because they are happy.' Karen and I would sing all the time – even when we were eating. We made tunes while we munched!

I cooked dinner for Sarah last night. As I served up spaghetti bolognese she shot me an appraising look and mouthed the words: 'Who says men can't cook!' After Sarah left, I used my quilt to wrap myself up like a double-decker Scooby snack and watched Nigel Benn, the dark destroyer, boxing like a true champion. If I could have my time all over again, this time with the right body, I could imagine myself as a boxer. I'm like a sewer rat. If you back me into a corner I always come out fighting.

This afternoon I watched the FA Cup football between Aston Villa and Tranmere Rovers.

Monday 28 February 1994

My endocrinologist is very perceptive and understanding, and I have his support. This was my first visit to see Dr Ellis Snitcher since he prescribed me hormones on 21 October last year. As I walked into his home-based surgery in West Hampstead he looked me up and down and said: 'You are looking great!' When I told him about my plans to study journalism, he said: 'I have a strong, intuitive feeling that you are going to make a living out of writing.' I inwardly hoped he was right! I promised to send him copies of my newspaper articles, and we made an appointment for me to return after my six-monthly blood test on 2 May. Talking to Ellis was important because it made me realise how much I have achieved since my last visit. It is only four months since I last saw him, and I seem to have achieved quite a lot in a short space of time. I walked back to Finchley Road tube station feeling taller than when I had set out that morning, confidence bursting from my pores like sweat on a humid day.

At my appointment at the Good Health Company in

Marble Arch the homoeopathic practitioner tested the resistance of my acupuncture points on my fingers and toes to 0.1 volts of electric current to decide which, if any, of my organs were under stress. I wanted to say, 'All of them.' He claimed that he had found several faults with my meridians, and consequently I came away with various homoeopathic remedies – as well as a considerably lighter wallet! I'm not sure what's in these remedies, but I really don't care as long as they work. They are supposed to cleanse the system and encourage the body's immune system to recognise toxins and throw them out. I have a repeat appointment in three weeks.

Saturday 5 March 1994

I have just checked my face in the mirror and stubble is creeping up my cheeks, just as ivy clambers up the trestles on the sides of thatched cottages. It will not be long before I have my own beloved thatch. As we push into March, the date for my visit to Mount Vernon Hospital is fast approaching . . . twenty-five days and counting.

The postman brought excellent news this morning. Four letters awaited me. I immediately went into town to pay in the two cheques which had arrived and then walked round the shops with an invisible sign saying 'rich bastard' tattooed on my forehead. I have decided that my life may well be a lonely one. But preferable to be rich and lonely than poor and lonely!

I waited for over an hour for a haircut at George's barber's and came out with a Gazza haircut, after some confusion with the stylist about how it should be clipped. I wanted my hair to be cut growing forwards, but my hair insisted on standing up, so the stylist let it do its own thing in the end. Elvis, the local nutter who is under the permanent delusion that he is The King himself, was obviously out on a good-behaviour bond. He was chatting away to all the stylists in his usual attire of gaudy velvet jacket with bad-taste yellow T-shirt and black pumps. Apparently, he had been arrested for singing 'Love Me Tender' in the high street. He is completely insane but totally harmless, and I often see him jumping erratically in front of traffic as I walk along the Oxford Road into town.

Sunday 6 March 1994

I have been a busy lad and put heart and soul into trying for a place on a one-year journalism course in September. I am applying for two courses, one photography, one writing. I have equipped myself with £275-worth of second-hand camera equipment, including a standard zoom lens as big as I'd wish my willy to be if I had one. I certainly felt great when I got my hands on it. It is now abundantly clear to me why photography is a male-dominated profession.

I took my tripod and Ricoh KR-10 to Prospect Park yesterday evening to catch the sunset. Unfortunately, manual photography is harder than it looks and takes quite a bit of concentration, so I am taking a day off today to relieve my cerebrum of this incessant pounding. This is a headache from hell; today marks its fifth day.

My father has been in hospital this week having tumours removed from his bladder. His condition isn't serious, which is a huge relief. I couldn't cope with any more strain at the moment. I have reached a stage where I am despairing of the future. I'm not even well enough to work my way out of trouble. I am putting all my hopes on getting a place on a journalism course in September; I am far too ambitious and talented to squander my life in a lonely bedsit with a flop-drop bed. My ego right now is the size of the smallest member of a group of Russian dolls stacked one inside the other. He is fragile, he is small, he is hidden, he is trapped.

Part of my mood is attributable to the letter I received yesterday. It dropped on to the mat and my mood along with it. It read:

Dear Mr Hewitt
We are sorry to tell you, you have not been selected for a place on the forthcoming croupier course. We hope you are not too disappointed, and we would like to thank you for the interest you have shown in our company.
Yours sincerely...

Bald and to the point. My misery is not about the job itself – I didn't want to make a career in casinos – but rejection of any kind always hurts. I take life a little too personally. I guess I'll never know the real reason why I never got the job, but I am pretty sure it had nothing to do with my transsexualism; more likely I was over-qualified. I refused to take the implied criticism lying down and summoned my courage to ring Reading Sporting Club and find out why they had turned me down. A small sliver of my soul keeps insisting that I am being paranoid. It is vital not to develop a defeatist attitude.

I rang the number and was put through to Mrs Marshall. Thank God for tact. She said very sweetly: 'I liked your application, and I liked you, in fact. It was simply a case of there being too many applicants and not enough places. You were very, very close. Please do apply next year if you would like to.'

I cling to the belief at times like this that there is a big plan for me. What doesn't happen is simply not meant to happen, and I will find happiness in the end. You've got to believe in something, haven't you? I certainly keep believing in my friends. They hold me together.

Today Debbie, my ex, and I set off for a photography field trip in the countryside in her red MR2. As we sped through the Berkshire roads with the velvet sounds of Sarah Washington playing at full volume, I spotted a bay mare and her foal. We reversed and they came over looking interested, but by the time I got my camera set up they had lost interest and wandered off. Over dinner we planned a field trip to North Wales. I need some good photos in my portfolio.

Monday 7 March 1994

Last night I did some weights in an effort to release some stress. I was relaxed until the moment it was time to turn off the light and go to sleep. Then unwanted thoughts began to force their way into my head. Suddenly I was thinking about my ex-football mates and how they have been treating me lately. I tossed and turned for hours, my mind encased in a blanket of paranoia.

I found myself reflecting on their recent reactions. About two months ago I sent a letter to Leila, one of our best forward players, asking her if I could make a copy of her football videos of the club. We'd already discussed this when I was still playing as a woman and she'd agreed to it without question, but we never got around to it. After my changeover these videos began to assume crucial significance. I wanted archive footage of myself playing the game I love because I may never get to play football for a team again. Leila didn't reply to my letter or my phone calls. The team captain, Jo, has also failed to respond to my request three weeks ago to have a kick around with them. When I saw another team member by the Ramada Hotel last week and she deliberately turned away as though she had not seen me, I realised that I was being treated like a social leper.

Disgusted that none of my ex-team mates had the balls to face me, I phoned Jo today to make sure I was not being paranoid. I wasn't. I am not welcome to train with the ladies, girls who used to be my friends because, and I quote: 'Lots of them are worried as to what the new players would think.' No wonder they are embarrassed to acknowledge me on the street. I'd be embarrassed if I too ostracised someone because of their transsexualism.

It is crucial not to let myself be haunted by melancholic thoughts. I have a new life now, but the pain is seemingly never-ending.

Wednesday 9 March 1994

It was time for injection number 'can't remember' today. I am becoming a dab hand at being jabbed in the bum with life-giving testosterone. I assessed myself in my long mirror. My boobs look like they belong to someone else, female appendages superimposed on a well-muscled and well-defined male torso.

My weight increased rapidly initially, but has been stationary at eight stone seven pounds since the sixth week of treatment. Hairs continue to creep like fine masculine vines all over my body, and even my buttocks are host to dark forestation.

Bored, I decided to look up some old friends. I flicked through the pages of my address book and settled on one particular number. I got straight through to an old school friend in Southampton who nearly dropped the receiver when I told her of my gender change. She exclaimed: 'How exciting for you!' Now that's just the sort of reaction I like. Then the phone rang for me. It was Dave Reynolds, the vice-president of the insurance company I was working for when I underwent my changeover. During our man-to-man chat, he said: 'You now sound just like my thirteen-year-old son. His voice is about to break too!'

Thursday 10 March 1994

Hangover city. I had thought I might find out what 'real

men' find so attractive about bitter. A pint and a half is only a warm-up and a bit of leg stretching, but it's knocked me out. I think it is now safe to assume that I'm allergic to alcohol. This has been a long and painful lesson to learn, with many headaches *en route*.

Is it my imagination, or are my feet getting bigger? My shoulders are looking more and more like haulage pivots. My body is like my mother's house: under reconstruction.

While I waited the required ten minutes in the waiting-room before leaving after my injection, my GP walked past and said, 'Hi.' Soul singer Barry White briefly hijacked my vocal cords and a bass 'Hello' boomed from my lips. My GP looked as surprised as I did. Feeling more manly than ever before, I watched Terry Venables make his début as England manager in the friendly international between England and Denmark.

As I walked along the Oxford Road this evening I lingered briefly to watch as a blind man with a white stick negotiated the busy road. I thought I had it tough, but it must be tougher living in a world of darkness where the sun never shines.

Saturday 12 March 1994

I met my mother for lunch in the Co-op today. She called me Martine, but did at least look guilty about it. It did not actually bother me too much at the time, as I failed completely to recognise this name as mine and totally ignored it. I have truly adopted Paul now. He is who I am.

Convinced that I had grown, I got the tape-measure out when I got home to check my measurements. I was right. I have gained half an inch in height since the beginning of treatment. Digging out my old boots confirmed that my feet have indeed grown one size. This is exciting news for me!

Sunday 13 March 1994

Karen and I went to Blackburn today. She was competing in the National Women's Cross-Country Championships. I hadn't counted on the coach being full of people known to me from running days past. Nobody recognised me initially, and I kept my head down as we got on to the coach at Palmer Park. I could not face embarrassing explanations of gender reassignment at six in the morning with my eyes only half open. But as the coach sped the 150 miles to Blackburn people began to realise who I was. Once we arrived, and each time I was out of the way, Karen carefully explained my situation to people as they asked. Fortunately, three-quarters of the party had not seen me before and accepted me as Karen's brother without question. I even got invited to run for the men's team. At the moment this seems like an impossible dream, but if my body were not crippled by illness I would love more than anything else in the whole world to be able to compete in my chosen sport alongside other men. This scenario would be more wonderful than words, and I have not given up hope that one day it will happen.

Soon, memories came flooding back of our competitive days as teenage runners for Reading Athletic Club. Karen and I made perfect training partners, so evenly matched were we. We would run stride for stride, both fiercely competitive. I honestly believe that Karen was the slightly more talented runner, but my determination was unmatched. I remember a county cross-country race once, where I was so determined to be the first Reading athlete home that I was physically sick when I had finished. But no matter, I had done it. Karen represented Berkshire in the English Schools Cross-Country Championships on the track, while I tended to have the edge in the cross-country races. We were very successful as club runners, and well known for our sprint finishes.

I digress here. Karen ran well and as she passed me I swelled with emotion as I cheered her on. I longed to be out there myself, pushing myself to the limit, instead of stuck behind the line, confined by my own physical limitations. I suppressed an outburst of tears which threatened, like the dark sky across the valley, to pour at any moment.

Monday 14 March 1994

I walked into town at lunchtime, extremely slowly. On the way I was overtaken by several white-haired pensioners speeding in their slippers to the post office to cash their state benefits.

There is a new breed of motorist on our roads. He is known as the 'superwanker'. Almost always male, he insists on driving everywhere at breakneck speeds. His car screams erratically from one side of the road to the other. I pity his wife if he makes love at the same speed at which he drives. He probably likes to call himself the 'love express'. I stepped on to the pavement and out of his way at a few minutes past one today.

In a paper bag under my arm was *The Complete Photography Course*. I went home to read it. I broke off to write a two-page essay to Berkshire County Council entitled 'Why I should get a discretionary grant from your piss-poor budget'. I hope I sold myself well; everything career-wise is hinged to this.

I telephoned my dad and we decided to go to Oxford Greyhound Stadium for the evening. My first bet – a modest £1 – was on a 5–1 winner, Could Be Worse! Dad and I sat together watching the European Cup Winners' Cup between races. We were in a lads' paradise with the bookies and track behind us and the football on the video screen in front of us. My father has acclimatised very well to having another son now, although I'm not sure I'm coping as well as he is. I felt the familiar old green jealousy well up inside me as Dad spoke with pride of Simon, his natural-born son and my half-brother, and his exploits on the football field. I wanted to shout the words of the soul record 'It Should've Been Me'!

Tuesday 15 March 1994

The dog-races left me in a state of hyperactivity. It took me ages to get to sleep and then I had another blood-pumping nightmare.

> *A long-haired, axe-wielding maniac was hacking through the door to my room. I was paralysed in my bed, watching the sweat pouring off his forehead, which I could glimpse as the flimsy wood split and tore. He had tattoos on his knuckles and I could see the dirt under his fingernails as the axe smashed up and down.*

I awoke with a start, too scared to get out of bed or go back to sleep. I lay remembering the nightmares that accompanied my childhood. Paralysed, I used to cry out for my mum to come and help me. But this time there was nobody there and I had to cope alone. Still, I'm a big boy now.

Friday 18 March 1994

I spent yesterday out taking photographs. With my interest in photography currently verging on the obsessive, I am Colorama's best customer. I am also becoming increasingly observant of my surroundings. I arrived home tired but at peace with the world, and I even did some more weights before my calm was shattered by an unexpected phone call.

I haven't mentioned Mick before, but I had to pick myself off the floor on hearing him at the end of the line.

Mick and I first met in the Railway Tavern in 1992. He worked behind the bar and I was a regular customer, along with the girls I used to play football with. It was an instant attraction, a meeting of minds which followed a convergence of smiles across a crowded bar on a Saturday night. Soon we had developed a strong friendship. I cannot say our relationship was purely platonic, yet it was not really a love affair. Mick is the most wonderful man I have ever met. He is also the only person I know who is as sensitive and introspective as I am, qualities that seem rare, or at least well suppressed, among men. Although he told me he loved me fairly early on, it was a relationship without direction. He was married, if unhappily, and he was soon to discover that I was transsexual and predominantly interested in women.

When we first met I had just come out on the gay scene and was having a long-term affair which was not bringing me a great deal of happiness. Although I loved Christine madly, she was nineteen, five years younger than me, and I found it difficult to talk to her about my inner feelings. I was her first lover. I was too intense, too strong, too independent, too passionate. I hated all the lies she was telling her parents about where she was going and with whom. She was supposed to be out with friends, but all the while was safely in my arms.

At about this time I was also beginning to question my own identity. The growing feelings of unease I had always connected with my female body had begun to formulate into something that could not be ignored. Stunned by what I was experiencing inside, I began a period of heavy denial. I might fancy women, but I was still intent on flirting with men, parading them as fashion accessories. I had a woman's body, society told me I should fancy men, so I was despising and denying what I feared about my true gender and sexuality. It was a recipe for disaster, and my relationship with Christine did well to survive a year.

Into this maelstrom came Mick, but he took my complicated life in his trainer-clad stride. I started seeing him a few months into my affair with Christine. He used to smuggle me back into the Railway Tavern after hours. I was working as a stripagram at that time and my hours were as unsocial as his. I would arrive at the pub in a coat hiding stockings and suspenders, and do a quick change into civvies while Mick would throw out the last of the regulars. Then we would disappear off somewhere, in convoy, his car following mine, just to be together. We once played football in Prospect Park at midnight, hardly able to see the ball, let alone kick it.

Sexually, Mick was sensitive. He never pushed me and picked up early on that my breasts were a problem for me. At that time I had no idea I was transsexual. When Mick took his shirt off and I ran my hands across his flat, muscular chest, marvelling at his masculine lines, my feelings were not sexual but ones of admiration and envy.

Mick soon discovered that I was seeing Christine and seemed to accept it. I poured out my heart to him one night, and from then on he was my confidant. He risked a great deal by staying out late with me. I justified my behaviour knowing that we weren't actually sleeping together, just spending time together and cuddling like fourteen-year-olds. We did not make a conscious decision to stop seeing each other; Mick simply seemed to pull away from my life as my gender reassignment programme began. I guess we had reached the end of the line, and that it was less painful for both of us this way. Few people have understood me as he did. I had not heard from him since taking hormones, not until last night.

His phone call has set my emotions in turmoil. 'I don't know how I'll feel if I see you,' he explained softly. 'The trouble is that I am worried I will still fancy you!' I explained my profound physical changes. He hesitated and said: 'My main concern is your happiness. I've seen you go through so much and you deserve to be happy.' I feel for Mick. It must be a nightmare to discover that the woman you fell in love with turns out not to be a woman at all – so deceptive were my feminine curves. We both knew that meeting face to face would be awkward. He loved my female body, and I don't think I could cope with his critical eye. But in time I am sure we will re-establish our friendship. It was never a relationship dependent on the bedroom.

I put down the phone and in the seclusion of my room burst into tears. It is at times like this I want to stick my head down the toilet and flush the chain. 'Goodnight, cruel world!' I find myself asking the question, 'Why is gender so damn pivotal to everything?'

So it's Friday morning and I feel like a square peg that has been forcibly squeezed into a round hole. Consultation of my pocket diary has revealed only twelve days until my appointment at Mount Vernon Hospital. I am crossing them off.

I lie still
Embraced by the warm sand
Knowing this fish is without water
As a mother who has lost her daughter

The sun's soft rays are small comfort
If at all
Just one thought keeps me standing tall

Every hurdle I face, every mile I race
Every sunset I feel upon my face
Brings me one step nearer my heart's abode

One bound further along my course
A river bank closer to the source

The future lies ahead, uncertain
But of one thing I'm sure

My heart will be allowed to exalt once more
Love's tap will resonate upon my door
Holding hands, sinewy bodies locked tight
Trading passion with the ladies of the night

I am still counting off the days
And dreaming up a million ways
To express myself in the cold confines
Of an unexpressive world

Saturday 19 March 1994
Oh, God, my hairline looks like it is receding and my head is thumping as a result of drowning my sorrows in several pints of Fosters last night. I was absolutely devastated to receive a letter from the London College of Printing yesterday, telling me that I was not even to be invited for interview. I wanted to cry my eyes out but, strangely for me, adopted the male tendency to suppress emotion. I will bounce back. It is not success or failure that defines the person but how we deal with either. I like to believe that success is only failure turned inside out. I still have two applications to hear about.

Fed up, I wandered in the direction of the launderette. With a burst of spontaneity I bought some flowers from a stall to give to Kathy, the launderette lady. I felt like letting her know how much I value our friendly chats every Friday afternoon. The expression 'salt of the earth' was surely created for her.

I went down to the Three Men and a Boat pub and was surprised to see an old friend, Nicolina, working behind the bar. She recognised me instantly and whispered across the polished panels: 'Are you still going through the you-know-what?' I nodded, and smiled at her choice of phrase, thanking my lucky stars she hadn't shouted M-A-R-T-I-N-E across a packed public house. At 11 p.m. my post-operative female-to-male friend Stuart and I moved on to Churchill's night-club. On my first visit to the dance-floor I was ambushed by a plump escapee from a hen party slightly the worse for alcohol. She grasped me in her clutches beneath the revolving spotlights, but I managed to escape into the safety of a darkly lit alcove.

I danced all night, but drink left me with sobering thoughts, as well as a hangover, to contend with in the cold light of day. I am a man haunted. Haunted by insecurities that I will not cut it in a male world. I have a serious hang-up about my diminutive stature and turn green with envy at pictures of well-muscled male bodies.

I watched three young lads in the disco last night. They were about nineteen years old, very drunk and uttering disgusting comments. Each was the football hooligan personified. But they were all beefy lads over six feet tall. I felt intensely angry that they should have the brains of a garden vegetable but bodies far superior than mine will ever be. I feel utterly cheated. I have to try to remind myself of what I do have, rather than dwelling on my shortcomings. I also harbour fears that my mastectomy could prove to be a huge disappointment. I have yet to see a good one.

I cut a picture out of the *Daily Express* this evening. Liam Neeson, bare-chested and wearing only faded blue Levi's and a smile. I have an all-encompassing jealousy of the male form, I desperately need to talk out all these feelings, but my male pride refuses to acknowledge that I am having trouble dealing with all this on my own.

Friday 25 March 1994

Hello, stranger. It's been a while, hasn't it, my love? Do you know why I love writing to you? Because you listen to me and don't crush my gentle spirit. I have had another injection and my marriage to the male way of life is rock solid. Testosterone and I are partners till death do us part. My homoeopath at Marble Arch has reviewed my meridians. He tells me that my liver is under particular stress. This would certainly explain my intolerance to alcohol. I came away, once again, with an empty wallet and still more remedies.

I did a quick shimmy down to Waterloo and met Beverley, a journalist from *New Woman*. I had fallen in love with her telephone voice. Being interviewed by her was a very relaxed affair. I returned home smiling, with red lipstick on my right cheek. She instantly became my friend when she told me that my shoulders look big. They are indeed bulging.

Wednesday 30 March 1994

I awoke feeling sick. The day of reckoning had arrived. Sarah drove me up to London for my 10.45 appointment with Dr Morgan at Mount Vernon Hospital. My nerves were contagious; Sarah was a wreck too. My name was called an hour late, and when the nurse did glance around the waiting-room with her clipboard she asked for 'Paula Hewitt' so I figured that had to be me.

I was left to sit in a small consulting room for about ten minutes before Dr Morgan, middle-aged and balding, came and shook my hand. I hoped he hadn't noticed the excess perspiration on my palms. I looked at him anxiously, feeling as though my whole future was a huge weight balancing on this moment. I hated sitting on the consulting bed as he prodded and gestured at the two space aliens dangling like helium balloons from my muscular chest. As I dressed with a heavy heart, the words 'It could be eighteen months' were not ones to create peace of mind.

I left the hospital feeling angry enough to start breaking

things. Yes, breast-cancer victims need urgent attention, but don't people realise that transsexualism is a life-threatening condition as well? Many people do not know that approximately one in five transsexuals actually commit suicide.

I am now supposed to play the patient waiting game again. But I won't. I won't rest from pursuing this. After I got home I spent the evening on the phone ringing private surgeons. I want to start my life. I want to be in control. I want to get these things off my chest, literally. If I cannot get my op soon I may have to stoop to the desperate measure of selling my story to the *News of the World* and use the money to go private. The longer I have to wait, the more depressed I get, and the less I want to stick around to see what my future holds.

I made Sarah turn off the bedroom light before we made love. I could not bear to see my own breasts. Catching sight of them beneath me totally throws me off my stride, throwing question marks on a manhood which, incidentally, the remarkable Sarah does not question. Making love is a rare form of escape for me, a time when the wheels of the world stop turning just for a moment and I can abandon all my troubles along with my pile of clothes at the side of the bed.

Thursday 31 March 1994

Beverley Kemp phoned me this afternoon; she really has the most wonderful voice to die for. I promised her I would not commit suicide. The water at Beachy Head is too cold this early on in the season and, besides, I'm not going anywhere until I've got through a few more women!

Sunday 3 April 1994, Easter Sunday

Yesterday I went into town to search for a new suit. Every shop contained a host of salesmen eager to encourage me to part with my cash, but finding a suit that fitted was a nightmare. Even the shortest trousers are too long for me, a fact that by now I take as standard! Not only that, but a thirty-six-inch, short jacket took a while to track down in a decent colour.

I went to use the Gents in Debenhams but turned around and walked back out again after finding the one cubicle occupied. Every so often this happens to me. I panic at the sight of the urinals I can't use and walk out instead of waiting for the cubicle. I guess it will be a while before I am entirely comfortable in the Gents.

Eventually, I came away from Burtons with a single-breasted suit by Centaur.

By the time I got home I had only half an hour to have a bath and meet my mum in town for her confirmation and baptism evening in the Catholic church. I had bought her a home-made cake for the occasion from Farley's Farm Shop, but I accidentally squashed the Easter chick sitting on three candy eggs as I climbed into the passenger seat of Sarah's van.

I thought Father Terry was going to drown my mother when he baptised her; he certainly looked as if he was giving her a bath. I wanted to stand up and offer him some Wash 'n' Go. The service meant nothing to me; so much for familial solidarity. I wish I'd taken a copy of *Mayfair* to insert inside my hymn-book. The only words I could relate to were 'Blessed is he who comes' and 'Blessed is he who comes in the name of the Lord'. Luckily, the service finished at 11 p.m. and the taxi got me home just in time to see Alan Shearer score two classic goals for Blackburn to beat Manchester United 2–0, bringing them within three points of the league leaders.

I had to laugh at my mum tonight. All the way to the church, and practically into the pew, she kept calling me Martine and referring to me as 'she'. Then, once seated, she pointed to the other side of the church, saying: 'The gents' toilets are over there.' She is so inconsistent! The funny thing is, I don't think she even knows she is doing it!

Wednesday 6 April 1994

Today was injection number twelve. Not only did Sister Ellen Lord put oily Sustanon 250mg into my bottom; she also put an idea in my head. On hearing about the frustration of my visit to Mount Vernon Hospital and the inevitable delay, she suggested: 'Why don't you write to the manufacturers of Sustanon and ask them if they will fund your operation? They seem to have plenty of money for their sales reps!'

Brilliant thinking. I have already drafted a letter and posted it to Organon Laboratories in Cambridge. They can only say no.

The next few weeks could be crucial to the complexion of my future. I have two written journalism entrance exams to take, I am awaiting the letter from Mount Vernon, and I will find out the decision from the appeals office about my grant. I am fighting hard for my future.

Friday 8 April 1994

I met my mother in town for lunch yesterday. We made a breakthrough. Walking through the packed-out aisles in Woolworths, she suddenly remarked: 'I think I like having a son!' This was beautiful music made specially for my ears.

At 9 p.m. tonight I was in an atypical dilemma. To go out or not to go out. While contemplating my exhaustion level I took a bath so as not to waste the 10p I had put in the electric meter. As I sat in the water contemplating the aphorism 'life is like a hot bath – it feels good while you're in it but the longer you stay the more wrinkled you get', I gave myself a good talking to. Whatever happened to the good old days when a nuclear holocaust would not have kept the boogie machine in on a Friday night? Where hides that party animal of days past who would look at his watch on Friday evening and shout, 'Oooh, I've been waiting all week for this'?

Saturday 9 April 1994

I did go out last night, although I practically had to contort my legs and kick my own butt to make it happen. I ordered a taxi and the controller at the end of the line said, 'It'll be with you in about ten minutes, mate.' As I put down the receiver and walked back across my room it dawned on me that I had just been taken as a man, no question.

During the taxi-ride the driver and I became engaged in a very male conversation, with him uttering a multitude of four-letter expletives he certainly would not have used in the presence of a lady. What would have amounted to thunderclaps to female ears was pure music to my own.

Once at the disco I was astonished to spot a male-to-female transsexual within seconds. Others may not have noticed her transsexualism, but my own physical shortcomings make me only too aware of other people's. I was dying to approach her to tell her how good she looked, but held back, sensitive to the fact that she might be offended that I had guessed her past. She towered over her two male companions, and was more slender than most male-to-female transsexuals. Slender and attractive, I thought. It was the shortness of her pale green skirt and the small handbag hanging from her shoulder which gave her away. She stood out immediately because it was a gay disco. Gay women, in my experience, do not wear mini-skirts. Never in a million years would you see a lesbian with a handbag. And this wasn't just any handbag – it was miniature, decorative and barely large enough to contain a packet of condoms let alone a hairbrush.

Today was Grand National day; no false starts this year. I walked into town to buy a paper to study form but the atmosphere in the smoky betting-shop didn't help me. My rank outsider, Fourth of July, fell at the first, and my other choice, The Fellow, was looking good until taking a nosedive about four fences from the finish.

Wednesday 13 April 1994
Tomorrow my Herb arrives – the secretary of the Female-to-Male Network who processed my order phoned from Manchester yesterday to say it was coming. I wished I had not been forewarned, as I could hardly sleep a wink last night with excitement. I have not been this excited since Hasbro patented Action Man. According to the card on the doormat the postman tried to deliver my parcel at 10.41 this morning but no one opened the door, so I will have to collect it myself from the post office tomorrow afternoon. Even waiting for Christmas Day to dawn as a kid was not this exciting.

Thursday 14 April 1994
I went to the post office in Caversham this afternoon to pick up my Herb. Call me paranoid if you like, but I am certain that the guys at the reception desk knew what was in my brown paper parcel. They seemed to make a real point of slowly and deliberately handing it over the desk to me, pausing to ask: 'Have you been expecting this?' I don't know how, but they certainly knew, judging by the smirks they were not trying hard to conceal. It was a little embarrassing but the beetroot colour in my cheeks quickly faded. Finally, I had my hands on the box that contained my trouser trident, girl-seeking missile.

I took it round to Sarah's and spent the evening trying to get to grips with it. I even took it into the bath with me to play submarines. I am delighted with its realism; it even has veins! I feel almost a complete man with it on now and I shall wear it every day, not necessarily as a sexual device but as a masculinising one. One thought troubles me. I feel that maybe I have a little more than I bargained for. It is not just large, it is huge. And not only is it huge, it is also semi-erect due to its rubbery nature. This effectively gives it a mind of its own when not securely strapped down. I poked Sarah in the eye twice without even getting out of the chair! Hanging loose in boxer shorts is a definite no-no. I can't dress left or right, just up and out. Even inside trousers I have a packed lunch bigger than any I ever had at school. If there's a guy out there with a bigger dick than I've got I'd like to meet him! Looks like I'm going to have to find a woman who's had six kids and been around the block a few times, lest Herbie and I should cause serious structural damage. Slack Alice, come on down!

Friday 15 April 1994
Herbie took up half the bed and I still couldn't sleep a wink last night. Today I went all the way to Harlow feeling like death to take the written test for the photojournalism course. All the other lads there were fresh out of short trousers so I didn't look a bit out of place. Right now my Herb and I would much rather be doing some serious shagging than sitting here writing this. All my trousers now seem to stay up without belts and I need bigger underwear to accommodate my new buddy. What am I complaining for? I wanted a large one and that's exactly what I got!

Saturday 16 April 1994
I am thinking about taking up pole-vaulting since I now have my very own designer pole. Phallic thoughts dominate my head, and I am currently being swept along by a momentum which is likely to keep me on a high for weeks.

Still no news of my mastectomy. Good job I have my

penis pal to take my mind off breast distractions. I certainly don't like being a pseudo-hermaphrodite with both sets of sex organs.

Unfortunately, I cannot get to grips with the peeing part of Herbie. I know it takes at least a week to master the art of not wetting yourself, but even if I crack that I cannot envisage being able to move around freely on the dance-floor with a medical catheter bowl wedged up between my legs. Nevertheless, I have to admit it feels good to stand and point Percy. As for the other parts of Herb, well I daren't go into detail since this is not a Jackie Collins novel. Herb has his own insertable, rod-like erection device. By the time you've done this part and lubricated it with a bit of KY jelly, your girlfriend will most likely have fallen asleep. But all is not lost, as Herb will stay up ... indefinitely. You simply wait until she awakes!

Chapter Seven

Monday 18 April 1994

It was a Monday morning in April 1998, and I was rushing around frantically in my one-bedroom apartment. I was going to be late for work – again. I scanned the rack running the length of my polished beech wardrobe with indecision. In front of me, all hanging neatly from their flesh-coloured harnesses, was a vast array of flaccid pink penises. My eyes alighted briefly on Cowboy penis, large with extra barrels, then moved swiftly on to Executive penis with built-in mobile phone and filofax. Too pretentious, perhaps? Decisions, decisions. Which one to choose today? My eyes scanned the whole selection from left to right. Yuppie penis made by Porsche. Man-About-Town penis with Gucci harness and gold lettering. Heavyweight Boxer penis – in black with optional silk shorts. Footballer penis coated with studs. Small, inadequate, hardly-tickle-the-sides penis. And lastly, Big-Boy-Rough-Rider, huge with bulging veins. This was worse than choosing which shirt and tie to put on. I pulled bulging Body-Builder penis from his peg and stepped into harness and shorts in one deft movement. Within minutes I was on my way to work.

Today on the Underground I began thinking about my

Herb and how large it is. Rather big in trousers and downright obscene in swimming-trunks. I might splash out and order another, smaller one when I get some cash. This will ensure I don't get charged with causing a public affray next time I want to slip into the deep end of the local swimming-baths.

I have decided to send off a pre-entry form for the 1995 London Marathon. I wonder if a transsexual has ever completed it? I want to be the first.

Tuesday 19 April 1994

Today I mastered the urinary device in my Herb; a standard 'male pee' without accident or splashes. Afterwards I went for a walk, and the distinctive aroma of summer – freshly cut grass and light, herbaceous air – wafted tantalisingly under my nose. The scent of summer brings pain as well as joy, as my gaze extends to green playing-fields and inviting-looking football nets. It is painful to know I am barred from these activities until I have had my mastectomy.

But my mood is most definitely one of optimism. It is such a boost to have a man's parts in my trousers; they are none the less significant for being artificial. I keep wondering what would happen if I were to get knocked over and taken into hospital, a male on the outside but hiding two breasts and an artificial penis beneath my clothes? This morbid line of thought follows a radio report I heard last week. Floating in the Thames was a body with both male and female sex organs, wearing a wig. It was obvious to me that this was a transsexual suicide. Sometimes I think it's not before we're dead that anyone realises what we are going through.

I have decided to grow my sideburns and will soon have to wet-shave as my stubble is thickening. My electric Hitachi Phase 2 is no match for it. I am also contemplating whether I will have enough beard growth to grow a goatee before they go out of fashion.

A middle-aged lady struck up a conversation with me on the bus yesterday. Half-way through she referred to us collectively as 'ladies'. We got off at the same stop and I resisted the temptation to point her in the direction of the optician's. Unimpressed of West Reading.

Friday 22 April 1994

Today I had my first wet-shave! With a white beard and moustache I stood with razor in hand. I didn't even cut myself. All these years of practice while shaving my legs have not been in vain. It struck me how funny it was that for years as a woman I used to struggle with make-up, yet shaving my face seems so natural. It seems to be an ability I was born with, rather than learned behaviour.

My GP phoned to tell me that Dr Morgan at Mount Vernon had written to say that despite the usual fifteen-month waiting-list he will try to call me in within two or three. This operation will be my liberation; it is the biggest obstacle on the transsexual assault course. I am anxious to rejoin the working population and begin the rest of my life.

Wednesday 27 April 1994

Today I received a letter from Organon Laboratories, the company that makes Sustanon. They have declined my kind offer to relieve them of a few thousand pounds for my operation. Being a pharmaceutical company apparently prohibits them from making donations to the public.

I am increasingly getting to grips with my Herb and his various functions and hope to be confident enough to show him off at a public urinal in a few weeks' time. I may air him in the Harrods Gents – somewhere momentous. Unfortunately, my sex life has died a death so I still have no idea whether Herbie is the Real McCoy.

Thursday 28 April 1994

Today I examined the brown envelope with the Sheffield postmark: too thick for failure, that takes only one sheet! I have indeed passed the photojournalism written test. It felt so good to be back on a winning streak again that I cried properly for the first time in ages. Since I have been on hormones I have felt as emotional as ever but, rather alarmingly, my tear ducts appear to have become somehow blocked.

Sunday 1 May 1994

Yesterday I took a taxi. The Alpha Cars' driver and I talked at length about championship boxing. When we got on to Mike Tyson, undisputed world heavyweight champion who is behind bars serving a long sentence for raping beauty queen Desiree Washington, the taxi driver said: 'What did she think she was going back to his hotel room at three in the morning for? Tea and cakes? He should never have been banged up.' I mumbled agreement with him to keep face but found myself, as usual, taking a woman's viewpoint. No situation can ever justify rape. Emotionally, I'm a woman's dream man.

When I arrived home yesterday I found a letter from a male-to-female Gender Dysphoria Trust member asking if I would like to meet her as she lives only six miles away in Crowthorne. Being at a loose end I phoned her and we met last night. Julie and I ended up going to River's night-club in Benson. She was really nice, but I feel ashamed to admit that I did feel quite uneasy with her in public. Two transsexuals out on the razzle together. Admitting this makes me feel a complete hypocrite. I shouldn't bother what people were thinking but I felt uneasy as people stared. It is not easy for most male-to-females like Julie to blend in. It took three pints of lager before I stopped worrying if people were looking at us. But I felt fiercely protective towards one of my own flock and would have decked anyone passing comment.

This afternoon I sunbathed my hairy legs for the second time this summer. The dark hairs are bleaching in the sunlight. I must be confident of my appearance, dressed as I habitually am in shorts and a blue polo shirt.

Friday 6 May 1994

Charing Cross Hospital in London have invited me for an appointment with a psychiatrist at the gender clinic. I realise that this is only a formality, as an NHS referral is essential for my operation, but this didn't quell my anger at receiving such a pointless letter. I crushed it in my hand and tried to score a basket. I missed the bin. I am sick to death of psychiatrists, most of whom seem less sane than I am. The appointment is not until 24 June. I was hoping to have had the operation by then!

Wednesday was my interview for the photojournalism course in Sheffield. I couldn't believe how scruffily everyone was dressed. I was the only one in a suit. I believe that in order to be taken seriously one has to dress seriously. Before my interview seven candidates and I stood in a workroom chatting. For perhaps the first time in my life I seemed to find my true personality with strangers. I made everyone laugh without really trying, something which would have been impossible in my early days of crisis and consciousness. I was basking in the fact that to everyone else I was just another guy. I left the interview elated, as I had managed to get through it without revealing my identity as a transsexual. If I can get a place on my course without anyone knowing my secret it will be wonderful beyond words.

Monday 9 May 1994

More good news. A letter arrived from the NCTJ telling me

that I have successfully passed the entrance exam for the journalism course in Portsmouth. I have been invited to interview on 25 May. It feels so good that things are finally going my way. Trying to stop me achieving what I want would be like attempting to stop a ten-ton truck falling off a cliff. I feel so powerful. I have a new haircut and a little beard.

Wednesday 11 May 1994

Woke up to Visible Male Puberty. I have spots on my face and shoulders and I'm not best impressed. Slung on my favourite T-shirt, bought in a shop selling juggling equipment; it reads: More Balls Than Most.

Went shopping today. I am starting to wonder if I have an 'ask me I'm a soft touch' sign tattooed on my forehead. Everywhere I go I get asked for money. I must look like a mobile charity. I bought a pair of size six boots from Oakland for Men which were reduced in the sale. They are a size too big, but I am hoping I will grow into them. I wore them out in Richmond on Saturday night, paranoid that they looked enormous. I went to the Gents after several drinks and practically skied down a flight of steps without stopping, aquaplaning on a layer of water I had picked up from the toilets. I heard a shout from behind me: 'Steady, mate, there's a step there.'

Friday 13 May 1994

What does it feel like to be a bloke? It feels bloody great! When I was younger I always thought that 'happy' was a state of mind you were supposed to be in. Yet I was the girl who had everything and nothing. I put on an outward show of happiness for the world's benefit – I was too proud to do anything less – but inside I was a vast empty desert. I felt empty and barren. Now I find it hard to believe I was ever female. I am my father's clone and it is eerie how much we are alike. I have all his mannerisms. I curl my hair in my fingers like he does. I even find myself telling jokes like he would. Stripped of my feminine disguise, the real me has been exposed. My hands, handcuffed for so long, are free. So is my soul, confined for two decades. For the first time in my life I am not dependent on anyone else for my happiness. I am no longer frightened to be alone.

I picked up some slides from the processing lab this morning and, as if by magic, the shop-keeper appeared. My twenty-seven-year-old cousin Ann, whom I had not seen for five years, was a mirage behind the counter. The last time I had seen her was at her sister's wedding when I was twenty-one and very much a woman, dressed in my black Lycra mini-skirt. When I saw her today I baulked slightly, not knowing how much she knew and what her reaction to me would be. She gave me a big beaming smile and said: 'Hello, how are you?' We talked like old friends. Her dad, my uncle, had told her about me and she was eminently supportive and sympathetic. 'You must have been through absolute hell,' she said quietly. She told the two receptionists that I was her cousin and instructed them to give me a discount on my photos. I walked out of the door into the sunlight.

Sunday 15 May 1994

I had a wild night out at Casper's wine bar in London last night. This is a novelty bar where there is a phone on every table. You decide who or what you fancy, then simply pick up the phone and dial the table number. Karen was on the phone before we had even sat down! She told me I would be irresistible if I were a foot taller . . . so I went to bed praying I would wake up six feet two. Alas, this morning I was the same size but with a hangover from hell. Too much Tooheys Export. Danny, Karen's friend, and I had a competition on the way home. We rolled up our trousers for Karen to judge whose legs were the hairiest. I won hands down! I thought this was hilarious. I have been taking testosterone for only seven months and I already have twice as much body hair as Danny, who's had twenty-five years to grow his.

Life is treating me well at the moment. My boobs are my major problem. I am binding them up with a vengeance. Karen says to me, 'Poor old boobs, they are meant to hang free.' They are shrinking a bit, but I can view them only with contempt. I think of them as cartoon breasts which someone has drawn on to my ribcage for a sick joke. I am absolutely desperate for a mastectomy – so desperate that I understand why others actually mutilate themselves. I am one op away from paradise, but I don't think I could survive another summer with these fleshy protuberances. Every time I see a guy with his shirt off I am overcome with jealousy. Still, my time will come and, although I have no special woman in my life right now, the night is still young.

On the down side I can feel a massive rift opening up between myself and my father. I am truly lucky to have a sister like Karen who is loyal without fail. Karen was supposed to be travelling up to Norfolk next weekend to visit my dad and his wife-to-be, but the point of this story is that I, the transsexual relative from hell, am not invited. Karen has told my father that if I am not invited she will not visit either.

I think my dad's girlfriend, Jill, has her reservations about me as a man, or at least that is what my dad would have me believe. My guess is that she doesn't want to face a barrage of questions from my inquisitive nine-year-old stepbrother. This is a great shame, as he may grow up with appalling indoctrinated prejudices. I am deeply disappointed with my dad for not fighting for me. It will take a long time to erase this hurtful slight. On days like this I would like to wave a magic wand and make him transsexual for a day. It hurts like hell. What can I do?

Tuesday 17 May 1994
I am now renting a room from Julie in Crowthorne. This morning I went bed shopping, but all practical plans went out of the window when my eyes alighted on the words 'child's racing-car bed' in the free ads of the Crowthorne *Times*. I have dreamed of having my very own racing-car bed for as long as I can remember. In my childhood dreams I would become Willard and his wheels, and my stationary bed would turn at night into Willard's dream racer. This afternoon Julie kindly drove me to High Wycombe to pick up the bed, a bargain at £40. I had to put on an extremely macho show by carrying it down the stairs with the guy who was selling it, and it nearly killed me. The trouble with being a man is that you are expected to have the strength of one.

I am now writing from my bed. It fits me perfectly. It is black and red and has the number seven on the side. As my nan would say if she were alive today: 'That's another thing out of your system!' Slowly but surely I am making things happen.

Thursday 19 May 1994
Last night at 10 p.m. Julie mysteriously disappeared upstairs. I could hear her rummaging around in her bedroom. Five minutes later she appeared with an armful of her old clothes which she threw downstairs for me to try on. For the next two hours I indulged in a fashion parade. It's not really me to like other people's clothes because I am extremely fussy, but it was as if Julie in her previous persona had chosen her wardrobe with me in mind. An Italian suit fitted me perfectly, as did a pair of blue designer trousers.

Saturday 21 May 1994
I couldn't sleep last night. My new wardrobe was filling my thoughts.

Sunday 22 May 1994

I am having so much fun being male, doing mundane things like shaving and admiring my newly acquired physique. Punch-drunk but not counted out, I went out with Julie to Ragamuffins night-club in Camberley. My confidence was riding high, and I had no fears that anyone would suspect my past. I felt good and boogalooed until my pants fell off. The place was heaving, wall to wall with luscious babes, and my hormones were racing and on red alert. Julie recognised two girls, so she went over to say hello. As soon as I was introduced I knew I would end up with either the luscious Alice or sinuous Sonia. They eyed me curiously, probably because I was not like any of the men there. Small and cute-looking, a real nice boy. I knew I had a chance. By coincidence, Ragamuffins is a night-club where I stripped two years ago; on my last visit I was disguised as a French maid, and here I was in 1994 chatting up the girlies.

I enviously watched a procession of men ask Alice to dance. She was quite short, with volcanic boobs which threatened to erupt at any moment from her low-cut blouse. I couldn't take my eyes off them. Although everything I say and do is natural behaviour – my transition from female to male has been smooth and effortless – there is one aspect of behaviour which I have had consciously to teach myself: male behaviour in the night-club dating arena. From being the woman waiting to be asked to dance, I now do the asking. This is the toughest part of all. As a woman I realise you never fully appreciate how much guts it takes to walk across the room to ask a girl to dance. Unless you have the hide of a rhinoceros a 'no' does nothing for one's ego. I try to force myself to overcome my natural shyness and apprehension. I like women too much not to have one in my life. If you don't go to them, you'll sit there all night. In this respect it is much easier to be a woman. With the exception of having the babies, they've got it easy.

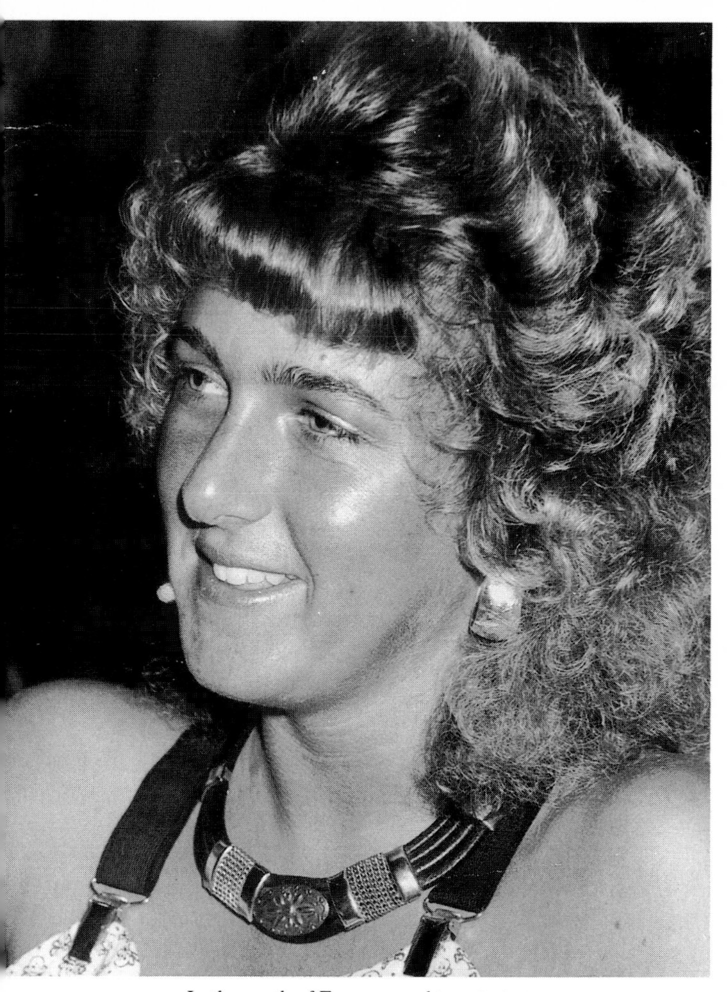

In the south of France, aged twenty-two

Our round-the-world trip . . . Hawaii

. . . Fiji . . .

. . . On a beach with Karen

I've always been mad about football

Hotshot Hewitt blasts Oxford

SUB Martine Hewitt made a sensational return as she scored four times in 20 minutes to set up a 7–1 victory.

Martine earns sweet revenge

A HAT-TRICK by Martine Hewitt helped gain revenge for a defeat earlier in the season in a 4–2 win.

I have quite a collection of cuttings like this

MARTINE HEWITT

PLAYERS PLAYER OF THE YEAR 1991

CLUB SECRETARY

3.MAY.1991

And was very proud of this

Glamour modelling test shot, 1992

More modelling shots – I feel as awkward as I look

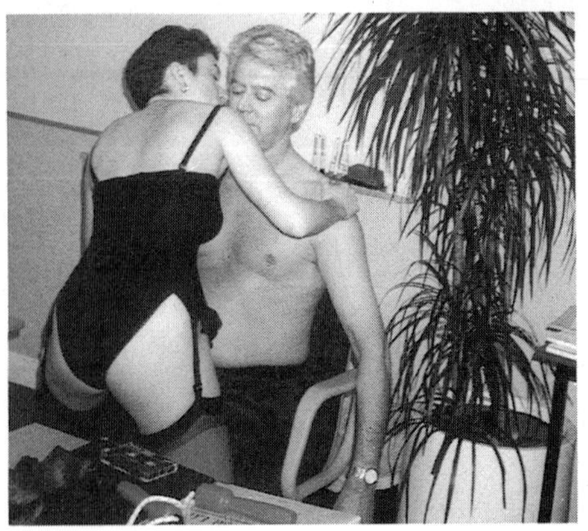

My last stripagram

At Wendy's house in October 1993, two weeks before
I began hormone treatment

At Karen's flat in Putney, October 1994 (*Debbie Humphry*)

Shaving is such a thrill (*Rebecca Meagher*)

My ambition is still to be a male model (*Rebecca Meagher*)

So when the slow songs started I tactically waited a bit, then caught Alice's bright blue eyes. I flashed my eyes from her over to the dance-floor. When she nodded and smiled sweetly I felt like I'd won Olympic gold. It has taken months to work up the confidence to ask a woman to dance. As I slid my hands around her hot little waist, she said: 'Aren't you short!' Unfazed, I whispered in her ear: 'Yes, I am, but I make up for it in other departments.' I snuggled her up close to my alert packed lunch. The size of my Herb really is a little embarrassing. She went back and told Julie that I was really randy. But she almost caught me out. As the music throbbed she ran her soft hands down my back. Noticing my chest binder she asked: 'What's this, braces?' Thinking on my feet, I replied nonchalantly: 'Oh that ... that's a support I have to wear since I broke a rib playing football.'

Alice refused to believe I was twenty-six. Apparently, I was too short and cute-looking! She and Sonia staggered out of the club shortly after our dance, rather the worse for alcohol. I wasn't too sad to see her go; she was married anyway. Still, I felt fresh with victory.

Thursday 26 May 1994

Yesterday I was interviewed for the journalism course at Highbury College, Portsmouth. It went well, my fingers are confidently crossed. Karen phoned me this morning in floods of tears. I was shocked. Life normally breezes over her. The problem was our dad. She had trouble composing herself enough to read me a letter she had just written to him. His prejudices have finally found a voice, yet his life has not been one of virtue. Karen is upset with him and I am angry at his passing judgement on me. Neither of us feels able to see our dad while he and Jill continue to snub my predicament. At the moment this rift feels too large ever to mend. It is a San Andreas Fault which occupies the space between me and the man who used to be my everlasting hero. I am not sure I can forgive and forget. All our lives Karen and I have been daddy's girls. Now I am for the first time my mother's son. She calls me her 'special son'. Time and hardship have united us.

After I had talked to Karen I sat down and wrote my own letter to Dad.

Saturday 28 May 1994

The last two days have been a living hell. Acute food poisoning has put transsexualism into perspective, and my bottom appears to think it has a new job testing toilet paper. Unfortunately, I have been laid out on the sofa listening to news reports every hour on Capital FM about a rampaging flesh-eating killer bug. Julie looked after me like an angel. She even called the emergency doctor, who was pregnant, never smiled once and left mud on our stairs.

Monday 30 May 1994

Dad rang this morning. He wanted to know if I was still alive. I don't know what Karen said to him, but it must have worked because he told me that he and Jill are considering seeing someone about the effect I will have on Simon. At last, he is requesting information and help, but this did make me laugh. I am just an ordinary, bog standard sort of a guy with a mountain of love to share with my brother. It is not as if I was ever a real sister to him; after all, it was always me who took him out to kick a football.

Friday 3 June 1994

This is my eighth month of hormone treatment, and I am relieved to hear that it has had no effect on my liver function or cholesterol level. Changes are now only discreet and filling in the physical gaps. I have almost completely left the suburbs of womanhood. There are two lines of hair on my chest. One begins high up and is moving down, threatening to meet the line which is moving from my belly button upwards. They are now only two inches apart.

Last night Herbie made his first test flight. I made love for the first time as a man. I was beginning to think it would never happen. When I awoke this morning next to Sarah the sun was filtering through the curtains. It seemed not to matter that I had no feeling in my penis; the feeling was all in my head. Making love with a false penis was better than making love with no penis at all, though the emotional pain was still there. But the earth did not move, it was far from momentous. I was scared of hurting Sarah and felt like a shy virgin making love for the first time. I just wanted to get the first time out of the way so that I could enjoy it next time. I had dreamed of the moment we could be a heterosexual couple together at last. I felt like a gawky schoolkid still in short trousers with the knowledge but not the practice.

Monday 6 June 1994

Karen told me today that I have a wide-eyed and scared expression on my face most of the time. I told her: 'You'd look wide-eyed and scared if you'd been through what I've been through.' And she laughed. I feel a foot taller and braver with Karen by my side. She is my guiding light, the female part of me, my personal, unpaid bodyguard.

On a visit to the kebab van this evening I could feel a spring in my leg muscles that I have not felt for years. The bearded 'bab man was just setting up. He turned to face me and said: 'Hello, mate, I won't be long now.' I experienced a sudden, overwhelming, all-embracing sensation of brotherhood. I, Paul, belong to the matey world of men.

Tuesday 7 June 1994

I visited my mum today. I had promised to help her sort out the house, as the family home goes up for sale next week. I found myself wanting to see her, and I even volunteered my lawn-mowing services. Today I was the lawn-mower man. I have never mowed a lawn before but felt really macho doing it. I also spent hours digging her garden. Undertaking these traditionally male activities is important to me. I remember how I used to watch my dad in the garden with envy, the sweat trickling down his muscled torso. I would wish I was strong enough to help. Until I was about twelve I was often asked the immortal question, 'And what do you want to be when you grow up?' I had set my mind on the dizzy heights of window-cleaning and, balanced carefully on the saddle of my purple three-gear Raleigh bicycle, would clean the garage windows.

Today, after a few hours of feverish garden labour, the lady next door, Mrs England, peered over the fence and shouted to my mum: 'I see you have a young lad there to help you.' I could have kissed my mum. She didn't say a word.

Mum and I are putting in the spade-work and building a relationship that never significantly existed before. She's told me she loves me more times in the past few months than she has done in the previous twenty-six years. She tried to give me some money for helping her but I refused to take it. It was reward enough to know that I had made her happy, and tears sprang into my eyes as she waved me off on the bus.

Last week I met up with Jane at the *Daily Express*. When I first met her in October last year and she interviewed me over lunch, she seemed to tower over me. I remember feeling very small and inadequate. But now I want to ask her if she has shrunk. These days she seems smaller somehow, or rather there seems to be less height between us. This I attribute to increased confidence on my part. I feel more confident and more significant. Adequate, rather than inadequate, for the first time. Of course, there could be a simple explanation; perhaps Jane had left her heels at home.

This afternoon I sat and cried at *Little House on the Prairie*. And all because a tall lady fell in love with a short man. She shouted across the playground, 'I love you,' and he said, 'But I'm not going to get any taller.' She replied: 'And I'm not going to get any smaller!' A few days later they were married. I need a woman who will share my dreams and fly with me. I have a mountain of love to give and expect a mountain in return. At the same time I feel like a dog on heat. There isn't a half-good-looking babe who escapes my attention. I'm surprised I can concentrate enough to write this diary.

Friday 10 June 1994
Today I bought my first naughty magazine, *Penthouse International for Men*. Well, strictly speaking it is not my first naughty mag. I used occasionally to buy *Playgirl* to look at the muscular male bods with envy. It was touch and go whether I would reach the top shelf or not.

Looking at these women in naughty magazines incites in me feelings of pure sex. But I prefer the more tasteful ones. I find pictures of semi-naked women more attractive than those women who are completely naked, performing the sort of poses you'd find in a game of Twister. I am beginning to discover how to use my sexuality as a fresh-faced young male to my advantage. When I was a flirty girlie I used to do this all the time.

Today I asked the young lady behind the steamy restaurant counter in Tesco: 'Are you still serving crumpets?'

'No,' she said with a smile. 'But I can make you some. I'll bring them over.'

Well in there, son, I thought to myself.

Sunday 19 June 1994, Father's Day
I have been offered a place on the reserve list for the photojournalism course in Sheffield, but it is really the

journalism course in Portsmouth that I want to start in September.

I went out and bought a signet ring and some new Guerlain aftershave by Heritage to cheer myself up. Wearing my new aftershave I felt like the sexiest man alive. My mood was a bit dented when I was told I would have to wait two weeks for my ring. It is being shrunk down to my size, and I am having my initials engraved on it. I cannot afford to get depressed too often – it costs me a fortune.

The lady on the front desk in the Army and Navy offered me a special Father's Day discount on a haircut. I didn't need a haircut, but I almost took her up on her offer anyway. I have two wishes. I want to be a father, and I want my very own, fully functional penis. It breaks my heart to know I will never have either. There are distant possibilities, though. I could go abroad for a phalloplasty, and I could adopt.

Friday 24 June 1994

So emotional, I could cry. I have been offered a place on the one-year NCTJ Newspaper Journalism course at Highbury College, Portsmouth. After so many years when success was something I took for granted, failure became a way of life as my feelings of gender dysphoria emerged. Now the tide is turning. I am striking out into my future. On 19 September I begin my new career in journalism. Most significantly, I will be beginning it as the real me. But certain members of the medical profession continue to thwart me.

I went to Charing Cross Hospital yesterday for my consultation and realised within minutes of talking to Dr Absolom that she would be absolutely no use to me whatsoever. I am sick to death of being grilled about my sex life and other personal details. Unfortunately, I became aggressive and surly when the best suggestion she could make, in order for Charing Cross to be able to treat me, was to come off hormones for six months to 'clear myself', as she put it. She's having a laugh, I thought to myself. She can't fuck around with my body and my mind like that. Three months I had waited for this appointment, and now these people were playing blackjack with my life. Suicide would be preferable to coming off hormones and losing all the stability I have strived to achieve. With deadly nightshade in my voice I explained that coming off hormones was out of the question and walked from the hospital ready to kill.

I immediately went to Earl's Court to see Dr Russell Reid at the London Institute. He is the first gender psychiatrist I ever saw and does have NHS connections. I found him to be most sympathetic. For a start, he told me how good I was looking. This is a doctor who understands that this is precisely the sort of comment a transsexual wants to hear. He suggested that my GP should refer me back to him and he will then formally interview me before writing to Mount Vernon Hospital on my behalf.

When I got home I sat down to write a letter.

Dear Dr Absolom
I am most disappointed with the outcome of our consultation. I feel as though I have wasted three months waiting for this appointment. I met Dr Morgan at his hospital on 30 March this year; we talked in detail and he seemed more than happy to treat me. He explained that a referral from a psychiatrist was necessary so that he could ethically operate. Dr Morgan led me to believe that this was no more than a formality as I am a genuine transsexual getting on with my life. I have been living successfully as a man for a year now, and my surgical completion is the only barrier to my future progress.

Following eight months of careful planning, hard work and determination, I have recently succeeded in securing a place on a highly competitive newspaper journalism course entailing three rigorous selection stages. I am also in the process of signing up with a publisher for a book I have written. The college have no knowledge of my transsexualism; I have gained my place on my own merit. Ritual chest binding is a mental burden which is severely reducing my effectiveness as a functional human being. Imagine, therefore, my feeling of desperation when the NHS is now the only barrier to my future success.

I am disgusted with the way I was treated. To suggest that I should go off hormones for six months to 'clear myself' is an insult to everything I have achieved. Not only is it an insult, it is downright dangerous. You may think you can play with people's lives but I will not mess around with my body in this fashion.

For all your medical and psychiatric qualifications, you obviously have little understanding of gender dysphoria. The medical risks aside, I dare not even imagine the effect that such a step would have on my mental health. It is eighteen months since my first visit to see Dr Russell Reid, when I was diagnosed transsexual, but you treated me as though I was a transient 'not sure' in need of psychiatric counselling.

Even the terminology you used during our interview indicated a lack of understanding. I did not 'decide I wanted to be a man'. I have always been one – it is simply a case of bringing my body in line with my mind and my self-image.

Luckily, I have found alternative help, but feel compelled to write this letter fuelled by my anger. I am probably the best example of a genuine female-to-male transsexual you will ever meet, but you made me feel like an experimental animal. I left Charing Cross feeling as though I would like to end my life there and then. I am intelligent enough to devise an alternative, but what of others not so fortunate? This is a

life-threatening condition which can kill as quickly as cancer if not properly treated. This is a fact of which you seem blissfully unaware.
Yours sincerely
Paul Hewitt

Friday 1 July 1994
Do you want to know when I feel most inadequate? It is when I am in the bath. Stripped bare, there are no clothes to swathe my shortcomings and I sit alone with them. As I look down – unless Herbie is bathing with me – I see only empty space between my legs where my male parts should be. I have in the past underestimated the importance of a penis to a man's self-worth and self-esteem. I see now that it is also deeply symbolic, the tool by which he can pass on his best qualities to the next generation. My eyes take in the shrinking alien protuberances I reluctantly called breasts. The trick cyclist at Charing Cross had asked me why I wanted a mastectomy. 'Why exactly do you want this operation, Paul?'

'Because I'm a man, and men don't have boobs.' Ask a dumb question, get an obvious answer.

This morning I had a meeting with Headline involving Jane, our agent Andrew Lownie, Anna Powell (senior editor, non-fiction) and Diane Rowley, publicity director. My stomach leaped as we travelled from reception to the fourteenth floor in a glass elevator looking out on the capital. For an instant I allowed myself to believe I was Charlie in his great glass elevator, Roald Dahl's creation. Once inside the office my new personality began to effervesce like a glass of Alka-Seltzer. It was obvious almost immediately that I was being tested for my suitability as a marketable product, but I found an unfamiliar confidence. Besides, I was being allowed to talk about my specialised subject: me! I was fairly certain the outcome would be positive because I am now experiencing self-belief with a passion. But more than that, I was happy to be there in a business situation in my own right. I also noticed that Andrew Lownie has very small feet. Yes! So there *are* real men with feet not much bigger than mine.

Martina Navratilova has reached her twelfth Wimbledon final. I will be rooting for her because she is a winner. She has the guts and integrity to live her life as she wants. That's my kind of woman.

Sunday 3 July 1994
Martina lost a dramatic final in three sets. I am temporarily gutted.

Tuesday 5 July 1994
I cooked dinner for Sally last night, the first time I have seen her in months. Nothing happened, but I felt as though it could have.

Wednesday 6 July 1994
While I stood waiting for a bus a stranger approached me. He seemed a genuine, friendly sort of a guy so I gave him a hearing. He was recruiting for the Christian Union in Sandhurst. I am not sure why I listened as I have never been vaguely interested in the Church, but my own hardships have opened up my heart and my mind to anything, I suppose. David, and his co-recruiter Richard, gave me a lift back to Crowthorne. I am tempted to go to one of their church get-togethers simply to meet new people who know nothing of my past. I have few male friends and suddenly I have two, even if they are Christians.

Dr Russell Reid is my saviour. He has written to the plastic surgeon to recommend that I am called in for a mastectomy as soon as possible.

His letter was terrific.

Dear Mr Morgan
re: Paul HEWITT dob: 15.9.67
I originally saw this person on 16.3.93. I saw him again on 24.6.94 at his GP's request in order to review his progress and recommend that he undergo bilateral mastectomy. I understand you saw him recently and referred him to Charing Cross for their blessing. He said he was seen by a Dr Absolom and was disappointed to be told to stop hormones for six months, then come back and they would think about it.

He said he was extremely hurt and angry at this, and pleads to be rid of his breasts as soon as possible on the grounds that he presently has to bind them tightly and this is very uncomfortable. It prevents him from swimming and participating in sports. It prevents him from having any sort of physical relationship with anyone, and adversely affects his self-confidence and self-image. The 'dislike' of his breasts has grown to 'hate'.

In my opinion he is genuinely transsexual, female to male, and stable, and has been successfully masculinised with Sustanon 250 fortnightly which he has taken since last November under the direction of Endocrinologist Dr Ellis Snitcher. I would recommend bilateral mastectomy as being in his interests socially, psychologically and vocationally, and that it should be done as soon as possible.
Yours sincerely
Dr Russell W. Reid. Consultant Psychiatrist

I phoned two transsexuals this week who have both had breast surgery by Mr Brian Morgan. He comes highly recommended as a caring and skilled surgeon.

Saturday 9 July 1994
Fed up. Fed up. FED UP. This 'having boobs' business is getting beyond a joke.

Sunday 10 July 1994
It is hot and sticky and my dislike of my breasts has turned to hate. The most important goal in my life is to be rid of them. I never anticipated that their presence would end up making me feel so wretched. It is very awkward when I stay at Karen's flat. Other people often stay too, some who know about me, and some who don't. I have to make sure I am first to the bathroom so I am not seen without my bandaging. I cannot bear to sleep with my chest bound, and anyway I think it would be dangerous. This hot weather makes the binding ritual an utter nightmare of sweat and constriction, and yet without bound breasts I cannot face the world. Mind you, I have speeded up. It used to take me several attempts to wind the eight metres around myself; now I can do it with deft agility. But why did we have to have a heatwave in the year when I habitually have several metres of excruciatingly tight bandage around my body?

I am wearing my new signet ring and it is gleaming. It is a present from me to me and marks a step forward. Spiritually my transformation is nearly complete.

Monday 11 July 1994
I dream of the day I can run free with the ball, swim the length of a pool, bare my chest with pride. I long for the day when all this inconvenience, mechanical detail and pain will be a memory.

I have a dream. I am lying beside a glistening aquamarine swimming-pool in some exotic land hotter than the hobs of hell. As I dive in, the ice-cool water washes around my flat, smooth chest. The first time I have swum in years, I am a dolphin released into the wild after years of captivity. I dive and somersault, at one with the water. I flip and jump, and smile, slicking my hair back off my face.

I went to an evangelical church with David and Richard

yesterday. We ended up having an argument about whether homosexuality is a sin or not, so I don't think I'll be committing to God. Not this century, anyway. This is my first and last involvement with Christians. David told me I was unusually polite for a man. It's those years of female conditioning again!

There was a male-to-female transsexual in the church – I had my suspicions as soon as I heard her deep voice. It takes one to know one. I could see she wanted to talk to me, but I'm not convinced she knew what it was we had in common. She gave me a lift home, and as I sat in the back of her Austin Montego I closed my eyes for a while. I listened carefully as she spoke to the guy in the passenger seat, trying to imagine whether I was hearing a male or a female voice. She was very convincing. Only a fellow transsexual could have spotted the special depth to her feminine falsetto. Other than her voice, Christine passed very convincingly. I know because I know, but I don't think anyone else would guess.

Monday 18 July 1994

I receive quite a few nice smiles from women now where I used to get them from men. I went to see Ellis the endocrinologist last week. He told me to try to focus on myself without breasts, but subconsciously I cannot help them getting me down. I have now reached a point where I believe further progress is impossible without surgery. I cannot move on until my physical transformation is complete. No doubt once I've had this operation I will crave an operation to make my genitals male. The lack of a penis is not an easy cross to bear; sometimes its absence feels like stakes driven into me with venom. But it is a question of coming to terms with what you cannot change. The paraplegic would probably commit suicide if he spent too much time dreaming about the things he could do with fully functional legs. But in order to survive you just have to learn to be grateful for what you have got, to be positive, not negative. This is pure survival. I am not even thinking about the hysterectomy at the moment. I have enough going around in my head to last me a lifetime and beyond.

I have decided to put some zip into my life by placing an ad in the Heart-to-Heart column of the local paper. It reads:

> *PASSIONATE MALE, 26, drop-dead cute, seeks intelligent, n/s female drop-dead gorgeous, to save the last dance for me. Box No. 9210.*

I have also answered three ads. That's the total number of women in my age-group who have not specifically requested tall men! Next week my post-box will be under constant surveillance.

Tuesday 26 July 1994
Another nightmare.

> *The church had the blackness of a pot-holer's cave and the stained glass showed only a dull, introspective gleam. The phantom of the opera was playing the organ; his hunched body plunging on to the keys created funeral chords. As I watched, he turned round to face me, then he shook his head and returned to his stultifying, hellish dirge. I knew that today was the day of my wedding, but I couldn't remember what I was supposed to feel and whom I was supposed to marry. As I was searching around my empty head for the right emotions, I heard the frenzied cackle of a gaggle of women. I realised I was naked and covered my penis in shame. The women were marching down the aisle and were ungraciously snatching a rag from hand to hand. As they approached me, I saw it was a floral sun-dress. A dull horror*

rose inside me as I realised that this was my wedding-dress. I imagined my hairy legs sticking out of the bottom. My mother followed the women. She was wearing a simple pillbox hat with a veil. She was dressed all in black and her face looked ashen. I glanced towards the altar. Standing there was a girl from my primary school ominously dressed in white robes. In her hands were orchids, in her face expectation. In slow motion I turned and bolted for the huge oak door of the church. I slithered out just before it swung shut with an oppressive boom...

Tuesday 26 July 1994
I went to see *Miss Saigon* tonight and got talking to two girlies, one of whom fanned me with her programme and lent me her binoculars.

Wednesday 27 July 1994
No more nightmares. All my life I have felt possessed by a force far stronger than my limited physicality. It drives me as a motor drives a car, working both against me and in my favour. It is this force which has predisposed me to physical illness, but it has given me strength to surmount seemingly impossible obstacles. This is the force I call 'never say die'.

It has been an interesting week, where the usual prejudices have reared their tinpot little heads. Three nights this week the young lads from next door have kept Julie and me awake. Smoking dodgy substances, playing anti-social music and wailing like demented animals, I can live with. What desperately angers me are the cowardly shouts of 'transvestite' and 'poofter' aimed at Julie. She has more backbone than they will ever have. We called the police but they were useless. All they did was politely ask our noisy neighbours to turn the music down. Being a transsexual is a lonely life unless you elect to fight to survive. But it ain't over 'til they put you in a plastic bag.

Thursday 28 July 1994

I have shot myself in the foot, metaphorically speaking. I told Ellen Lord, the nurse who so kindly sticks a twice-monthly needle in my butt, that I had found out it was safe for me to self-inject. I meant this as just a bit of interesting chatter, perhaps a fact to put into practice next week. Certainly, I was not prepared for her response.

She snapped off the top of the capsule and began to draw up the oily testosterone derivative into a syringe. 'Here you are.' She smiled sweetly. I wanted to be master of my own destiny but I felt sick. Now I had to be brave or risk losing face completely.

Afterwards, I sat in the waiting-room for fifteen minutes with my head between my legs feeling faint. The pain still stretches all the way down to my ankle. I am dragging my right leg around like a piece of wood.

I have been on a strict diet for ten days, but my will-power is being severely tested by a piece of banana cake in the fridge. It keeps looking at me and whispering, 'Go on, take me, you know you want to.' Bloody too right I do! Sometimes I think life just ain't no fun any more.

Chapter Eight

Friday 29 July 1994

I am having a crisis. Somehow I have managed to spill ink on my Herb. I don't know how I managed it, but it now looks as if I have some exotic venereal disease. I don't know how to clean it. If I use a detergent to try to remove the stains I will probably end up disintegrating the sensitive rubber material. I knew it would not be long until I damaged something of real value.

Karen told me on the phone last night that as well as being stressed out at work she is also stressed out about me. 'I feel all the pain you're going through,' she told me. This concerns me. I have my lot in life, but it breaks my heart to think of Karen suffering because of me and my problems.

I have to admit that I am feeling rather stressed out myself at the moment. I have a low pain threshold and I wonder why I am bothering to self-inject? It is my self-destruct personality showing through again.

I haven't heard a word from the hospital about my operation. By the time I get a date it will probably be slap-bang in the middle of my course. I desperately need to be able to put all of this behind me.

Wednesday 3 August 1994

An unfamiliar woman flopped through my letterbox on

Saturday morning. She had replied to my letter in the Bracknell Heart-to-Heart column. A black-and-white photograph fluttered out when I unfolded the neatly typed page. She looked lovely, a sweet, heart-shaped face framed by feathery hair. I immediately wrote back, leaving out any mention of height or transsexualism. No point spoiling the romance of the century before we even get past the preliminaries.

Anna Powell, my editor at Headline, phoned to ask if I had a good photograph of me for the book's cover so I sent her a caricature of Arnold Schwarzenegger which I'd cut out of the *Guardian* and a little note saying, 'Will this do?'

Sunday 7 August 1994

I went out to a gay disco on Friday night to say goodbye to the friends I have made during my years on the gay scene. It's an open, non-judgemental environment where you can be anyone you want, but it's no place for a heterosexual man like me. Shortly after I arrived and sat down with a pint, a boyish-looking woman in her early twenties leaned towards me while her girlfriend was out of earshot. Her shiny-pink lips mouthed something I couldn't hear above the pulsating beat of D-Ream. The sweet irony here was the song – 'Things Can Only Get Better'.

I got closer. 'What did you say? I can't hear you,' I shouted.

'If I weren't a gay woman and you weren't a gay man I could go for you,' she repeated stridently.

I told her I wasn't gay.

Later on I strode across the dance-floor towards the toilets and was stopped by a young man in tight denim jeans with a half-filled pint glass in his right hand. 'I just had to tell you,' he said. 'You really are cute!' I made a quick exit, fearful that he would think I fancied him. This place was doing my head in. But, perversely, I find it a compliment being chatted up by gay men. It is proof to me that I have arrived as a male but, strangely, the roles are reversed and I become the hunted rather than the hunter once again.

Monday 8 August 1994

There are new bristles on my face. While carrying out my usual late-night analysis in the bathroom mirror yesterday, I noticed that my beard and moustache are starting to join up. But, unfortunately, the new growth also heralds the arrival of spots. This was not part of the deal. I never wanted to be an advert for teenage acne. I wanted to be a man. Instead, now I look more like a game of join the dots.

As I stood scrutinising my fur I noticed a long curly hair on my left shoulder. I started to brush it off and realised it was attached ... I have hairy shoulders! A closer analysis confirmed there were three in all, each about two to three centimetres long.

Tuesday 9 August 1994

Jo, my lonely heart, has written back to me already. She liked my photo and wrote: 'Is that photo really of you? And if it is, why are you single? Your picture made me curl at the toes (and the rest of my bits tingle).'

Apart from both being frustrated poets, we have more in common than I first imagined. She is a student at university and boldly tells me: 'There is something you must know about me right from the beginning. There are two things I hate and just cannot abide. They are (1) Prejudice of any kind. (2) People who sit on mountains of money, watching it grow while other people starve.' She also adds that she believes 'everyone is equal'. I have no intention of mentioning my transsexuality until I know her better. Then I will be curious to see how her cosy belief system will stand this revelation.

I just phoned Mr Morgan, my saviour surgeon. I reckon

that if I keep ringing up they will sort me out just to get me off their back. My persistent approach is working. His secretary told me I will receive notification of my op shortly – this is a transsexual's equivalent of winning the national lottery.

Wednesday 10 August 1994

Today I awoke to the mad rattling of the first tube into East Putney station, but with a sense of new-found freedom. It is my first morning living in Karen's flat in Putney and life is already infinitely better being in close proximity to my twin. When I was in the kitchen Karen slunk up behind me and gave me a hug, wrapping her cute little arms around my neck. 'Whatever happens,' she whispered, 'I don't think I'll ever love any man as much as I love you. I'm so proud of what you have achieved. All my friends are proud of you. You are revered by everyone.'

We are two inseparable hearts which seem almost to beat in unison. This is true whether we are in the same room or a thousand miles apart. I take great strength from knowing she is a solid rock in my life.

An old girlfriend wrote to me today. I bumped into her at a night-club recently, and her letter contained warm, affirming words.

Dear Paul,
Mel, the girl I was with at the night-club, said she couldn't tell you used to be a chick! I must say, though, that I still find it difficult to adjust to calling you Paul and seeing you as a man, but I suppose that's natural considering what we used to have together. But what the heck! You're still the person inside that I used to know (cute, cuddly and caring) so I'll definitely keep in touch...

This was just the tonic I needed. I walked into Wandsworth

feeling like a new man. Everything I need for my life is just within walking distance, both literally and figuratively. The air was humid and the soft rain collected on my squad cut. As I walked, I felt proud. Yesterday I mastered the art of self-injecting at my regular appointment in Reading. The trauma of a fortnight ago has now vaporised.

Penny was the nurse on duty. She looks just as comic-book nurses are supposed to, plump and nicely rounded with a perfect complexion, rosy-red cheeks and blonde hair neatly tied back in a ponytail. She softly talked me through the injection procedure, then sat up beside me on the padded bench as I stabbed the needle into the skin on my left thigh. It was a strange sensation, the syrup-like Sustanon floating cold into the muscle. I have never met a nurse who has given me such confidence as Penny. 'Not many men would be brave enough to inject themselves,' she told me afterwards. I will see her again in two weeks just to check I am proficient enough to go solo and to collect a batch of needles. I have become something of a celeb at the local surgery. There are half a dozen receptionists but I am never required to give my name. I attribute this to the curiosity factor. I guess it is only natural for people to talk.

Sunday 14 August 1994
Love is in the air. I have had two letters this week from my Heart-to-Heart correspondent and each one keener than the one before. Her phone number was strategically placed at the top of the last letter, so on Friday I plucked up the courage to ring. She sounded so young – she is only twenty – but interesting and talkative. We are going to meet on Wednesday.

Tuesday 16 August 1994
Hot date tomorrow!

Wednesday 17 August 1994
Jo has blown me out. One minute she was desperately keen and protesting that she couldn't bear a whole week without hearing from me, the next I receive a letter telling me she doesn't want to write or phone any more. I feel disconsolate. This doesn't really make sense, and I have a nagging, discomforting suspicion ... she has discovered my secret. But how? I feel like I've developed bubonic plague overnight, but I have my pride and I will not cry. (Instead I am silently weeping inside.) So much for her non-judgemental, open-minded attitudes. That's women for you. They build you up then cut you down.

Friday 19 August 1994
A letter. From Jo. I tore it open, eager to digest its contents. How was she going to justify her appalling, unfair, demeaning actions?

'I'm fat,' it said simply, then continued: 'That's it. That's the problem. I'm frightened that once you meet me you won't like me any more.'

I didn't know whether to laugh out loud, shout 'silly cow', or cry. I'd been totally paranoid and pathetic and all the time she had her own agenda forcing her to battle against insecurities of image. There is a lesson in this for me.

Aware that I would feel a bastard if I allowed her to pour out her heart without being honest myself, I have written back, telling all. I've no idea what the outcome will be. All cards are now on the table. This is where we separate human wheat from chaff.

Monday 22 August 1994
It is Karen here, writing in Paul's diary. Little Miss Perceptive, they call me. In fact, I have always been Little Miss Something, born as a quite blatant and stark contrast to you, Little Mr Hairy Legs. I asked you today if you had

been putting heated rollers in your leg hairs, and if you realised that your rise to manhood was personified by the immensely groovy pop group, Boyz 2 Men?

I think I have an idea of what you are going through because I felt your pain when Jo wrote you that strange letter, and, yes, I live and breathe your excitement at every increase in your confidence.

You may well be having to work twice as hard as normal people to achieve the same thing, but then is that so bad? After all, a Hewitt twin without a challenge is not really a Hewitt twin at all. There is no shame in falling, only glory in rising again. I'm not religious, you understand, quite the opposite in fact, but this mantra helps me through life's tribulations. Love Karen. x.

Tuesday 23 August 1994

I feel smugger than a rabbit in a field full of carrots. I phoned the hospital and was told that the surgeon has set a provisional date for my first operation. When this news sinks in properly I will take my fated boobs to one side and warn them that their days are strictly numbered. In less than three months I will have the body I have been waiting for. The date is bang in the middle of my course, but at least I won't spend another summer in purgatory. Next year I will be able to ride the waves in my Rip Curl shorts.

Wednesday 24 August 1994

Another letter from Jo this morning. Following my confession I opened it with a stone in my stomach. 'You certainly know how to let the cat out of the bag,' she said. We have no secrets now. Our ink and paper love-affair continues. This is definitely safe sex.

Monday 29 August 1994

Karen and I went partying on Friday night. I am no longer

strait-jacketing myself and have become a rather outrageous male flirt. I have my moments. One friend, Trish, pointed to her cheek and indicated that she wanted me to kiss it. She got more than she had bargained for when I gave her a big, noisy, squeaky kiss and she responded by hugging the air out of my body. I decided to kick my no-drinking ban into touch.

Suddenly we were spotted. An old friend, the brother of one of Karen's best friends at school, was loping over. I squirmed. I feel confident with strangers when I can reinvent myself, but faces from the past alarm me. I fear the inevitable comparisons with who I was.

First he spoke to Karen, then turned to ask me what I was doing and whether I was happy. It was obvious that he knew all about me and seemed to have no problem. I relaxed. He kissed Karen goodbye, then moved in my direction. A concrete block dropped into my stomach as expressions of horror crossed both our faces simultaneously when we realised what he was about to do. Just in time, he managed to manipulate his arm. A hand was thrust into my face before his dry lips could graze my cheek. Gratefully I clasped it and shook it, feeling my colour rise. Karen roared with laughter to fill the awkward gap. Kevin and I smiled rather limply. He had retained in his head a female image of me which at that moment had become stronger than the reality of the man in front of him. I did not find this funny.

Later on I was standing just to the side of the dance-floor, my hormones on babe-alert, when a stocky man came over to talk to me. He was well bevied. 'Don't be shy,' he said.

Oh, god, I thought, not another middle-aged gay.

'Go and chat the women up,' he finished, then limped off, staggering slightly. Minutes later he was back. 'Are you a jockey?' I was just about to laugh and say no when a naughty light lit up in my head, as it does when you've had a few bottles of Fosters Ice.

'I'm an apprentice,' I told him. 'The lads take the mickey out of me because I'm the only one there who still has all my teeth.' He was taking it all in, so I told him I was National Hunt jockey P. J. O'Neil, and he disappeared in the direction of the bar to get a pen. He was going to write down his phone number so I could supply him with some hot tips. There's one born every minute!

Yesterday Jo (Heart-to-Heart) phoned. She has decided that she *does* want to meet me. I am kicking myself for my moment of impassioned honesty. I wanted to meet her as a real man. It was my ultimate experiment. But hot date scheduled for Tuesday the sixth. Watch this space.

Saturday 3 September 1994

Here I am on the 10.50 Intercity service from London Euston to Manchester Piccadilly, wedged between a dusty window and a fat lady devouring rounds and rounds of British Rail sandwiches. My destination today is the gender conference and Female-to-Male Network annual dinner at Manchester University. As I glance out of the window, as much to avoid having to watch the fat lady munching as to admire the scenery, I see a heron splash-landing in a river running parallel to the train tracks, sheep dotted through the fields like blobs of cream cotton wool, and grey smoke billowing from chimneys.

Fifteen months ago I was in Reading for this transsexual get-together and I can now realise just how far I have come in that time. Back then I was living with Lisa in Tilehurst, selling insurance and getting more disillusioned with myself daily. I was in love, but not with myself. Lisa was my sole *raison d'être*. She was survival. The thought of hormones terrified me, and I wasn't even binding my chest. I was a mess. I had invented the persona Paul but was having great difficulty implementing him with confidence. I remember being overwhelmed by the other guests and how they really looked like normal men, not freaks. I felt so empowered by them, and to this day I find it hard to believe that female-to-male transsexuals once had women's bodies.

In a few hours' time I will be sitting in Hulme Hall listening to a talk on phalloplasty and the campaign Press For Change, which is lobbying for improved legal rights, headed by Lib Dem MP Alex Carlile QC. No doubt there will be some people present in the same limbo I was in last year. But today I, Paul, will be one of those masculine-looking men I could once only admire and envy. There may be others like me in this carriage, but I can't spot them.

Monday 5 September 1994

The weekend was a success, but my head is full of images from the explicit phalloplasty slides. The skin grafts used to create an artificial penis are so horrific they made me want to settle for what I've got. This is the stage of surgery which tests just how far you want to push the surgeon's scalpel. It is a high price to pay for unrealistic manhood. Yes, you can have a grossly inadequate penis created by a surgeon, but you offer up other parts of your anatomy as a sacrifice: a horrendously scarred arm or leg, from which the radial section of skin, nerves and blood capillaries is taken, or a badly scarred chest. I question the mental stability of anyone wanting to mutilate themselves in this way, at least until surgeons refine the technique.

I met Andrew and Joanne, a sex-change couple who appeared in the *Daily Mirror* recently. They are my kind of people: quiet, courageous and down-to-earth. I recognised them instantly, and Andrew came over to introduce himself. The best thing about them is that they are really very ordinary – this is quite an achievement for two such unusual people. When I had almost reached the bottom of my first pint at the disco in the evening, I saw the famous Dr Montgomery sitting in a corner, besuited and looking rather out of place. It is to him that I have penned a letter of complaint about my treatment at Charing Cross Hospital. Suddenly I wanted to confront him, to ask him how he could justify his treatment of transsexuals. I thought better of it, but later I met two other female-to-males contemplating the same action and one of them did eventually force a confrontation. Dr Montgomery is in charge of the Gender Identity Clinic at Charing Cross Hospital. He operates a standard procedure which every patient must follow. Under this system transsexuals may wait years to be recommended for operations.

Several people approached me to ask if I was Paul from the newspaper articles. Apparently, the photos added extra inches to my Dinky toy frame. I was made to feel immensely proud of having transformed so well within such a short space of time. Eventually, at 2 a.m. I staggered around the corner to my cheap hotel. When I opened the bedside cabinet I discovered a cache of naughty mags, so I stayed up chuckling to myself at pictures of women shaving their pubic hair.

When I got home, Karen and a friend had hijacked the living-room for a step aerobics session. Since they were both wearing tight little bodysuits I decided to sit and watch them for a while.

Tuesday 6 September 1994

Today was my blind date. As I approached Jo's rounded figure outside Reading station I felt as though I had known this girl for years. I kept my distance, not knowing how to play it. She was very sweet and very tactile, but I'm not sure if she fancied me or just fancied the idea of love. The afternoon sped by. We walked, talked and fed the ducks at Caversham bridge, and then at four o'clock I had to leave to see the nurse for another supervised injection. We stood in Union Street outside Marks & Spencer, neither of us knowing how to proceed, so I took the initiative and kissed her soft, youthful rosebud lips.

But this is not to be the love-affair of the century. Jo is too young, too sweet, too innocent for me.

Sunday 11 September 1994

Today my clothes were badly rumpled. I got out the iron and the board and attacked my creases. Karen's flatmate Pam was astonished. 'I've never seen you iron a thing before.' I recalled how I had failed my ironing badge as a twelve-year-old. I was never a natural woman.

This weekend was something of a breakthrough. After so much angst and indecision, Karen and I spent the weekend in Norfolk with our dad, Jill and our ten-year-old step-brother Simon. Apparently, the whole affair had been a misunderstanding. 'There had never been any question of you not being welcome,' Jill told me insistently. It has been a difficult situation all round, as much for them as for me. My dad has taken a while to realise how much I need him, but is beginning to move closer to me now.

This was the first time I had seen Jill and Simon in nine months. Jill was the perfect hostess, as always, and I was chuffed to mintballs when she told my dad that 'Paul has a pair of big, hairy legs, just like you'. Only a blind woman would have failed to notice the changes in me. I find Jill really easy to get on with. In fact, if she were not my dad's girlfriend, I could fancy her myself. I definitely relate to women much better than I do men. I am a woman's man, and suspect I always will be.

Simon immediately took to me, more so than to Karen. In fact, he wouldn't go near her in case she kissed him with her sunset-coloured lipstick on. At the moment he believes all girls are universally silly.

On Saturday night we had a meal in a hotel by the sea. My transsexualism wasn't mentioned once throughout the weekend, and I almost prefer it that way. I can get on with being the man I am rather than being a curiosity. I played pool with Simon. He is very much like a younger version of me, and this is uncanny.

When I hopped up to go to the toilets, Dad said: 'Simon will show you where to go.' He led the way and then followed me in, no doubt curious to see whether I had a willy or not. He walked in the direction of the urinals, testing me, seeing whether I would follow him, and of course I darted into the single cubicle.

The toilet light was flickering. Simon was silent. Then, in a high-pitched voice, he said: 'You have to sit down, don't you?'

I did not reply. I was a bit taken aback. What could I say to that? I afforded myself a half smile as I shut the door of the cubicle behind me. This is one ten-year-old who knows how to hit where it hurts. I didn't know whether to laugh or cry. But I was impressed with his grasp of my mechanics. His youthful innocence has allowed him to bring up a subject which is apparently taboo to the adults in our family.

We played football together on Sunday morning, and he proudly told all his mates ... 'My big brother is outside. He's going to play football with us.'

We had a play fight in the lounge, bundling around on the soft, green velour chairs. I wrestled Simon to the ground as *101 Great Goals* played on the video. He had jumped on me once too often. I told him: 'One day, little brother, one day soon, you will be bigger than me. But for now I'm bigger than you, and I'm going to make the most of it.'

Thursday 15 September 1994

My twenty-seventh birthday. Paul's first. And all I really want is a fully functioning penis. It's those damn hormones again.

Karen took me to the Theatre night-club in Wandsworth,

the same club where we celebrated twelve months ago, only last time the doorman called me 'madam'. Last night the bouncer stopped me inside to tell me that I was approaching a 'ladies only' bar. I was forced to stand on my own looking like a spare part while Karen went off to buy the drinks. I boisterously shouted instructions from the sidelines. The evening was a wild, inebriated success. Karen was dancing as if she had a firework in her knickers.

Friday 16 September 1994
My sideburns are coming along nicely. I think I will have some proper ones down to my ears by Christmas. I met Jo after work in London this evening. We held hands in the cinema and are now on snogging terms.

Monday 19 September 1994
The real test is beginning. I am launching myself into the realms of the unknown. My new life beckons and I have not been this frightened since Dr Who first met the Daleks.

My first day at Highbury College in Portsmouth was a success. After the usual collection of initiative tests – such as finding the entrance to the college itself – I started to lighten up a bit. In our first journalism lecture in the afternoon we had to interview one another in pairs. Our brief was to gather as much information as possible in ten minutes. 'You never know,' said our teacher, Chrissie Barrow, 'you may uncover some real news stories.' Yes, indeed, I was a dirty great big news story sitting right in front of their noses.

I interviewed Vicki Walker and she interviewed me. I admitted to having worked as a stripagram and a life assurance salesman. She told the group: 'Believe it or not, this baby-faced man is in fact twenty-seven years old.'

I signed up for Highbury College football team at

lunchtime. I don't know whether I will be fit enough to play or whether I will be able to compete physically with natural-born males, but I couldn't resist putting my name down anyway. This is great. A whole new world opening up for me.

Friday 23 September 1994
My confidence is expanding exponentially. This course is putting the L back into my life. I get such delight out of being referred to as 'one of the guys' in class, although it still surprises me. After all, I have not changed dramatically as a person. It is only other people's perceptions of me which have shifted perspective.

A twenty-one-year-old guy called Chris has befriended me. This does not unnerve me unduly, but his accompanying me into the toilets does. Many more times and he is liable to think there is something odd about my disinclination to use a urinal.

Nessa, my new landlady, is seeing through my quiet moods. She has persistently questioned me about a message she intercepted on the answer-phone from a photographer, Debbie Humphry, telling me that my photo will appear in the *Observer* this Sunday. I don't know how long my secret will remain intact. For now, Nessa probably finds me the most polite man on earth, since I never leave the toilet seat up. But I am having to be quite meticulous to ensure that she never sees me without bandages on, using the bathroom after she has gone to bed so a heavily boobed Paul doesn't collide with her on the landing.

I am proud that I injected myself alone in the house on Tuesday afternoon. I was nervous of my maiden flight with a needle and syringe, but managed to inject without injury. I hope Nessa doesn't go looking in my room. My sharps box is hidden in my bedside drawer. She might think I am a junkie.

I have still not received anything in writing from the hospital about my mastectomy. My consolation is that I am now so busy I cannot spare the time to get depressed. My body is in shock. I had forgotten that there were two seven o'clocks in one day.

Monday 26 September 1994

Last night I had carefully unwrapped my miles of bandaging and climbed into bed when the doorbell chimed violently – my landlady had assured me she would be out for the night. I grabbed the nearest jumper and, heart thumping, ran downstairs to answer the door trying to ignore my jiggling breasts. It was Nessa. We chatted and I kept my arms folded across my chest, praying she wouldn't notice my two bulges.

My mate Chris is from Tamworth. This is my first experience of genuine male bonding. I wonder what his feelings would be if I were to admit I used to be a chick? I have no plans to find out.

My chest and stomach are getting hairier. Thankfully, spot crisis is over.

Thursday 6 October 1994

The past three weeks have been a maelstrom of mixed emotions. Exaltation and despair go hand in hand, and I seem unable to feel joy without experiencing excruciating pain. But a huge chunk of me feels triumphant; I have achieved the impossible. I am living successfully as a man in Portsmouth, where a whole new world has opened up to me. I have only to look over my shoulder to appreciate how far I have come.

Despite this I seem unable to break free completely from the miserable chains that continue to confine me. I have received a letter from the NHS Trust in London explaining that it will not fund my gender reassignment because I have not lived in its area for five years. Once again desperation and desolation are swamping me. Another door has slammed shut in my face. My mastectomy is receding into the distance; I try to reach out to grasp it and realise it is just a tantalising mirage on the horizon.

I have had two panic attacks in the past fortnight. I had fought all week to keep my feelings of despair in check. I tried to sleep on Saturday morning, but thoughts were flying around my head like heated atoms in Brownian motion. Feeling panic-stricken, I got up and went downstairs. My body was overcome with palpitations, and I badly needed to talk it out. There are times when I feel utterly defeated and so alone. Without really thinking about it, I blurted out 'my secret' to Nessa. 'What's up?' she asked. 'I think I'm going to have a panic attack' was my reply. Head in hands, it was a full five minutes before I could communicate what was going on in my head. Then suddenly my secret was out, like cards on the table, and I had told her everything. 'I knew there was something you weren't telling me,' she said, 'but I would never have guessed this. If you want the truth I was expecting you to tell me you were either gay or HIV positive.'

I also told my course tutor, Cleland Thom. Clel is small, like me, which is comforting. I would guess he is in his thirties, but he seems even younger. I didn't know how I expected him to react, and his support and understanding took me slightly by surprise. 'I will back you completely should anyone else on the course find out,' he told me reassuringly.

I told Clel because I was finding it very hard to keep a smile on my face and keep handing in work while my flesh-eating despair was chewing away at me from the inside and working its way out.

On the positive side of life, I am a billy whizz with a needle. I feel flushed with the success of achievement. Being able to inject myself, without the need to attend a surgery, makes me feel like less of a patient. I am self-contained and capable. As a diabetic needs his insulin, I need my testosterone. Jo and I are still writing. I feel older and tireder than in previous relationships, but I'm still waiting for Claudia Schiffer to kick illusionist David Copperfield into touch and look me up in the phone book.

So here I find myself down again, but not out. I feel I have more chance of getting an England call-up than getting the NHS to fund my op. If things do not improve I shall contact my MP. I have struggled too far to give up now.

We have started writing for the Portsmouth *News Chronicle* this week. I have to wait until Monday to see if any of my stories make it into the paper. I have given up the idea of playing football at the moment. Miracles we can do at once – the impossible takes a little longer. What kills me more than anything is to have to watch the lads go off to play football on a Friday afternoon – without me.

But the way I'm feeling at the moment I wouldn't last five minutes on the football pitch without either collapsing or getting one of my legs broken. And, as a pre-op female-to-male transsexual, using the same changing-room would be an experience from hell. Patience here is the key. Everything comes to him who waits.

I am dreaming of the day when life does not feel just like survival. I need a hug.

Sunday 9 October 1994

I watched *Rocky II* on video last night. Rocky is one of my heroes, along with Tarzan. As I watched, I realised that my dreams of being a huge, streamlined, lithe, aerodynamic, athletic force are no more than foolish fantasy. In the mirror I could see my puny, female body struggling to contain my world-class aspirations. After the credits had rolled, I jumped up and shadow-boxed in front of the mirror, screwing up my face in pain and pounding the air with left hooks.

I have been trying to trace back to the exact moment when my illness and unhappiness first started. I now realise that these symptoms coincided with the arrival of secondary sexual characteristics. This happened very late for me, when I was seventeen, delayed by my punishing routine of club athletics and cross-country running.

Every time I look at my body in the mirror I experience grief. Each glimpse is a reminder that my dreams will always be out of reach. This frustration is making me more of a bastard each day. Fired up on testosterone, my internal tormented aggressor aches to escape and express himself. I may have balls but they are only illusory. I will never forgive the world for the fact that it took my balls away from me.

It is only work that is keeping me sane at the moment. I go on, because we do go on. My sideburns are improving, and so is my stubble. This gives me strength. So does knowing I have women who love me despite my shortcomings.

Monday 10 October 1994
Today my first news story appeared in print.

Tuesday 11 October 1994
This evening I went to Havant Gymnastics Club near Portsmouth to write a piece. A troupe of fourteen-year-old girls were waving at me, trying to attract my attention, but I could only watch the male gymnasts with envy.

Sunday 16 October 1994
My mood has elevated considerably since last weekend. Bashing away on my computer, I worked my way out of it.

The administration error that is my operation still gnaws away at me like a cannibal on a leg bone, but I am trying to place things in perspective. I have waited twenty-seven years, and it seems sane to suggest to my subconscious that I can wait a little longer.

Jo has blown me out for good. She has done me a favour. I couldn't afford the train-fare anyway. She has met someone else at university and can't decide who she wants. I have made up her mind for her by making the decision not to write to her any more. I'm not playing second best to anyone.

On Wednesday I saw international clairvoyant Kate Lomax. She was a blowsy woman with cascades of flowing hair and was sitting behind a desk in the Meridian Shopping Centre, Havant. Chris and I had time to kill, and I was insatiably curious to discover whether a clairvoyant could spot a transsexual. Kate knew only my first name. She shuffled the cards wistfully and then looked me directly in the eye, asking me to split the well-fingered cards into three piles.

She ruminated on these for a while, moving her hands up and down above the table and rubbing her fingers together as if trying to dispel dust from between them. Then she asked: 'Who is the woman with the broken heart?'

'Is there only one?' I quipped, but inside felt alarmed. Had she sensed Martine's pain? I sent Chris away from the desk, worried that Kate would get too close to the truth. We maintained eye contact as she looked at me for confirmation of her findings. I gave nothing away.

She continued: 'I can't see you at Highbury College at all. You will move on somewhere else, but it will not be a disaster. You will go on to something better. You are an emotional war zone, very strong-willed and liable to get very stressed out.'

Yeah, well, tell me something I don't know!

Tuesday 18 October 1994
In exactly four weeks' time I will be out of savings. As I consider this rather desperate financial situation, the words shit, creek and paddle come to mind simultaneously. I have applied for a Career Development Loan. Life is a bit of a roller-coaster ride – your knuckles certainly turn white and your hair stands on end.

Oh, yes, while on the subject of hair, I feel I must mention the sudden arrival of a dark sprout of hairs on each of my little toes.

Tuesday 1 November 1994
It is exactly one year ago today that I began taking male hormones. My sideburns are now taking on a life of their own. I injected myself tonight, as I do every fortnight, relieved that this is not a daily routine since the needle strikes the fear of God into me each time I see it.

But now there is a new spring in my step. For the first time in seven years I feel I have taken control of my life; I have finally sorted out the ridiculous and frustrating scenario surrounding the funding of my mastectomy. My life is once again worth living. My dreams remain possible and my goals intact, but this has taken great perseverance. Each week I have been phoning Mount Vernon Hospital to get an update on my case and allowing myself to be fobbed off by an overworked secretary. Yesterday I decided enough was enough; my patience, like the grains in a sand-timer, had run right out. I asked to be put straight through to the department dealing with funding. Valerie Jenkins will never know the importance of what she did today. Within twenty minutes she had phoned back to confirm that Berkshire NHS Trust had agreed to pay. Now I do what has become second nature – sit back and wait. A date should follow shortly.

Saturday night was Hallowe'en and Karen introduced

me to a colleague of hers, Tatiana. Instantly I realised she was my kind of woman. A real live wire and beautiful with it. Soon it was not only the pumpkin soup with hot chillies that was bubbling over. As everyone else gradually passed out in a drunken stupor around me, passion between Tatiana and me was burning like a fire in a petrol station. Several pints the worse for wear, I found myself in a compromising position, but while I was a sexual timebomb waiting to explode I had to hold back for fear of discovery. As Tatiana's hands felt their way down my back, they alighted on the harness holding my Herb in place. Why did this have to be so complicated? Nervously, I shifted her hands to a new location by shrugging my shoulders and squirming. I was desperate to have sex there and then but my common sense was still fully functional ... Do not pass go, do not collect £200...

We abandoned the foreplay and forgot our frustrations as we fell asleep in each other's arms. I will never know what she was thinking, but as far as I am aware Tatiana has no idea I am a transsexual. Unfortunately, we didn't get that far.

Twice last week I was asked to show an ID in a pub. This is pissing me right off. I am twenty-seven years old. I wish I looked it. I yearn to be treated with respect and not called 'lad' all the time.

Tuesday 15 November 1994

Never, even in my worst nightmares, did I imagine that my life would turn out to be so tough. Having offered me a Career Development Loan – my last pennies are slipping away – Barclays are now faltering. They have discovered a delinquent bank account. This is all I need. It is the outstanding loan which fell into arrears when I became too stressed out to work last year.

I skipped college today after I had been to talk to a

counsellor. I just couldn't cope any more. It was a case of the straw which broke the camel's back. I came home and cried and cried.

Still, all is not bleak. My legs seem to be getting even hairier, and this provides comfort big time. I was talking to James in New Zealand last night. He is a fellow female-to-male transsexual who started writing to me after seeing a syndicated *Daily Express* article in the Kiwi *Woman's Weekly*. We talked about the simple things which natural-born men take for granted. Like walking out of the bathroom with a towel around the waist instead of covering the top half. Sometimes I do this if there is no one else in the house, and it feels like heaven. It is a basic difference between the sexes which no one but a frustrated transsexual would ever devote time to contemplating.

It is difficult to feel good about yourself when you are a man who has the remnants of womanhood clinging on like groupies. The worst piece of advice I routinely get is to 'keep your pecker up'. The chance would surely be a fine thing.

I had a Manchester haircut today – named after the Manchester United players with smart barnets. It is seriously short.

Sunday 20 November 1994

At last I have a date for my bilateral mastectomy. This marathon of endurance is due to end on 27 January. I have put a chart on my bedroom wall to enable me to tick off the days. I feel like a small child eagerly opening the windows on an Advent calendar, desperate for the delights of Christmas.

Sixty-seven days to go, and counting. Now I am completely focused.

I have got a firm grasp on my college work and feel powerful, able to dodge life's constant shellfire. I had another piece published in the *News Chronicle* this week.

Also I sent an anonymous note in shorthand to Lindsay Coulson, the tall, bespectacled, sexy student I have got my eye on. It said: 'You remind me of Miss Moneypenny. Can I be your James Bond? I'm saving my best looks for your eyes only.'

Within minutes every journalism student got wind that Lindsay had a mystery admirer. I am sure she suspects me. She keeps giving me long, penetrating looks across the classroom.

Friday 2 December 1994

Fifty-four days to go and I feel more focused than ever. Last night I dreamed I was a sick albatross with a broken wing taken in by a mysterious brunette. She fixed splints to my broken wings and gently and lovingly fed me hot toddies by the warm glow of a restorative fire. The days skimmed past and time drifted. Gradually my wing mended, then my mobility returned overnight. Suddenly I could fly. Once again I was a viable aerodynamic creature, in control of my environment. I moved through the air like music, master of the thermals, maestro of the updraughts.

But these positive affirmations mask a nagging feeling which nibbles at my gut. I remain haunted by my predicament. I live with profound sadness, but it is vital to rise above these negative emotions; they are useless to me, a waste of energy. I try to control them – until a pretty girl enters the room and I wonder why I haven't got a penis to stand to attention. Most men are embarrassed to suffer from premature ejaculation . . . I would be delighted.

Still, life isn't all bad. There are four women waiting in the living-room downstairs and I am about to join them. Don't wait up for me.

Monday 5 December 1994

It is an odd feeling, abandoning one's life and setting out

again on a completely different path. My fresh-faced looks hide the maturity of the person I am inside. I have gained wisdom from my unique perspective. I have crossed the gender divide and it has given me insight. But sometimes I fear I will never recover from the trauma induced by the warring factions lurking inside me. They fight constantly, my incompatible body and mind, aching for resolution. Yes, the body-shock has been devastating and complete.

Last year I thought I had lost that winning feeling, that magic touch. Yet here I am doing more than just surviving. My mind remains precision focused and the motto 'Never say die' is chiselled like a granite inscription inside my head.

Every day that passes propels me onwards towards my goal. Every twinge of joy, however, is accompanied by a splinter of pain. It seems I cannot reach dizzy heights without experiencing the pangs of barren despair.

Today I feel a sense of well-being which I have never experienced before. I am content in the knowledge that no one can prevent me from achieving my goals and finding my destiny. Tears track down my cheeks as I write, but they are tears of sheer relief. My metamorphosis is reaching its climax. My passions and my convictions burn like lasers through my head.

I have a new companion. My new ProSport jock-strap. It is strange what can make one person discover inner contentment. I have never had a jock-strap before. I am like the South African man in the Arctic who has never seen snow.

Thursday 8 December 1994

The *Sun* carried a news story today entitled 'Cop Swop'. It tells of a San Francisco policeman, Stephan Thorne. This forty-year-old was born Stephanie. But his gender reassignment has been given the official blessing of San Francisco police bosses. Police chief Anthony Ribera said: 'Sergeant

Thorne was a fine female officer – and now he is an equally fine male officer. What he did was a personal decision that in no way affects the quality of his work. We are delighted with his decision to stay with the San Francisco department.'

The story continued with an explanation of Stephan's background. 'He was the younger of two daughters who lived with a single mother in Lincoln, Nebraska. She played football with the boys and was called Mike by close family friends. But when she attended her local high school her life became a nightmare. She hated dresses and had eyes only for other girls. Stephanie knew she was never going to become a married woman. She spent five years as a gas-pipeline maintenance worker and fourteen years ago joined the police. Two years ago she decided to have a sex-change operation. Now Stephan says the process is almost complete and he is manly enough to engage in a normal sexual relationship with his girlfriend of nine months.'

Stephan said: 'The difference between me and being a tomboy was that I felt I was a boy being made to wear dresses. Puberty was awful. I felt as if my body was betraying me when I developed breasts. I dated a few boys but it was very uncomfortable. I think I make a great boyfriend because, having been Stephanie, I understand all my girlfriend's womanly needs.'

Saturday 10 December 1994

Another strange thing has happened to me. I can whistle. Now I know that nature designed us to wolf-whistle at women. I couldn't whistle until my voice broke!

I am staying with Karen in Putney for the weekend. I borrowed her white dressing-gown as I travelled from her bedroom to the bathroom this morning. She later told me at that moment she had had a vision of me. A vision of me in the shower with a penis. I asked her, 'Was it a big one?'

What does this prove? I would say it proves that she sees me as a man completely. She can no longer imagine me as anything else.

Chapter Nine

Wednesday 21 December 1994
I went into the men's changing-room for the first time last Friday after I played football with the guys from college. I thought I was going to have a panic attack as I walked into the realms of the unknown to experience male bonding first hand. To say it felt strange would be an understatement. I felt like an impostor, a mole planted to convey information to 'the other side'. My eyes nearly popped out of my head as a hairy bottom plunged in front of my face. Then a colleague with Big Daddy's frame took off his shirt to reveal saggy breasts. What am *I* worrying about, I thought to myself.

Another first was actually playing in an all-male match. I felt certain that I would be stretchered off with broken bones, but I survived intact. There was no real competitive edge to the game and I was hardly outclassed. But although I even came close to scoring on several occasions, I felt a shadow of my former self. I was so stiff the next day that I could hardly walk, but being back on the turf had been a wonderful liberation.

My self-confidence lurches precariously up and down. For days at a time I feel lower than a wriggling worm, then something happens to boost my confidence and I fly high for a while. I never anticipated that being transsexual would leave me feeling so insignificant.

Today, though, I am on an up. I am delighted to have survived my course to the end of the Christmas term. Even a few months ago I had no idea I could be achieving this much this soon. The countdown to my operation continues, but it is now only a matter of weeks until I am rid of these wretched dangling protuberances for ever. When I get out of hospital I anticipate the sort of high which can normally be achieved only by injecting illegal substances.

Wednesday 25 January 1995

I awoke at 5 a.m. this morning with pains shooting through my left side. I reached for the green towelling dressing-gown my mother had bought me for Christmas and staggered downstairs in search of a cup of tea and a hot-water bottle. I lay on the sofa, hidden beneath a blanket, until the pains began to subside. Not appendicitis, but a legacy of the last six days, which have thrust me brutally through an emotional mangle.

This time last week my mind was on countdown. My operation was a virtual reality, just days away. I was obsessed by the belief that soon my boobs would be history. I couldn't concentrate on my work, and my life was like a dart on target, zooming towards an inevitable bull's-eye.

Then my mother rang and my world was rocked.

'Paul, a letter arrived for you this morning. I opened it because it looked important. Shall I read it?' Her voice worried me. She sounded so sad and hesitant.

'Sure,' I said, sitting down.

'Dear Mr Hewitt. We regret that it will be necessary to cancel your admission on 27 January under the care of Mr B. D. G. Morgan. We apologise for any inconvenience this may cause and will contact you with regard to a new admission date as soon as possible. Yours sincerely, Admissions Officer, Plastic Surgery Centre.'

My mother read out a footnote which added that 'Mr Morgan will not, unfortunately, be at the hospital on the above date'.

The shock was immediate, as dramatic as a thunderclap. My dream had disappeared from view and the wailing began. I slung the phone back into its cradle and began shaking, dropping on all fours, unable to hold myself together. I thought that testosterone had dried up my tears, that I had lost my ability to cry, but instead the accumulated grief of extinguished expectation spurted out of me like blood from a pierced vein. I wanted to bang my head on the floor, on the wall, against anything. Then, when every emotion had dripped from my body, I flopped into the armchair by the telephone in a hypnotic, exhausted trance. I have never felt such feelings of complete devastation before. I also had a frightening sense that I would not have the strength to pick myself up and carry on after this disappointment. I always thought that I was invincible, that my spirit was basically uncrushable, that the only way was up. Now I was all alone and childlike, scared of the dark and of my own shadow.

I had no clue as to when I would be called into hospital again, and the awfulness of that took the form of a sickening void in my stomach. I limped through the afternoon, managing to call Chris, my best mate from college. He came round like a shot, knowing how much the operation meant to me, and stayed over, sleeping on the sofa.

We walked into college together the next morning, but lessons did not go well. As the shorthand teacher began to read out the two-minute dictation, panic bubbled up in my body like hot water filling a bathtub. I scraped my seat over the vinyl floor and fled the room for the safety of the Gents. I sat on the cold tiles inside the cubicle, dethroned and abandoned, until the lesson was over and I could go back to collect my things. When I arrived home I tore my Seven

Days To Go chart off my wardrobe door in disgust and hurled it, tattered, into the bin.

My operation date had been the only thing keeping me going, for the nightmare is infinitely easier to bear when it has a definite end. The platform upon which my whole life rested had been my forthcoming bilateral mastectomy. Now it had crumbled into dust and I was free-falling into oblivion.

I spent six days of desperation crying, not caring whether I lived or died. When I wasn't crying my heart out I was having a panic attack, and if I wasn't doing that I was reading Armitage Shanks at close range. Everyone kept telling me that I had to pull myself out of it, that I had to go on, but I didn't want to. I no longer cared. Every man has his limit, and I had found mine. My will to survive had packed his bags and left. On Friday morning, after another troubled night, I said to Chris: 'I feel like I've spent the night in a bus shelter.'

He replied with his natural honesty: 'Sorry, mate, but you look much worse than that.'

But, as suddenly as my distress had begun, it was over. Just as I was contemplating the least messy form of suicide, Jane phoned from the *Daily Express*. 'I've got you an operation. In three weeks.' I couldn't believe it. Jane had pulled rabbits out of hats before, but even Paul Daniels couldn't have extricated this one. 'It's true,' she continued. 'I've phoned round several private surgeons to see if anyone would do the operation for £2,000, and I've found a Harley Street surgeon.'

Jane is to lend me £1,700 and I have to find £360, since the surgeon will operate for £2,060, including hospitalisation fees. Jane is one of those people who are very persuasive, a woman of action, and since I would find it difficult to say no to her, I could well appreciate his predicament!

I didn't know what to say to Jane. 'Thank you' seemed so inadequate. She was the one person who had never once said 'snap out of it' because, since we have written this book together, she knows my feelings almost as well as I do, and realises I am fighting for the body I need to survive. The first time Jane ever spoke to me, in the Express Newspapers foyer at Blackfriars, London, in November 1993, my instincts told me that she was pure gold-dust. My opinion has not changed since.

The only thing that could rescue me from my particular clifftop was hope, and Jane and the surgeon had given that back to me.

Karen had written a powerful letter to Dr Morgan at Mount Vernon Hospital. It might have done some good had he been there.

20 January 1995

Dear Dr Morgan

I am writing to you with reference to Mr Paul Hewitt, who was due to have a double mastectomy with you on 27 January, and which was recently cancelled for the second time.

I have spoken to Mrs Moore, and she has informed me of the problems you have with keeping a date for Paul's operation, due to the number of recent malignancies and also the fact that you are the only consultant able to carry out the surgery.

I do, therefore, very much appreciate the poignancy of your position, but as Paul's twin sister, am extremely concerned for my brother's welfare – he is, I would say, extremely depressed, and do not feel he is able to wait for an operation which is so vital to his existence, and even if he could wait, the trauma of another possible cancellation would be just too much to bear.

Paul has been so strong, and I have tried to keep him strong, but his distress at this recent cancellation frightens me so much that I am writing to ask if there is anything at all in your power to help Paul – although it is difficult for some people to grasp, anyone who has done their homework knows as well as I do that transsexuality is as life-threatening as cancer.

I would be so grateful if you could do anything at all to help Paul.

Yours sincerely

Karen Hewitt

Jane's boyfriend, Richard, also phoned Dr Morgan. 'I need to speak to Dr Morgan urgently,' he said.

'Sorry,' said his assistant. 'He's not here.'

'Can I get hold of him at another hospital then?' Richard asked.

'No,' she said. 'Unfortunately, he's on holiday.'

Not that it mattered. He was just getting on with his life. How could Dr Morgan know that he had just pulled away the last support that was holding me up?

I've never felt disappointment like it. So frustrated, so angry, so crushed, so helpless, so absolutely nothing. I feel like a physical wreck, as if my body has been ripped apart and then reassembled with vital components missing.

I'm going back to college tomorrow. It will be a tough day because it was to have been the date of my admission into hospital, the day I thought would never come. When it finally did it didn't matter any more: how bitterly ironic. I feel as if I have glimpsed death during this last week, but I've now got my smile back and feel like the luckiest bloke alive to have such sincere and loyal people around me. The vision

I had in my head of my whole life going down the toilet has disappeared. My game-plan has slipped back a few weeks, and my body feels it has been beaten to a pulp, but let the whole world know 'the fight is back on'...

My crazy dream of being able to walk along the beach on a hot summer's day, with my shirt tied around my waist, now feels like a distant possibility again.

Thursday 26 January 1995

I went back to college today, but it took more courage than I had expected to face the world again. The emotions of the past week have left me feeling as if my legs are going to fall off, a sensation I remember from running a hard cross-country race. Only all I've done is go to college for the day and come home again.

But it's great to be back in the land of the living. I seem to have taken more bashes, albeit psychological ones, than Frank Bruno. My life at the moment seems to have developed a rather surreal quality to it. It makes me think of a little scenario involving my fictional friend, Fred. Fred had lost his head in a road accident, and his mate said to him, 'Just think, Fred, one day you'll look back and laugh about all this...' Only poor Fred didn't have a head, so the poor bugger could neither look back nor laugh.

Started thinking about women again today, so I must be feeling better. But I don't feel able to build up my hopes again about this private operation. My fighting spirit has gone into hiding. I've had about as much as I can take.

Saturday 28 January 1995

Got a card from the House of Commons this morning and was tickled pinker than a baby's bottom. It said: 'All the best for your operation – we hope you recover well. From all in Alex Carlile's office.'

It's been a funny old week. I've bounced back with a

vengeance, but the scars are still healing and I am depleted of energy reserves . . . like a fast car with a flat. Although I'm motoring again, this baby has far from reached top cruising speed.

On Friday I persuaded Chris to have his hair cut like the Crystal Palace yob who was karate-kicked by Eric Cantona last week. While Chris was losing hair at a vast rate of knots, I chatted to sexy Simone who cropped my locks last time. My confidence had not deserted me. Why am I totally hypnotised by tall women? Because they feel the rain before I do? This one was at least six feet and towered over me. In between bouts of showing off I was spellbound.

I am once again finding it really hard to motivate myself to do any work with only seventeen days until my operation. I'm experiencing a sense of *déjà vu* – haven't I been here before? But the operation still seems like such a distant possibility that it might as well be seventeen years.

A great number of masculine urges are rising up inside me like molten lava journeying upwards from the core of a volcano. To hell with sitting behind a computer trying not to suffer from screen blindness; I think I fancy being a builder with his bum hanging out, or a plumber or a mechanic in greasy overalls. Better still, I fancy joining the Territorial Army or the Foreign Legion. (My mother would never forgive me.)

Sometimes I feel as if I am little more than a walking, talking collection of unfulfilled dreams. There isn't a sniff of a woman in my life at the moment. Even my cuddly gorilla is starting to look attractive.

Mick, my ex-boyfriend, phoned me out of the blue this afternoon. The last time I spoke to him was on New Year's Eve. When I replaced the receiver I suddenly had a strong sensation of loss. I really miss him, but could never tell him that. He called me 'love' when he said goodbye, and I smiled as I replaced the receiver. He still has a picture of

Martine in his head, an image which my deep voice has been unable to erase. He was my best friend for a time, someone who loved me unconditionally, warts and all. Though completely heterosexual, he never ever demanded that I behave like a woman. He just wanted me to be happy.

Thursday 2 February 1995
I didn't make it into college today as I was once again totally exhausted. There is no middle ground for me. I am either up or down. I am trying not to think about the operation. I feel unable to take another disappointment as severe as the last one. I have taken to listening to the theme music from the *Rocky* films every morning to fire myself up and force myself out of bed on those mornings when this feat feels quite impossible. I have to remember 'The Eye of the Tiger', the lyrics of which state, 'I took my chances, now I'm back on my feet. Just a man and his will to survive.'

I have now developed a full-blown lust attack for the woman who cuts my hair in Just Gents in Cosham. She waved through the window at me yesterday as I walked past. My legs went to jelly, and I gave her a huge cheeky grin which remained fixed to my face for the rest of the evening. Simone is as tall as I am short. I can only hope that Christmas comes early this year and she likes diminutive men.

I am now getting my hair cut every two weeks.

Thursday 9 February 1995
Last night I had the nightmare from hell.

I got dressed in a hurry for college and ran for the bus. When I arrived at college, students in corridors giggled and pointed at my legs. I looked down and realised I had pulled on a clinging black mini-skirt by mistake. My rampantly hairy legs poked from beneath my skirt, each one anchored by a

Caterpillar boot. A wave of non-reality passed over me, and although I knew something was wrong I couldn't work out what they were laughing at. Whispers of 'weirdo' and 'poofter' suddenly filtered through on the currents to my ears, and sweat broke out and beaded on my brow. I looked again in horror at my legs, my skirt looking as out of place as an Armani shirt in an Oxfam shop. I rushed to the toilets to tear off the skirt, hoping no one had seen me, but it was too late. They had.

I awoke, feverishly gripping the sheets. The clock said 3.30 a.m. That was the end of my night. I sat touching my chest hair and contemplating how stressful life has become. It seems tragic that all my chest growth will have to be shaved off by the surgeon next week after months of careful cultivation.

Karen says I look a bit effeminate in my baseball cap so that has gone straight in the bin. I may go into Just Gents and visit Simone, the sexy scissor lady, tomorrow – if this spot on my chin has receded, that is. If I ask her for her phone number I wonder whether she will shave it into the back of my hair with her clippers?

A blob of fear and excitement sits in my stomach as I wait to visit the Harley Street surgeon tomorrow for my private consultation. I will find out whether my boobs will be having their last breakfast next Thursday. Once again I am facing the final countdown: 3 . . . 2 . . . 1 . . . NO BOOBS!

There were so many cute Valentine cards in the shops this afternoon that I couldn't help myself and ended up buying four. I am working on the principle that you reap what you sow. I am also exchanging erotic letters with Marie in New Zealand. She is the flatmate of James, the female-to-male transsexual who read the article about me and struck up a correspondence with me. I have promised to visit them later this year when I take a well-deserved holiday.

Sunday 12 February 1995
Just when I thought it was safe to go back in the water it was back – Desperation, The Revenge. I don't know how much longer I can keep going when there is just an empty shell inside me occupying the space where my fire used to be. On Friday I travelled from Portsmouth to Harley Street in London for my appointment with the consultant plastic surgeon. He was a really nice bloke wearing a hideous green tie, the loudest in the history of the planet, but he could not tell me anything to provide me with hope. It cost me £60 to see him, and his secretary booked me in for surgery on the twenty-third of this month, but I had an intensely uneasy feeling as I stepped out into the squally rain falling from a lead-grey sky.

He had talked of scars, and incisions, and of 'not being able to go swimming, ever'. My heart sank as I sat on his white-paper-covered bench naked from the waist up. I realised there was a world of difference between removing female boobs and creating male chests. This examination was an ordeal in itself. I felt at best awkward, like a Guns 'n' Roses fan at the Royal Ballet, at worst ugly and exposed. I have nothing but hatred for the body parts which a monster has designed.

There are two techniques for bilateral mastectomy for transsexuals, one that involves crossed incisions and leaves scarring, and one that doesn't – instead, it involves lifting away the nipple, sucking tissue out, and then contracting the skin. The doctor felt that my breasts were too big, with too much skin for me to hope for no scarring. This did not tie in with what Dr Morgan at the NHS had told me.

I felt weak and faint as I trekked across London to meet Karen from work, like a pack-laden donkey crossing the Himalayas. I looked in a mirror in Top Man and was shocked to see that my face had erupted in pink blotches, showing the strain. I decided I had better call Stephen

Whittle, organiser of the Female-to-Male Network in Manchester, for his opinion. 'If he says you will be left with scars, don't touch him,' was Stephen's advice. 'If you're going to go privately, you may as well have the best!'

My heart sank like the sun going down. I would have to cancel surgery on the twenty-third. There was no point making a rash decision, the results of which I would have to live with for the rest of my life. My last remaining flame of hope flickered and went out. I could see only darkness. Just last night I had pulled myself out of depression and was the life and soul of the party, cracking jokes all night at the World's End pub in Camden Town and flirting as if my life depended on it. I have developed the skill of 'snapping out of it' into a fine art. But for now it is all gloom again and I am frightened. Why does this depression feel so final?

I am going to see the doctor on Tuesday to ask him to prescribe some anti-depressants. I am in a deep, black hole and I need a helping hand to climb out. 'Go on, treat yourself if that's what you need' is what my sister said, bless her. I find myself caught up in a vicious circle of not sleeping, and I am pinning my hopes on drugs to give me the lift I need. Perhaps I could hire myself out to funeral processions: £20 an hour to set the mood for everyone else. 'Rent a sombre bastard.'

I have been trying to contact a Dr Bannerjee in Essex, my last hope, as I am told he is the best private surgeon for transsexuals. But without a win on the National Lottery it is unlikely that I will be able to afford his fees. Mind you, I got three numbers right last night. Only another three and all my prayers could have had the lucre to come true. I am putting all my hopes on my lucky six numbers: ONE, my favourite number; EIGHT, the number of legs on a spider; TEN, the number of women I've slept with; SEVENTEEN, my door number; THIRTY-SIX, my friend Joanne's bra size; FORTY-ONE, the number of hairs on my chest.

Whoever said that money can't buy you happiness obviously didn't know where to shop! Life wouldn't be so bad if I had at least a little romance to take my mind off things, but it's work, work, work. And who wants to go out with a manic-depressive anyway? My game-plan is being systematically flushed away, like a spider down the toilet which keeps coming back for more, and I am powerless to do anything about it. I am like an astronomer gazing at the stars; I can still see all my dreams, but I can't reach them.

Wednesday 15 February 1995
I am sitting on a cold platform at Winchester station waiting for my train to Reading to arrive, feeling betwixt and between, in emotional and physical limbo. I've got an appointment to see my old GP, Dr Dodson, in Reading this afternoon. I feel that if anyone can help me, it is him. Sarah is coming with me, and I am going to tell him everything that has happened, the whole sorry tale. I've hardly done any college work, and am now moving backwards instead of forwards. It seems absolutely crazy that I am being treated for depression rather than for its easily identifiable cause. The only thing that can cure me is the operation. I feel almost as bad as I did in July 1993 when a psychiatrist attempted to pack me off for psychotherapy when I told her I was transsexual. There is absolutely nothing wrong with my head.

My new GP, in Portsmouth, prescribed me anti-depressants yesterday when I saw him and explained how desperate I was feeling. I felt anger welling up inside me as I left his surgery, his words haunting me: 'Is this really all that's depressing you? When it comes down to it, it's only a couple of lumps of fat that have to be removed. You won't be a different person afterwards.' In a couple of dismissive sentences he had totally belittled everything I was going through. When I explained that my operation was considered second to the cancer cases admitted to the hospital, he said: 'Well, of course.' I tried explaining that if he was transsexual he too might understand the extent of my desperation. Then, as I heard my voice rising, I just stopped talking. There was absolutely no point in arguing with him. Now I feel like a caged lion at London Zoo, pacing anxiously up and down, frustrated that I am powerless to take control of my life.

Jane has been making enquiries abroad for me and has found a surgeon in Switzerland who will operate for the exorbitant fee of £5,670. It may be hideously expensive but Switzerland is the best place for surgery for transsexuals. I have been provisionally booked in for 9 March. I have no idea how I am going to raise the money, but I know I can't sit around wallowing and waiting for things to happen. I have just written a grovelling letter to Captain Cash of the *News of the World*, telling him: I need to raise £5,670 and so far I've got 27p. Can you help?

My life has become a stomach-churning nightmare. I don't feel I can cope with much more. My journalism training is slipping away from me, and all I can do, from my vantage-point of deep depression, is watch.

I have realised something else rather crucial during the past couple of weeks. Although some female-to-male transsexuals may be able to live without eventual phalloplasty, I am not one of them. Despite the fact that genital surgery is risky and expensive, I can't live without functional parts. Again, surgery in Switzerland is probably my only option. I want to see a body that is as male as possible when I look in the mirror. I yearn to rectify what nature has miscreated. One day I will have to raise £20,000.

Thursday 16 February 1995

I feel a little happier today. My old GP in Reading, Dr

Dodson, listened sympathetically and allowed me to pour my heart out to him. What many other GPs don't appreciate is the courage it takes to make an appointment and admit to how you are feeling. He is unable to make any promises but said he will phone Dr Morgan, the NHS plastic surgeon at Mount Vernon, to see if they can squeeze me in soon. I'm not expecting miracles, but at least I'm doing everything I possibly can.

I feel drugged up to the eyeballs at the moment. So much so that I couldn't work out where I was when a strange woman brought me a cup of tea this morning – it was only Sarah. And I threw my second tea of the day all down my trousers when I ran for my train (it was the wrong one and I ended up in Salisbury).

It's 10.30 p.m. and I'm sitting in front of the fire watching my clothes dry out after being battered by the Portsmouth gales. Chris Rea is playing 'Fool if You Think it's Over' on the radio, which is ominous. On the phone today Jane said: 'I don't understand how you can be so down yet still be so funny!' No, I don't understand my sick sense of humour either.

My life is a piece of shit and 1995 has been for me, so far, a living hell. God help the world should I ever get a penis; I wouldn't be impossible, I'd be downright dangerous.

Saturday 18 February 1995

I have been on Amitriptyline for four days now, and although I feel like a zombie until about four in the afternoon I have certainly pulled myself up a few rungs on the depression ladder. I went into college on Thursday and Friday and felt a shadow of the real me, but at least I was there. All I can do is soldier on until things get better.

Wednesday 22 February 1995

This morning was spent madly stuffing my head with local

government finance for our public affairs exam in the afternoon. In between revision I was trying to phone my GP in Reading to try to sort out the details of my operation. I could do with my own personal secretary to cope with all the letters I have to write and phone calls I have to make. My life is an administrative nightmare. Nevertheless, the exam went very well – just think what I'd be able to achieve if I had the time to concentrate properly.

I got £50 in the post this morning from Victoria Wood. You are probably wondering what Victoria Wood is doing sending me money! Last Friday I came to a decision. I could not watch myself getting sicker and sicker – I have hardly recognised myself during the last six weeks of sheer hell – so I drafted a form letter asking for help in raising money for a private operation. My mate Chris went to the library and copied from *Who's Who* the names of fifty celebrities who we suspected had large cheque-books and might be sympathetic towards my plight. Over four pots of tea in Sunny's restaurant in Cosham High Street, we addressed and stuck stamps on envelopes. During our hour of inspiration Chris suggested we write to, among others, Stan Richards (Seth in *Emmerdale Farm*) as the *News of the World* recently reported that he had had an affair with a transsexual male-to-female. Then I remembered that Desmond Lynam had asked Caroline Cossey, the Bond girl, model and famous male-to-female, to marry him. So we sent a copy of the letter to him as well. Other than those we tried to select the kind of enlightened, liberal types who might attempt to understand rather than judge me. Mailing off the letters made me feel much better. I felt as though I was doing something constructive and taking control of my life once again.

Here is the letter I sent out:

Dear ....
I have never written a letter like this before, but there are

many things we find ourselves considering when we become desperate. As a lifelong admirer of your work I am asking for your help. This is a letter about sex. To be more correct, it is a matter of gender, but now at least I have your attention.

I am a pre-operative female-to-male transsexual, that is to say I was born female, but after fifteen months of hormone treatment I am successfully living in the male role. I am a trainee journalist at Highbury College in Portsmouth, where no one knows about my past.

For the past eighteen months I have had to bind up breasts which I have grown to hate. I knew I was male, and not female, from a very early age. I have been a prisoner in a body which does not belong to me.

I have made great progress these past eighteen months, after suffering physical and emotional breakdown in 1993, including gaining a place on an NCTJ newspaper journalism course and writing a book of my experiences which is being published as a Headline lead title on 13 July, co-written with Daily Express *feature writer Jane Warren. It has a thousand-word foreword written by Alex Carlile MP, who is fully supportive of my personal battle.*

In spite of the recommendation of two independent psychiatrists, who say that bilateral mastectomy is in my interests socially, vocationally and psychologically, I continue to wait to be called in for the operation on the NHS. So far I have had dates which have been cancelled twice, most recently on 26 January this year. The news has almost finished me.

I am now in a state of clinical depression and my progress has slipped backwards to the state I was in when my transsexualism first reared its head. I am too depressed to do my college work and I can see everything I have worked for slipping away from me. It seems crazy that I am being prescribed drugs for depression rather than anyone attempting to treat its cause. Getting this operation as soon as possible has now become a life-or-death issue for me. As such I am trying to raise £5,670 for a private operation in Switzerland on 9 March. So far I have 27p and would be ecstatic if you could help in any way.

I am happy for you to contact Jane Warren at the Express *if you want to check me out (phone number as above). She is desperately keen to help me but neither of us has this sort of cash. Thank you for reading this far.*

Yours very sincerely

Paul Hewitt

I was really excited when I saw Victoria Wood's name on the cheque. It seemed strange that she should be the first to reply as she is one of the women I most admire – I have always found her side-splittingly funny. This morning my post also included a letter from Sir Clive Sinclair saying he had only limited funds.

Jane has found another operation for me in Belgium. Dr Monstréy has told me that I have a good chance of claiming back the £2,100 cost on the NHS by making a request for an E1–12 form, on the basis that my operation is not available in the UK 'within a reasonable time'. I drafted a letter to Berkshire Health Commission and faxed it over to Dr Dodson this afternoon. Things may be complicated, but at least I am actually smiling now.

Tuesday 28 February 1995

I now have my own little army of fourteen-year-old admirers in Cosham. I went into the newsagent's to buy a paper on Saturday and I heard the hushed whispers of two females in collusion. 'How about him, Julie? He's about our height,' one girl whispered to her mate just loudly enough for me to hear. I was still chortling to myself as I walked past them and out of the shop, paper under one arm. Just as I was almost out of earshot, I heard a raucous shout. 'N-I-C-E B-U-M!'

This I could hold up as conclusive proof that I am living in a time-warp. I look like a teenager yet I am a twenty-seven-year-old man. I laughed my head off as I was assailed with shouts of 'Phooarr!' Was this to be the full extent of my pulling power?

Saturday 4 March 1995

I expect to look back on 1995 as being the toughest year of my life. Certainly the first two months have been a nightmare of Freddie Kruger proportions. Now I find myself with a new dilemma. Dilemma is my middle name. In the post this morning I received a letter from Mount Vernon Hospital with a new admission date of 27 April. Do I still go to Belgium or do I cancel and leave myself at the mercy of the NHS once more? If I go to Belgium I will have to fund the operation entirely myself, since I can no longer claim that it is not available within a reasonable time. But what if they cancel again at the last moment?

My mind is made up. I can't cope with any more disappointment. My mind and body are fragile creatures at the moment, incapable of withstanding any more stress. Even if I have to sell my body and my Garfield collection I'm boarding that plane to Brussels on 23 March. And when I've made up my mind, changing it is like trying to shift blocks of concrete.

Wednesday 15 March 1995

Work. Sleep. Work. That's the pattern of my life at the moment. Still, it blocks out all the pain, confusion and anger which threaten to run amok in my head. I have just completed my nightly ritual of taking my bandages off and winding them back up again ready for the morning. If all goes to plan, this time next week I will be able to burn them.

I don't know how I'm surviving at the moment, but the important thing is that I am. The only thing that could crush me now is a fifteen-foot African python.

My hair needs cutting again. But Just Gents seems to have lost a great deal of its allure now I have discovered that Sexy Simone has a bun in her oven. Still, at least I can't be blamed for that one.

Fundraising is still very much on my mind. Jane's mum has been an absolute diamond, agreeing to lend me her £2,000 savings for my operation. By the time this is over I'm going to have more debts than Barings Bank.

Saturday 18 March 1995

I looked at my pile of Belgian francs this afternoon and felt my first twinge of excitement. Can it really be only three days until I fly out to Belgium and only five days until my operation? This is the closest I've ever been to paradise. Surely no one can pull the plug on me this time? But I forced myself to calm down, refusing to get too excited. I have already built myself up for a big fall on two previous occasions. This time around I'm doing my best to protect my fragile emotions. I don't think I'll believe I've actually made it until I look down and my boobs are no longer there.

Meanwhile I have plenty to keep me occupied. I swooped like a Lancaster bomber on Portsmouth this morning and cleaned the travel agents out of Belgian currency. Nessa, my flatmate, has just given me a Biggles bear, as I leave for London tomorrow. He keeps winking at me and giving me knowing looks. I am wearing my thermal long johns – another present from Nessa. They are arguably the best thing to happen to me this week, but you'll laugh if I tell you that the reason I love them so much is because they've got a flap to tuck my willy into. (The next best thing to having a willy is having a flap to put it in!)

I had the back of my head seriously shaved yesterday. I

now look like Robbie's dog – Well Hard. The joys of being male, Part Two. I was followed home by a little kid on Thursday shouting a torrent of abuse at me. As he ran past me he spat at me. I wasn't in a very good mood anyway, so I retaliated by shouting 'arsehole'. He exploded in an obscene vocabulary, all flailing arms and expletives, before eyeing me and spitting defiantly: 'I'm going to get my dad to break your arms and legs.'

I was certainly not going to be out-talked by a twelve-year-old. 'Go on, then,' I said. 'Run home to Daddy and tell him how you spat in my face!' He shrank a bit and much of the venom exited his youthful face. I sensed surrender as the kid from hell slunk off into the distance. Phew, I thought, close shave. Okay, he *was* smaller than me, but only just. This being a bloke business is not all it's cracked up to be.

Sunday 19 March 1995

Richard Thorpe (Alan Turner) from *Emmerdale Farm* phoned at lunchtime. Nessa was avoiding her ex-boyfriend so I picked up the phone, poised to tell him to quit while he was ahead. When I heard Richard's voice I sat down quickly in the nearest chair. He was the last person I expected to call. I recognised his voice because he sounds exactly as he does on television. His compassion and warmth astounded me. He had received my letter and wondered if he could help in any way. He suggested sorting out a documentary to raise money, but I fear it will be too late for this. We tried for months before. Nevertheless, I took his phone number and intend to call him back when I've thought it over.

I arrived at Karen's flat to find a pile of Good Luck cards and, shock of all shocks, a letter from Jo. She was the girl I had been writing to before Christmas who blew me out big-time. I had not heard from her in four months. What could she want after all this time?

Dear Paul
How's this for a blast from the past? I want you to know I'm not proud of myself, but rather disgusted at running out on you when things began to heat up. I think I kidded myself at the time about how easily I was coping with everything you were telling me. When I got back to Southend the reality hit me with a thud...

I've kept all your letters and read them sometimes when I'm thinking of you. You told me after a few months of knowing you that all the revelations are by the by. I've come round to your way of thinking. It's you I like. Everybody's opinions got the better of me. I couldn't compromise the small-minded views of other people with my growing feelings for you. I felt like I was being pushed into a corner. If things developed between us then I would have to tell my friends and family, and possibly be forced to choose. Begrudgingly I felt I had no choice at that point but to end it all before it had barely begun. There wasn't really another man; that was just a convenient excuse.

I really trusted you, but began to have nagging doubts about everyone's feelings except ours, which I didn't even consider it seems...

My suggestion that you should come and stay with me was great in my mind, but the reality scared the shit out of me. Now I just want you back...

This letter, apart from coming completely out of the blue, made me think back to the time when I first discovered a name for my transsexual feelings. It had taken me a year to come to terms with these feelings myself. How could I have expected Jo to take it so easily?

Chapter Ten

Monday 20 March 1995
I am lying in bed feeling reflective. It is the eve of my departure for Belgium. In the general scheme of things I may have sacrificed a great deal, but it barely compares to what I have gained. My quality of life is far richer than before, and the calibre of my friends unsurpassable. All my acquaintances at Headline treat me like a superstar, and that means so much to someone who has spent his life deflecting his self-hatred into himself. As a teenage athlete I would run so hard, punishing myself until I was physically sick, running to numb my emotional pain with physical pain. It took me two decades to realise that escape from myself, like Alcatraz, was impossible because my real self was an unshakeable shadow. My body was an island with its own treacherous tides which isolated me from everything I wanted. Now I have developed a new self-acceptance, and I can allow people to reach out and touch me as never before.

I popped into Headline this morning and afterwards went into the NatWest bank two doors along to buy some foreign currency. Standing at the counter, I heard a voice next to me. 'Hello, Paul. How are you?' I tilted my head towards the voice and recognised the woman who had sat on my right at the sales conference on 1 December. I told her that I was buying Belgian currency and was flying out for my operation. She held out her china-doll hand to mine in the most caring way imaginable, and the warmth in her eyes touched my soul. 'I'm so glad I've seen you before you go. Good luck and bless you,' she said and then disappeared out of the door. Bless you too, I thought to myself; for every bigot in this world there is someone like you. I don't even know her name, but I am carrying the image of her face in my head. It makes me warm inside. Perhaps I'm just a soppy old romantic, too soft and sensitive for this tough old world. I feel even more melancholy than usual on the eve of this great event in my personal evolution. I feel like my body is an over-stuffed suitcase – the bulging clothes are my emotions. I have to keep squashing them down, but they keep bulging out. I've wanted so long to be free, I can't believe I soon will be.

I had dinner with Jane and Richard last night. As I said goodbye on the doorstep, the light of candles flickering and dancing in the doorway, Richard pressed a piece of paper into my hand. I opened it out. A cheque for £50. 'A present,' he said. 'For everything you are going through right now.' I wanted to cry again. This is a very emotional time for me.

Today I had lunch with my mother. She cried when I gave her a Mother's Day card a week early as I will be in Belgium on the twenty-sixth. She kept looking at me as if I was the prodigal son, and I had to fight with myself to stop my own tears welling up.

A lump sits in my stomach as I prepare to turn out the light on my last night in England with breasts. I keep remembering the motto which is written on Nigel Benn's hat – NO FEAR. I must have no fear.

Tuesday 21 March 1995

Well, this is it. No turning back. No regrets. Just pure unadulterated expectation and soon-to-be liberation from female parts. I am sitting on the British Airways plane to Brussels, nervously awaiting take-off. There is a cute chick sitting on my left. I do feel a bit excited about my impending adventure, but mostly just plain ill. Jane dropped me off at Heathrow's Terminal One this morning. She had brought me a little furry creature wearing a backpack, bobble hat and scarf, and carrying a plastic ice-pick. 'He's an explorer,' she told me, 'just like you.' She gave me a hug and I didn't want to let go. From now on it's just me versus the rest of the world. I wish I was going into the hospital today; instead, I have to overnight in a hotel. The operation can't happen fast enough for me now. I never imagined that my life would come to this, but it's amazing what you can adjust to, given time.

I was stopped by Customs on the way through for a routine passport check, and the bearded official asked me if I was travelling for business or pleasure. He looked foxed when I cheekily replied, 'Neither.'

'Do you want to let us in on the secret?' he asked me sarcastically.

I smiled enigmatically. I wasn't going to give anything away.

Today is an epic journey for another reason. This is the first time I have travelled abroad in four years and the baptism of my new passport. Today I am travelling as a man.

Wednesday 22 March 1995

I am sitting on my rock-hard bed in the hospital at the University of Ghent, Belgium. There is a Belgian man sitting next to me in his underpants dragging around a can full of liquid attached to his kidneys by a tube. Strangely, despite the clinical surroundings, I feel as cool as a cucumber. I'm totally exhausted and eager to proceed as soon as possible. The nurses are hilarious; they walk around with little springs under the heels of their *click-clack* clogs. All I can hear in addition is the rattling of trolleys, the hum of a radio, Flemish gabblings and the gurgling of the contraption of the man next to me. I'm bored and I wish I had someone to talk to. I am in a small ward with two other men, neither of whom is very communicative. Everything seems hyper-efficient, nothing like English hospitals. Mind you, I've never been to a private hospital before.

My feelings about my impending ordeal are rather like this environment, clean and clinical. I want the job done as successfully as possible so I can just get on with the rest of my life, belatedly streamlined.

A nurse has just been in to give me an electrocardiogram, and she indicated that I should take my top off. I froze as she gestured at me. We can't communicate, and I thought she was going to pull it off in full view of the other occupants in the room. At the last minute she translated the look of panic on my face and decided to draw the curtain across. I felt like a freak as I lay in front of her on the bed looking completely undignified, my boobs hanging out from underneath my Lycra top.

2.40 p.m.

It has just occurred to me that the way I was treated by the nurse doing the ECG this morning was actually a compliment. My male face is now so convincing that she forgot that there was anything other than a male chest under my jumper. It wasn't until the panic flickered across my features that she remembered my transsexualism.

I should delete my comment about the Belgians being super-efficient. I have just spent two hours on a trolley in a dusty corridor waiting to see Professor Monstréy. A nurse flapped around me apologising and justifying the delay. 'A lot of emergencies today,' she said. During this time spent in limbo I was able to analyse the other patients being whisked around on their trolleys. They had one common denominator: boobs. Gigantic ones or none at all. I couldn't take my eyes off one girl, she had the most expansive chest I have ever seen. We are talking battle of the planets in a jumper here. Poor girl, to have those swinging round her waist. I wonder if any of the patients realised that I too am here to shed my breasts. After all, everyone pronounces my name: Meester Who-it!

The prof is much younger than I imagined he would be. He looks only about thirty. A statuesque man with thick dark hair and suntanned cheeks, he strides authoritatively up and down the corridors of power in his white clogs. Jane would adore him. Of all the consultants I have seen regarding breast surgery, he impressed me the most. Very kind, very efficient, very intelligent. The good news is that I am to be first down to the operating theatre tomorrow morning. Eight o'clock is my deadline.

My porter has a ginger goatee. As he wheeled me back to my cell I felt icy calm. Rather than the sense of nervousness I had anticipated, instead I feel a glorious sense of destiny.

8.05 p.m.

Waiting. Bored. But can I really be on hourly – rather than monthly, weekly or daily – countdown? In only twelve hours' time will I really be taking a trip on a trolley? I should have brought something to read. The pump next to me is doing overtime. Unfortunately, some time between now and tomorrow morning a spring-loaded nurse is going to approach me with a razor to shave my chest hair. Poor old Bob, my initial one hair. He and his hirsute family face a sudden execution at the hands of a Belgian razor-blade. This thought has got to me and made an unfamiliar species of butterfly flap gigantically in my stomach.

8.45 p.m.
Well, that's the chest hair gone. Gulp! I almost shed a tear. God, I've waited so long for this moment, my eyes are filling up with tears. It was a male nurse who shaved my chest. He looked at me as the hairs slid off beneath his fresh Bic razor and said with an encouraging smile: 'Don't worry. It'll grow back.'

Thursday 23 March 1995
It's only 6 a.m. I have been awoken at this ungodly hour by nurses wanting to take my temperature and my blood pressure. Why couldn't they just have given me a nudge at 7.55 a.m.? That would have suited me.

I feel all spaced out ... it must be the pre-med...

Monday 27 March 1995
I have briefly found the energy to write a diary entry, after a horrific five days, now that I am back home in Karen's flat. What has happened to me since last Thursday I would not wish on my worst enemy. I am laid out on my back, looking rather yellow and gaunt, feeling as though I could not fight my way out of a paper bag if I were given one. I'm so glad to see Karen and England again that I'm not letting them out of my sight. Not this week anyway. Let me tell my story of my escape from my female body and all the tears I have shed on my way out.

It was eight in the morning when I was scheduled to go down to theatre on Thursday 23 March. When Professor Monstréy told me I was first on his programme I remember thinking, 'Oh great! At least his knife will be nice and sharp then. It's later in the day you've got to worry.' I had an incredible, overwhelming feeling of excitement as I counted down the last twelve hours until the chop. All the mental preparation took place months, even years, ago now. This was just a job that had to be done.

Because of the big build-up the nurses give you, waking you up at the crack of dawn and preparing you for your op as though they're preparing you for your early-morning execution at the hands of the firing-squad, I thought I would be terrified, a real coward. But the reality was that I was surprisingly calm. When the nurses came down to collect me ten minutes before the operation I tried to remember the words – NO FEAR. Whatever happened to me, I had decided I was going to take it like a man. I must be true to what I am.

When I reached the end of my trolley journey to the operating theatre, wide awake and trying to peer out from under my blankets, the anaesthetist took my left hand and stuck a catheter in my vein. It hurt like fuck so he pulled it out again. I couldn't believe he'd put me through that pain only to stick it in my other hand in the end.

My legs felt like lead as I was asked to clamber on to another trolley at the entrance to the operating theatre. I made it, but after the pre-med my legs felt like giant water-filled wellies as I heaved myself up on to the table. When I looked up, at least a dozen pairs of eyes seemed to stare back at me. Green hats and green coats bobbing and weaving, silver instruments seemingly floating in mid-air. A yellowing opaque mask was held near my face, and I was encouraged to take deep breaths. 'Are you feeling dizzy yet?' asked the anonymous voice.

'No,' I said defiantly.

The next thing I remember was being in a bed with barricades on each side, like a baby's cot, which made it impossible to fall out. I was wide awake, but everyone else seemed to be sleeping. I pulled off the oxygen mask covering my face, and a vision of Professor Monstréy appeared before me, wearing clogs and singing 'Edelweiss'. 'I've got a message for you,' he whispered softly. 'Jane Warren phoned and sends her love!' Several hours later I was still not sure whether this was a dream or not, but it turned out to be real and a truly treasured memory. My eyes filled up with tears and a little river trickled down each side of my face.

My bed was parked in the waiting bay in the recovery room for what seemed like an eternity. I just could not comprehend why they were keeping me there so long. I didn't want to sleep; I wanted to have a long chat with someone over a cup of tea. But the recovery room was cold and clinical and no one talked to me, so I welcomed my room 323A like a long-lost relative when I was finally wheeled back into it.

It must have been mid-afternoon, but under the influence of anaesthetic you are unaware of the day of the week, let alone the time of day. Three fuzzy figures drifted in and out of focus at the end of my bed, each with his own clipboard. Professor Monstréy came closer and leaned over my bed to examine the bandages covering what used to be my breasts. He pulled them apart to examine further and I yelped. I squealed again, like a spaniel puppy with its paw trodden on, as he pulled at the soft gauze covering the left nipple. Damned painful.

'They're looking a bit black,' was his verdict. 'There's a possibility of blood clots developing under the nipples. We'd better not take any chances. Let's get you under again for another fifteen minutes to aerate them a bit.'

Disbelief. I couldn't believe I was going to have to go through it all again, another operation, if only for fifteen minutes this time. But I had put my entire trust in the professor when I first met him. I knew he was acting in my best interests, and I felt too tired and ill to put up a fight.

So, still nauseous, wobbling and weak from the first dose of anaesthetic, in I went again. It all seemed incredibly surreal and inter-galactic the second time around. Once again my bed was pushed through the doors of the operating theatre, which opened out into a cavernous dome which reminded me of the cockpit of a spacecraft from another planet. There were mirrors all around me, and it was the one covering the ceiling above my head which gave me my first glimpse of my chest. Lying horizontal on a bench, I looked up at myself, naked except for a towel strategically placed over my private parts. My right hand was taped up to hold the catheter tube in place, giving it the appearance of a boxer's hand bandaged before a title fight. As I gazed in wonderment at the male chest Professor Monstréy had created for me, I could see the next Prince Naseem Hamed on the table. I felt tears spike my eyelashes. For the first time in twenty-seven years I saw the real Paul, the man I had been searching for and thought I would never find. It felt like watching a miracle.

It was now eight o'clock on Thursday evening and twelve hours since my first visit to theatre. 'You must be tired,' I said to the prof.

He looked back at me. 'I'm OK.'

My next memory was of finding myself in my 'carrycot' in the recovery room again, being pushed into my parking spot by Marc, the nurse who had taken me down earlier in the evening. I thought he was kidding when he said I would have to stay there all night as I had come into recovery after nine in the evening. 'You're joking,' I said.

'No, I'm not,' he said, grinning at me.

Total disbelief again. I couldn't believe I was going to have to spend the whole fucking night in this place. It was the longest night of my life.

Drug-induced snores created gentle background noise as patients with faces covered by oxygen masks slept around me. Once again I was wide awake, taking a keen interest in what was going on around me. There were two nurses – one male, one female – sitting behind a desk illuminated by two overhead fluorescent-green strip lights. All the other lights were off, leaving the rest of the room dull in semi-darkness. The nurses walked around from time to time, checking patients, then returned to their desk under the light to pour coffee from a huge red thermos and exchange a few quiet words in Flemish.

Time seemed suspended as I watched the hour-hand on the clock creep slowly round. Every time I did drift off, my sleep was cruelly short lived. My blood pressure was monitored hourly.

I had a throat like Gandhi's flipflop in a sand storm. My skin was yellow and sweaty, my nipples felt as if they had been seered by branding irons, and the ultimate indignity was yet to come. At 3.20 a.m. the male nurse came over to see me. He had decided that, since it was six hours since I'd had major surgery, it was time for me to go to the toilet. He stuck an ice-cold bedpan underneath my bottom, which was like being asked to park your bum on a pile of crushed snow and pee off the end of a glacier. The most unnatural position possible. No joy. He then tried lifting me out of bed and perching me on a chair. Still no joy. I was going to empty my bladder when I was good and ready. 'I'm going to have to empty your bladder,' he told me. He stuck something sharp inside me and all my troubles came flooding out. Why couldn't I have a willy like any other bloke? After the experiences of the last twenty-four hours, things could only get better.

But, strangely, intermingled with indignity and pain was joy of the most rapturous order. At 9 a.m., still parked in the recovery room, I decided I wanted to go to the toilet again, so I told the nurse who had just come on duty, the pretty one with the orange tint to her hair. Yes, even at death's door I still had an eye for a looker! As anyone who has spent any time in hospital will be aware, blokes are given a vase-shaped jug to put their thing in, while women are given ice-cold toilet-seat-shaped pan things. I watched orange tint reappear from beyond the door at the other end of the room and head in my direction with one of the male vases in her hand. I wished I didn't have to, but as she arrived at my bed I looked up at her and said: 'Sorry, but I can't use that.' She initially apologised profusely, but when she saw I was helpless with laughter started to laugh too. 'Don't worry,' I said. 'It's a compliment!' What other proof do I need that people view me as completely male? I loved her assumption that I had the right tackle, particularly as she had washed me only half an hour earlier. She had already completely forgotten.

My next two days in hospital were a misery. I lay still, feeling sick and helpless. My only entertainment was watching the liquid drip through my volumetric pump on the left-hand side of the bed. This provided my body with glucose, painkillers and antibiotics through the vein in my right hand. I had a drain coming out of each side of my chest, near the base of the arms, each one leading to a bottle on the floor collecting blood and fluid.

This didn't give me much mobility and getting up to go to the toilet was a feat in itself – my trolley of tubes and bottles had to come with me.

On Saturday I was moved to tears because I felt so ill. I was trying to drag myself out of bed every five minutes because I had a bladder infection and was still labouring under the combined effect of two anaesthetics. I felt so horrendously lonely in this strange hospital where hardly anyone spoke my language that I started to talk to myself. Huge plates of food kept arriving, but they looked distinctly unappealing. I felt so down that I got the phone next to my bed connected and started to phone England. I had to speak to someone English.

On Saturday night a young man from the Norwegian navy was wheeled in from the recovery room . He had been stabbed coming out of a pub in Ghent. He was throwing up next to me every twenty minutes for the whole night, and I kept ringing the bell for him. We were a formidable team. 'You chuck it, I'll ring for the nurse.' It was at that point that I decided I could not spend another night in a Belgian hospital.

I discharged myself on Sunday afternoon, knowing I was nowhere near well enough to travel, but I was going home if it killed me. At least I could feel like shit in the comfort of my own home. Professor Monstréy came to say goodbye to me on Saturday evening. It was obvious that he was off duty and had come in specially to see me, a gesture which I greatly appreciated. 'Will we meet again?' he said in soft Belgospeak.

'Probably not,' was my reply.

'Maybe we'll meet in a pub somewhere in London.' He smiled before leaving.

I didn't even see a doctor on the day I left. I just got up and went. I had to spend 3,500 Belgian francs (about £80) to get me from the University Hospital at Ghent to Brussels Airport as I was too weak to take the train. Earlier in the morning a nurse had changed the bandaging on my chest and taken the drains and the drip out. Tears were streaming down my cheeks as I felt so ill. It was all too much for me.

Yet in contrast to feeling so weak and awful, mini-waves of euphoria began to ripple inside me as I realised that I was free of bottles and tubes, that I was going home, and that I'd be leaving my boobs on the operating table. I have visions of some flat-chested cleaner going into the operating theatre, spying my boobs in the bin, picking them up, trying them on and thinking, Hmmm, these will do for me!

I was so excited, but my body refused to support my excitement. When I got up the most I could do was shuffle around, I felt so dangerously weak. My first stop was the mirror to get a proper look at my chest. 'How does it look?' I asked the nurse.

'It is beauty,' she smiled, struggling for the right words in English.

'You liar!' I said.

'No,' she insisted. 'I mean it.'

I couldn't wipe the grin off my face, then suddenly I was crying again, this time with happiness.

As I sat in the taxi heading for Brussels International Airport I found myself having to grimace to hold back the tears. I had to wait until I had checked in before I received confirmation that I really wasn't well enough to travel; I virtually collapsed in the airport lounge. I swallowed my pride and staggered up to a nearby British Airways official for help. Luckily, once I explained I had just left hospital after major surgery, BA couldn't do enough to help me. I was crying my eyes out in a rather un-macho manner and helpful Joe Public just sat and stared.

A wheelchair was arranged to ferry me on to the plane and I was given a row of seats to myself. I felt half-way healed when Jackie, the BA stewardess, put her hand on my shoulder and said: 'Are you all right now, love?' Her accent was British, so familiar and comforting. I felt safe for the first time in days. I knew that in less than an hour I would be in London with Dad.

Friday 31 March 1995

I feel like a new man today who has been welcomed back to the world after three years' absence. I am back and have just eaten a huge breakfast to confirm it. Eggs, bacon, beans and toast. Mmm, don't mind if I do.

Mum has sent me a wonderful card. It says: 'To my dearest son Paul. Wishing you all the love, peace and happiness in the world. I'm proud of you. Love Mum x. Get well soon.'

Her support means a great deal. She was very emotional on the day of my operation and spoke to Jane on the phone.

'I regard today as Paul's birthday. It is his first day of being a man. It's been a very difficult two days. I feel like it's me going through it. I love him so much. I went to church last night and I cried when I got home.'

Nurse Tracey took out my stitches this morning, which was quite a delicate operation, I can tell you. Her visit was a tonic in itself, as she was lovely. Now I feel like a pollinated plant, ripe and ready to burst. Top-priority mission is to shop for a pair of swimming-trunks, and when I get them – well – watch out, world, I'll be dangerous.

I can feel this little ripple of euphoria inside me about to erupt into a huge Mexican wave. I have found a new record which signifies how I feel at the moment. It's by Barry Manilow and is called 'I Made it through the Rain'. I made it through the rain, and found myself respected by those who got rained on too.

My chest is currently a little yellow, as the bruising is coming out, and it is also a bit crinkled, but I could not expect perfection. I am hoping that my body hair will cover up any imperfections in the skin, and it seems to be sprouting up thick and fast. All I have to do now is to wait for the scabs to drop away.

Even at this early stage following the operation, the clouds are starting to clear in my mind, and I realise why I have been so ill these past eight years. In fact, it is a wonder I have been able to function at all. I consider my health to be a direct reflection of my emotional state, and there have been huge negative influences in my life for so long. All the things I love I have been unable to do, and this has depressed me severely. No matter how strong the spirit fighting upwards has been, the negative forces pushing down on me have been too strong.

I can now start to think of all the possibilities before me. In just a few weeks I will be able to go for my first swim. I haven't been able to swim for at least three years, yet I used to be a qualified lifeguard. The prospect of submerging myself in the water fills me with so much excitement I feel set to explode. Swimming is the safest way for me to build up my chest without tearing anything. I'm going to be like Flipper the dolphin when I first dive in, flipping over and over in sheer delight and splashing water everywhere.

A revival of my football career is also a definite possibility. Football used to be my everything, and I have felt deprived without it. I can feel an abnormal high flushing through my veins like being on some wonderful substance. My nips are still giving me jip and I've got pains in my drains, but they will soon disappear. Thank you, God, for getting me this far. Right here is where we start living, baby!

I predict a massive and dramatic improvement in my health and huge strides for Paul from this day on. It's goodbye hot, sweaty bandages for ever and hello Speedo swimming-trunks. There is one message I would like to send out to the world, and it is this: 'To those who said I'd never get away with it, you were so wrong. I plan to get away with it for a whole lot longer. If you believe in it and want it enough, it can happen. And if you're asking, yes, I'm dancing!'

If anyone can read this book and still believe I'm some kind of freak, then I truly believe that it's not me who's got the problem. If an atmosphere of greater understanding has been created for transsexuals in the future, then this project will have been worth while. At this point I have only half the body I need to survive, but it's more than enough to make my life worth living again. I'm glad it wasn't easy. If I'd been given everything on a plate I wouldn't feel half as wonderful as I do right now.

Epilogue

Wednesday 1 November 1995
It is exactly two years since I had my first life-saving testosterone injection, and I have the throbbing arm to prove it. I had my annual blood test this morning to check my liver functions and my cholesterol and testosterone levels. Unfortunately, my arm swelled up a bit under the vein and I had a funny turn and ended up laid out on nurse Sarah's crisp and clinical white bench. I feel like a bit of a pin cushion today, what with my bruised right arm hanging limply by my side and my right thigh stiff and aching from last night's injection. As I lay faint and panting in the nurse's room at the surgery this morning, I couldn't help but think to myself, 'the things I have to go through just to be me'.

A hell of a lot has happened since I had my breasts removed back in March, in a lonely hospital in Belgium. Changes to my life have been dramatic and most rewarding. My new manly chest is the best present anyone could ever give me, and not a day goes past when I don't admire it in the mirror. The gather marks are fading, I have the seeds of a pair of pectorals and a generous covering of hair which women seem to adore. It is still growing, as is my stubble, and my chest hair has set up camp on both shoulders. I still get shooting pains through my upper body, and I swear my nipples will never be the same again, but any discomfort is a small price to pay for the peace of mind surgery has given me.

Within three weeks I was in the swimming-pool. I could hardly stretch my arms out to form the strokes, so tight was my chest, but I had dreamed of this moment all my life, and could not wait any longer. I was convinced everyone would be looking at me, but nobody did. This was a mission which carried feelings of both fear and excitement.

Following my first trip to the swimming-pool, there was no stopping me. I began to swim as if I was in training for the next Olympics. Duncan Goodhew had nothing on me. I returned to college after the Easter holidays having missed only one week of the previous term and felt like a new person. Everyone else noticed it too. At my end of term tutorial in June this year, my tutor told me that the difference in the quality of my work since my surgery had been incredible. 'Of course it was always good before,' he told me, 'but your work has been first class this term'. I asked him if he'd noticed that I hadn't had a day off sick this term. He had.

A huge wave of euphoria swept me through the final term and through my journalism exams. I had become extremely depressed and withdrawn for the few months prior to surgery and life had become an ordeal. I had wanted to tell my colleagues of my predicament. I sensed they knew something was wrong, but I knew that once I started talking I wouldn't stop, and the whole sorry tale would come gushing out.

Now the whole world seemed to be responding differently to my thoughts and actions. As I had a ready smile for strangers and friends alike, people seemed to have a ready smile for me. While my mate Chris and I were having our regular greasy spoon breakfast in Sunny's Diner one afternoon, I noticed that the petite dark-haired waitress with the pretty face was taking more interest in me than usual. 'We haven't seen you in here for a while,' she remarked casually while thrusting my fry-up in front of me. I was flattered by her interest and asked her out for a drink two days later. Within weeks we became lovers, and it felt good to be in a relationship again.

I kept Andrea at a distance for as long as my hormones could realistically stand. She was starting to think I didn't find her attractive due to my reluctance to get her into bed, but of course I knew that once the relationship became a sexual one, my secret would have to come out. I was not really in a hurry to shatter her illusions as to what I kept tucked away in my trousers. However, I decided she would have to know if our relationship were to continue and I worked myself into a right state for over a week. Once again we found ourselves in an intimate situation and finally the moment had come. I pulled away and struggled to get the right words out. I had imagined that her facial expression would change to one of contempt and confusion and that she would make a hasty departure. But she took the revelation that I was born female totally in her stride, so calmly in fact that it was unnerving. I thought to myself, 'I must have drama in my life'. She said she loved me just the way I was, and then we made love for the first time and it was surprisingly good.

During my last few months at Highbury College in Portsmouth, Andrea was very good for me. She gave me back my confidence and I am indebted to her for that. But I knew that once I left Highbury, that particular chapter of my life would be over. And I certainly went out with a bang, in every sense of the word. Three days after the last day of term, my face appeared in the national press as my story was serialised in the *Daily Express*. I had kept my secret until the bitter end, which was no mean feat in the company of a bunch of journalists.

Unfortunately, I had to come back to resit one of my exams as my computer disk with my story on it was unreadable. That very day my face was in the paper but I had to put all thoughts of how the world would react to me out of my head to enable me to concentrate on my resit.

After my operation I did some work experience on the Showbiz desk at the *Daily Express*, and ended up doing one or two shifts a week in the run-up to my exams. Suddenly, after nearly two years of being in awe of my co-author, we were working virtually side by side on the newspaper. I felt that I had come of age, and that the huge professional chasm between us had almost disappeared.

I thoroughly enjoyed my shifts at the *Express*, though the pace was quite hectic at times, but once my book came out it became a whole different ball game. My face was all over the paper and suddenly everyone knew my secret. I felt as though all eyes were on me. A couple of people on the staff were unnecessarily nasty to me and I couldn't help but wonder if bigotry was behind their comments. I felt ill and stressed out from having to give daily radio and television interviews to promote my book, and once again life felt like survival. I began to dislike working at the *Express*. I made mistakes because I wasn't well and hated being a small fish in a big pond.

It was looking increasingly unlikely that my shift work would continue as rumours of redundancy within Express Newspapers were rife. So I made good my escape, away from all the prying questions, by flying out to Finland for a five-week journalism scholarship which I had won earlier in the year. The timing was perfect and it had not come a moment too soon. Once I was in Helsinki I was anonymous once more and it was bliss.

My trip to Finland was paid for by the Ministry for Foreign Affairs in Helsinki. It was a time of great joy, a time for making friends from different countries, a time for falling in love and also a time for me to face great pain. The group of eighteen students was rather unbalanced, in the sense that there were only five men, including me, compared with thirteen women. The women swarmed around me and I could hardly believe my luck. I spent half the time trying to avoid a Ukrainian girl who I was convinced was trying to seek political asylum in my underpants.

But I had eyes only for Isabel, one of three Spanish girls on the trip. We got talking on our second night there and I was captivated by her huge brown eyes. I fell for her big time and I was gutted to have to leave her at the airport.

I was also confronted with my own weaknesses time and time again. You try and get on with your life, and live as actively as possible, but it seems that in doing this, as a surgically incomplete transsexual, you have your nose rubbed crudely in your own inadequacies. I love swimming, and nothing will stop me going, but in doing so I come face to face with what I haven't got, each time in the changing-room, and I can hardly contain my own anger and resentment. Large willies, small ones, fat ones, flat ones, bent ones, shrivelled ones. I swear I'm going to get punched on the nose one of these days for staring. My need for genital completeness grows stronger each day, and I now find myself having to detach myself mentally from my lower body in order to preserve my own sanity. And this is no easy task with the constant throbbing in my groin brought about by hormones!

In this respect Finland, birthplace of the sauna culture, was the worst place I could be. In England you are expected to wear your shorts. In Finland you are expected to go naked and you look very odd if you don't. Rather than miss out on the joys of the sauna, I had to content myself with looking odd, a complete dick in fact, and this was a ritual which almost reduced me to tears. But I didn't let my incompleteness stop me, and was quite proud that I would not let something as 'minor' as not having a penis stop me from mixing with the other guys.

Most of the time I would have the sauna to myself as I would go early, at the very beginning of the evening shift, in order to avoid confrontations. I kept my towel wrapped round me and prayed it would not slip out of place. One particular weekend, when the whole group of us were lost in the wilds of Lapland, staying in a remote log cabin, the sauna became a big issue for me once again. The girls took the first shift and as the men waited for their turn, I began to feel panicky and resentful. Anger surged up inside me and I hated my creator for putting me in this situation. I had two choices: to make up an inadequate excuse or to get in there and look stupid. In the end I had a few beers to block out the pain and I stopped worrying about looking stupid. Besides, I wasn't alone. Brett, the American guy, was naturally shy and wouldn't entertain the idea of going into the sauna without his white boxers. So, we looked stupid together. While we were waiting for the girls to come out, Brett kept winding me up and asking me if I was going to go naked. If he had asked me just one more time I swear I would have punched his lights out. But I couldn't really blame him; how was he to know?

Later that evening, some of the guys made trips down through the forest and into the icy lake to cool off. I went with them and began to enjoy myself. As the bottles of beer began to disappear, so did my inhibitions. We even went skinny dipping, though I was careful that no one should see my front side. I always jumped in first and grabbed my towel close to me before getting out.

I had a rather nervous moment when the girls played a joke on us, deciding it would be jolly funny to steal our clothes. As one girl tried to pull my towel away from me, I legged it into the forest. I had a hell of a lot to lose that night and looking back, I can't believe the risks I took and that I was so daring. But it had been exhilarating and fun and the fact that I did join in made me far less suspect than if I had decided to sit the evening out. No one had the faintest clue about my transsexuality.

But, not counting the sauna thing, I had a great time. Isabel made a comment about trying to get near me, but it was difficult because I was always surrounded by women. As usual, I found them the best company, though I did enjoy a practical joke which Yan, the French guy, and I masterminded. As an act of vengeance for having our clothes stolen, Yan and I went through the girls' rooms while they were drinking and singing downstairs. We stole any items of underwear we could lay our hands on and strung them across the front of the team bus as a lingerie washing line. 'Operation knickersnatch' was almost terminated when one of the Spanish girls started climbing the stairs. Yan and I escaped across the roof, via the balcony window. I nearly broke my neck jumping off the roof into the undergrowth below. A quick inspection confirmed I was still in one piece, though covered in lingerie, and Yan and I fell about laughing. The girls were livid when they saw the bus the next morning and wouldn't speak to us for the rest of that day.

About a week before I was due to return to England, I began to get depressed, thinking about all the financial responsibilities I would have to face up to when I got home. I didn't even have a home. And my debts would now become due.

The last two months have been hell on earth with the pressures of finding a decent job, somewhere to live, and trying to pacify the people I owe money to. My health has suffered, but as usual, I seem to have fallen on my feet. I have been offered two jobs in the last month, and have accepted one back in Portsmouth as a technical author, with the sort of salary which will enable me to pay off my debts and have some semblance of a life again. I made up my mind that I wanted it, I researched it and after two lengthy interviews I got it. It was a nail-biting time, but now I couldn't be happier about it.

I have also learned in the past month that not only did I pass all my journalism exams, but I also received the Highbury Diploma, a certificate awarded to those students who achieve a certain standard in all areas of their studies. I cried when that arrived in the post. The relief. After all the hell I went through on that course, I had come out of it with flying colours, once again against the odds. Sometimes it frightens me to think what I could achieve if only I had been given the most precious of all gifts, the gift of the right body.

Friday 3 November 1995

I move down to Portsmouth this weekend to start my new job on Monday, and it feels like the start of a new life once again. I will hardly recognise myself with money in my pocket. My new employers have no knowledge of my transsexuality, and I have no plans to tell them. Not because I am ashamed or frightened of their reaction, but because it is important to me to have got this job in my own right. And I have had enough attention this year to last me a lifetime.

I still face a huge fight to gain physical completeness, not to mention pain and a lot of risks, but I know now that I can never be happy without being able to look down and see male genitals. As Raymond says in his autobiography, 'What took you so long?' It's a matter of personal safety, about feeling safe and comfortable in your own body.

As far as women are concerned, I have never had so much attention, and I can only hope my good fortune lasts. It seems there is a huge market for the sensitive man. Currently I am having a serious relationship with Laura. She took a fancy to me after watching me on the Richard and Judy show and we have been together ever since. She is so understanding, and is more supportive than I deserve. I am fearful of long-term relationships right now, because I feel like a child who has been let loose in a chocolate factory, and one whose personal evolution is not yet complete.

Thursday 4 January 1996

Learned an expensive lesson on an extremely drunken Christmas Eve: never lift up a girl's skirt, not when she's wearing stilettos anyway. A tall, feisty blonde came into Murdoch's, the pub where we were drinking, and I laughed because she was wearing a short, red, Miss Christmas number. 'She's really made the effort,' I chuckled with my friends. But you know that old saying, 'He who laughs last laughs longest?' Well it was certainly true that night. About two hour later, I noticed out of the corner of my eye that she was standing right next to me, her skirt flaring out temptingly in my direction. I don't know quite what came over me, too much testosterone perhaps, but I reached out my right hand for the investigation: what exactly did she keep under that white furred skirt? I didn't have to wait too long to find out. The festive smile turned into a grimace of pure fire and a mule kick flew in my direction. I could hardly walk. The smiling blonde had turned into the snarling, kickboxing, killer bitch from hell. My look of pain and surprise was met with her fury: 'try that one again matey, and I'll kick you somewhere where it hurts'. Karen was doubled over trying to contain an exploding fit of the giggles. 'That must be the biggest ego boost of all time,' she screeched helplessly. But I could only slink off in the direction of the toilets, dragging my poor lump of wood cunningly disguised as a leg with me. I think it's this second youth thing, because every time I see a boob these days I get the urge to grab it.

My New Year's resolution is never to lift up a girl's skirt again in my lifetime. The pain of that night lives on in my memory. I've still got big plans for this particular life, and since I seem to be on a bit of a roll at the moment, perhaps 1996 could be my year. My new job as a technical author has helped to give me my confidence back and allows me to continue achieving those important little firsts, such as wearing a dinner jacket to our Christmas dinner dance at the Marriott hotel. Suddenly all things seem possible.

I've got a lot of surgery still to face and fight for, but it is true what they say about hard times making strong men. The flesh is still weak, but in my head, where it counts, I feel indestructible. The news back in September that Berkshire Health Authority, as a result of its new cash crisis, will no longer fund 'non-essential operations including sex-change surgery' came as quite a blow. This is surgery I must have to live. But I'll fight any way I can to get it. Currently I am on the waiting-list for a hysterectomy – apparently the battle for funding begins when a date is given for surgery – and I have an NHS appointment to see a urologist about phalloplasty in February. A long and tortuous journey still lies ahead of me.

I have started playing football again, indoors with the lads from work on a Monday evening. At the first session I nearly hung up my boots before I had scarcely started. I came home fighting back the tears. I was broken hearted because I had played so badly, someone had laughed at me and the game was so much more competitive than ladies' football. But, only seven weeks on and I am playing as well as anyone else, scoring a few goals and feeling much more confident in general. This year I plan to start training with a local team, the City Exiles, and now I really know I can be good enough. After all, Maradona was scarcely bigger than I am. I always disappear quite quickly once we have finished playing, since nature has poorly equipped me for the changing-room camaraderie. I make my excuses and leave and it always seems a lonely walk back through the corridors as I head for my car. Yes, I've even got a car again;

I certainly am going up in the world. I haven't paid for it yet, but that's just a technical formality. But returning to that lonely walk, this is the very reason why I must have phalloplasty, for my own protection and to feel good about myself as everyone deserves to. It is not a God-given right to be born with the right body, it is a privilege.

Life is treating me very well now, thank you. I've sweated for it, I've cried for it, I've even prayed for it. And now it's almost here. I sit just 'one large willy away from paradise . . .'

This is not the end, it is just the beginning.

Bibliography

Harry Benjamin, *The Transsexual Phenomenon*, The Julian Press, New York, 1966
Caroline Cossey, *My Story*, Faber and Faber, 1991
Caroline Cossey, *Tula: I Am a Woman*, Sphere, 1982
Duncan Fallowell, *April Ashley's Odyssey*, Cape, 1982
Liz Hodgkinson, *Bodyshock*, Virgin, 1987
Liz Hodgkinson, *Michael Née Laura*, Columbus Books, 1989
Jan Morris, *Conundrum*, Faber and Faber, 1974
Janice Raymond, *The Transsexual Empire*, The Women's Press, 1979